"THE HIGHER CHRISTIAN LIFE"

SOURCES FOR THE STUDY OF THE HOLINESS, PENTECOSTAL, AND KESWICK MOVEMENTS

A forty-eight-volume facsimile series reprinting extremely rare documents for the study of nineteenth-century religious and social history, the rise of feminism, and the history of the Pentecostal and Charismatic movements

Edited by

Donald W. Dayton
Northern Baptist Theological Seminary

Advisory Editors

D. William Faupel, *Asbury Theological Seminary*
Cecil M. Robeck, Jr., *Fuller Theological Seminary*
Gerald T. Sheppard, *Union Theological Seminary*

A GARLAND SERIES

PROMISE OF THE FATHER

Phoebe Palmer

Garland Publishing, Inc.
New York & London
1985

For a complete list of the titles in this series
see the final pages of this volume.

Library of Congress Cataloging in Publication Data

Palmer, Phoebe, 1807–1874.
PROMISE OF THE FATHER.

(The Higher Christian life)
Reprint. Originally published: Boston :
H.V. Degen, 1859.
1. Women in church work.   I. Title.   II. Series.
BV4415.P3   1985   262'.14   84-28659
ISBN 0-8240-6434-8 (alk. paper)

The volumes in this series are printed on
acid-free, 250-year-life paper.

Printed in the United States of America

THE. PROMISE OF THE FATHER.

PROMISE OF THE FATHER;

OR,

A NEGLECTED SPECIALITY OF THE LAST DAYS.

ADDRESSED TO

𝕿𝖍𝖊 𝕮𝖑𝖊𝖗𝖌𝖞 𝖆𝖓𝖉 𝕷𝖆𝖎𝖙𝖞 𝖔𝖋 𝖆𝖑𝖑 𝕮𝖍𝖗𝖎𝖘𝖙𝖎𝖆𝖓 𝕮𝖔𝖒𝖒𝖚𝖓𝖎𝖙𝖎𝖊𝖘.

BY THE AUTHOR OF

"THE WAY OF HOLINESS," "ENTIRE DEVOTION," "FAITH AND ITS EFFECTS," "USEFUL
DISCIPLE," "INCIDENTAL ILLUSTRATIONS OF THE ECONOMY
OF SALVATION," ETC.

And it shall come to pass afterward, that I will pour out my Spirit upon all
flesh, and your sons and your daughters shall prophesy. —*Joel* ii. 28.

And behold I send the promise of my Father upon you ; but tarry ye in the
city of Jerusalem until ye be endued with power from on high. — *Luke* xxiv. 49.

This is that which was spoken by the prophet Joel. — *Acts* ii. 16.

BOSTON:
PUBLISHED BY HENRY V. DEGEN,
No. 22 CORNHILL.
1859.

PRINTED BY
GEORGE C. RAND & AVERY.

ELECTROTYPED AT THE
BOSTON STEREOTYPE FOUNDRY.

PREFACE.

Our theme is novel, and addresses itself to all Christians, irrespective of sect. We are disposed to think it the most important that can, in these last days, claim the attention of the religious world. We may seem to overrate our subject, but if the reader will suspend judgment till he has prayerfully weighed the doctrines of this volume in the balances of the sanctuary, we shall be satisfied. Many years have passed since the magnitude of this theme has been pressing upon us. We have repeatedly been solicited, in behalf of common Christianity, to give our views to the public, but have declined, and, in turn, urged others, whom we deemed more competent than ourselves, to undertake the work. We were at last unexpectedly constrained to present what we believe to be truth on this subject, by the following circumstance : —

At a large social meeting, where ministers and people of various denominations were assembled, a lady of strong and influential piety, known to some in that circle to be an individual of more than ordinary mental and cultivated ability, rose to speak. The privilege of being placed in circumstances where she might open her lips in testimony for Jesus before her brethren, was of rare occurrence. Her testimony was most memorably affecting. But we must pause only to glance at its special indices, which were about thus : She had, with unutterable longings, been seeking that the Promise of the Father to his daughters of the last days, might be fulfilled in her experience. As the Marys and " other women " assembled with their brethren on the memorable morning which ushered in the dispensation of the Spirit, she had resolved that she would obey the command of her risen Lord, and wait in unyielding faith for the promised tongue of fire. But, lo, the strange and affecting dilemma in which, through church ordainments, she had been placed ! In coming to the decision that she would, in unyielding, humble prayer and faith, wait for the promised baptism of fire, she drew nigh unto God ; as ever the day of the Lord is near

in *the valley of decision.* And now the Spirit, whose grace she supplicated, drew nigh unto her, and in unmistakable terms assured her
if she would have the promised grace, she must comply with the
obvious conditions. When Mary and the other women disciples
received the tongue of fire in answer to the Promise of the Father, they
at once *used* the gift and spake as the Spirit gave utterance. She now
felt that she had entered, as it were, in audience with the Deity. The
Holy Spirit was demanding of her acquiescence with the condition,
whether she would be willing to pass through the crucifying process
of speaking, as the Spirit gave utterance, in the social assembly,
though those utterances were in danger of being withstood by the
church. And here, though intellectually and piously strong, she
stood and wept over the dilemma. And what a dilemma ! The will
of the church and the will of Christ in conflict ! We need not say,
that the entire of that waiting company were in sympathy with the
scene. What could be done ? We knew that not only the church to
which this lady belonged, but many other churches, in like manner,
would withstand the utterance of a Spirit-baptized Mary in the
church assembly, though they had seen the tongue of fire descend
upon her.

Though in love with church order, we concluded where church
ordainments conflict with the manifest order of the Head of the
Church, it were better to stand up with TRUTH. We therefore
stood up, and gave what were our convictions of the mind of the
Spirit in accordance with the lively oracles, believing that where
church order is at variance with divine order, it were better to obey
God than man.

Our defence, though humble, seemed to be received with favor.
An elder of the church to which the lady whose affecting dilemma we
have stated, belonged, rose and made a motion to the effect that our
views be embodied in writing and given to the public. A congregational minister seconded the motion, and by the unanimous concur-
rence of the meeting, we were pressed to a service which we had long
desired that a more able hand might perform. We believe the error
contemplated lies at the foundation of wrong-doing, immensely detri-
mental to the upbuilding of Zion in well nigh all religious bodies.

Since we commenced the preparation of our volume, we have
received letters from persons of various denominations, in connection
with the interests of our work, a portion of which we will present to
the reader.

PICTOU, Nova Scotia, September 25, 1858.

MRS. P. PALMER.

Dear Sister: I have had sufficient time to examine your new work, "The Promise of the Father," to get hold of your idea. It is a grand one, and, I have no doubt from your manner of treating the subject, the universal church will see and acknowledge that the gifts of the Spirit are "special," and not partial. I have often sighed over the prejudices of the church in relation to woman's exercising her gift in speaking. Think of it! Woman held in bondage by the church! Well, after all it does seem appropriate and significant that, having lost to such a degree the power of love, the church should imprison its form in the person of woman.

Man is regarded as the head of the woman: it is no less true that she is the heart of the man. If man is capable of uttering words of wisdom under spiritual inflatus, it is also apparent that woman can speak in words of love which breathe and burn into the souls of men. If man can enlighten and instruct, woman can do more ; she can warm and melt into penitence the dead and frozen sensibility of the sinner, when her own affections are sanctified under the "baptism of fire."

What is the want of this age? Is it not spiritual power? Where is that power to come from? From men and women filled with faith and the Holy Ghost, under whose blended testimony, like the union of heat and light, the wilderness and the solitary place will yet blossom as the rose. We need instruction, but need power more ; but love is power, and woman is a form of love. What can she not do, when she is sanctified?

The church has been truly in a winter state, in which there has been no lack of light and intellectual splendor, increased a thousand fold as it came reflected in prismatic glory by snow and ice. But with all this glitter was there warmth? Was there the beautiful forms of vegetable life? No. It required the mingling of the woman's love, set on fire by the Holy Ghost, with man's sanctified intellect, to give us the beauty, the glory, the power of summer, and the fruit of glad, rejoicing autumn.

Bless the Lord, the winter is over and gone, the time of the singing of birds is come, and the voice of the turtle is heard in our land. The turtle, beautiful emblem of love through the voice of womanhood in the service of the church.

A fresh instalment of spiritual power is coming down upon us. Its first tokens are seen in the part which woman is taking in the humanitarian movements of the age. Her sphere will widen and embrace the service of the sanctuary. Then shall wisdom and love stand before God's altar, and be united in the sacred and inseparable bonds of holy marriage. O, sacred wedlock of faith and charity ! What prolific and luxuriant fruits of holiness will appear as the result of this Heaven-approved union ! Power will be the result — mighty power. Zion shall travail and bring forth children, comely and fair, walking in the beauty of holiness ; and the church will be a diadem in the hand of the Lord. God bless and prosper you in your work and labor of love, and may he make your book a blessing to the church.

Yours, in the bonds of gospel love and truth,

ALEXANDER MCARTHUR, *Presbyterian Minister.*

BRUNSWICK, Me., December 20, 1858.

Dear Sister Palmer : I recognize the divine hand in the work you are called to publish, having relation to woman's position in the church. Such a work is greatly needed. No Christian denies that the Spirit of the Lord descends with like power on man and woman ; that this Spirit is subject to no human limitations ; that the grace of God is diffusive, and freely to be imparted as received. And yet a large proportion of the church, by reason of the law of custom, sit in silence at every social gathering of her members for prayer, praise, and exhortation. Thus the church suffers loss. "The eye cannot say to the hand or foot, I have no need of thee." Each member of the body of Christ, deriving life from the same vital source, has a work to accomplish, a breath of life to diffuse, which no other member can impart.

Woman's *heart*, which, in an important sense, may be considered the *heart* of the church, must be developed in its naturalness and strength, under the operation of holy love, before the church arises in her majesty and beauty, and has power to conquer the world. The women brought of their offerings to build the ancient tabernacle. They have an important work to do in building the New Jerusalem church. "Whosoever shall do the will of my Father, the same is my mother, and sister, and brother." The *mother*, the *sister*, are thus placed on an equality with the brother. The laws that appertain to the kingdom of this world, to Satan's kingdom, or the dominion of selfishness, do not obtain in the kingdom of Christ. In his kingdom there is no usurpation of man or woman, Christ alone being the Head, and each one deriving his or her power and commission from him, and responsible alone to him.

It gives me pleasure to add, that my husband, who has given no small degree of attention to this subject, coincides with these views.

I doubt not the Spirit of the Lord will accompany the truth, and make this volume subserve the good of the church and the glory of its divine Head.

Your friend and sister in Christ,

P. L. UPHAM.

———

PORTLAND, December 20, 1858.

MRS. PHŒBE PALMER.

Dear Sister : I had the pleasure, a few days since, while in Boston, of examining the *proof-sheets* of your forthcoming work — "*The Promise of the Father.*"

Permit me to express my unfeigned gratitude to God for the assistance he has rendered you in the production of a work of such soul-stirring interest. I regard the subject of incalculable importance to the Zion of God at this time.

What part has *woman* in the great work of human redemption? How far is she to exercise her gift in the church of God? How far is it her right to prophesy? How far may she receive the *tongue of fire*, and use it for the salvation of the world? These are questions which have divided the "*sacramental host of God's elect;*" but I rejoice that these questions are answered in this volume, *clearly, fully, scripturally,* and *practically.*

When the mantle of Miriam, Deborah, Mary, Priscilla, Lois, Eunice, Elizabeth, Anna, and the daughters of Philip, shall fall upon the daughters of Zion as it fell upon Miss Bosanquet, Lady Huntington, Hester Ann Rogers, and others, whose record is on high, then will the story of Jesus, who saves to the uttermost, be *felt* and *proclaimed with tongues of fire*, as in days of old.

I can but believe that this volume, so replete with the spirit of holiness, will do much, under God, to produce these much-to-be-desired results.

Wishing it all the success which shall be for the glory of God and the good of the world, I subscribe myself,

Yours, in the bonds of a pure gospel,

WILLIAM McDONALD, *Minister of the M. E. Church.*

BROOKLYN, N. Y., December 23, 1858.

Dear Sister Palmer: I am glad to learn that your new book is about to issue from the press. I believe it will prove a great blessing to the church, conveying to them just views of a most important subject, and encouraging many to "stand up for Jesus," whose testimony might be lost in their silence. I was greatly pleased with those portions of the book which you permitted me to read. Your citations from the Scripture were apt and forcible, and your comparison and explanations of them seemed to me very clearly to harmonize with the letter and spirit of the divine teaching.

When God says, "Ye are my witnesses," he addresses his people, and lays a responsibility upon every one of them. He reveals himself to them, and they are to make him known. As they believed through the word of others, so they are to speak, that others may believe through their word. Every man, woman, and child, who knows the love of Christ, and has a tongue to speak, can and ought to tell of the blessedness they know. In the several situations and spheres of action in which God has placed them, let each one confess Christ, and give to others, by their word of testimony, all that they know about him. None can be silent without suffering loss. If we do not speak to the praise of God, and publish abroad his grace, the light within us will fade away, and God will withhold those soul-gladdening assurances of his approbation and favor, which he is wont to give in abundance to those who speak for him boldly and faithfully.

All this applies to women as well as men. That common sentiment which forbids females to speak in the gatherings of Christians is not only depriving them of precious blessings, but it is robbing the church of those benefits which it might have, and withholding from the world a vast amount of valuable testimony. Considering the fact that a large proportion of the church is composed of females, and in the meetings of many denominations these are restrained to silence, I think I am warranted to say that *two thirds of the talent* of the church is buried and smothered. I do not think it would be scriptural or proper to ordain women to the office of the ministry. The apostle Paul, as I understand him, has shown that they are not to act as authoritative teachers. That office is reserved to men called of God and solemnly ordained of the church; but there is a wide interval between the positions of the ordained teacher and the silent hearer, into which any and all of the members of Christ's family may step and exercise their talents. Once I was an advocate for the silence of women; but when the Holy Ghost came down and converted many to Christ, and females as well as others were ready, out of the fulness of their hearts, to tell what the Lord had done for them, I could not forbid their testimony, and I found it greatly promotive of the work.

In meetings for the promotion of holiness I have found the testimony of women equally valuable with that of men; and, in addition to the great benefits which I have known others to derive from it, I can say truly that it has been greatly helpful to me, by bringing me more fully into the knowledge and love of Christ, and strengthening me in every Christian grace.

In the love of Christ, your brother,

HENRY BELDEN, *Congregational Minister.*

CONTENTS.

CHAPTER I.

CHAPTER II.

CHAPTER III.

CHAPTER IV.

(xi)

How the weak may be made strong. Whole burnt sacrifices required. How used, exemplified. Unspeakable triumphs. The effect or fruit of salvation. The ordination. What holiness again. Is that all? Fifty saved at one meeting. Minister's perplexities. The lost saved. Saved on earth as in heaven. That is the question. Ten months' seeker. The baptism of fire. The young lady. Reachings of faith. Letter to Mr. E. W. All consecrated but the will. The question settled and the witness received. The open testimony. Letter to Rev. H. V. D. An eventful evening. The promised gift retained, and how. Manifestations of spiritual life. Doctrines of the cross unpopular. Exemplifications of power. A Wesleyan minister's opinion. The tongue of fire received and its effects. Do I walk worthy of my Father? An incident in my experience. Can one made meet for heaven remain on earth? Saved after she had ceased to weep. Cost of faith's superstructure. The Tuesday meeting. How to become a model Christian. Two steps to the blessing. A holy call and a holy heart. Popular favor a trying test. The present dispensation and its responsibilities. Letter to Rev. W. H. D. Outpouring of the Spirit in H. Letter to Rev Mr. F. Effect of a pentecostal baptism in L. Bands of soul savers. Letter to Dr. B. Letter to Dr. S. Letter to Dr. H. Revivals extraordinary. Letter to Mr. D. Letter from C. A believing meeting. Letter to sister L.

CHAPTER XIII.

Request before the minister and church session. Decision. Seeks an asylum from persecution in another denomination. Family gathering. Wife and daughters sit in silence. Worldly and Christian courtesies contrasted. Minister's text and deductions. Sudden outpouring of the Spirit. Female instrumentality. Miss Miller. Hundreds of charmed hearers. Mr. Bramwell's appreciation of female laborers.

CHAPTER XIV.

Amazed listeners. A church acknowledging the gift, but not using it. A daughter of the church turned away. What ought to be anticipated. Psalm lxviii. 11. "Of the female preachers there was a great host." Incredulity anticipated. Self-imposed blindness. Who have been the crucifiers? Last act in the drama of the world's redemption.

CHAPTER XV.

Who are called to preach? Grace tested and proclaimed. What class of truth most effectual in the conviction of unbelievers. Female witnesses called forth. Forbidden by the church to speak. Revolting revelation. New pastor. All invited to speak. Women not a part of all. Crucified by an official enactment. The most pious the greatest sufferers. What would rectify the error.

CHAPTER XVI.

Deacon's daughter. Husband's mortification. Injustice to his Saviour and his wife. A potter's field. The church estranges herself from woman's gifts. Lady of superior mental endowment. Gifts brought within the church pale. Sepulchred in the midst. A libel on the religion of Jesus. God will require the return of woman's gifts with *usury*. Who will meet the demand? Particle of old leaven. The church buries the gifts of three fourths of her members.

CHAPTER XVII.

Early visitor. Not insincere, but mistaken. Man of business waiting for the baptism of fire. The minister resolves not to leave his study till the full baptism is obtained. Revival succeeds. Where faith is not needful. The way in which many sin. Weighty truths. The point where the tongue of fire falls. Claim to discipleship may be lost.

CHAPTER XVIII.

Wonderful testimony. Scriptural searchings. How to open heaven's windows. No responsive chord. Divine sympathy. Religious and social courtesies contrasted. Efforts of false religions. Remarkable change of opinion consequent on a change of experience. Portrayings from real life promised. Impious doubtings.

CHAPTER XIX.

Symmetrical holiness contemplated and desired. Good news. A question better not asked. Eight weeks' study. Fasting, weeping, and praying. New emotions. Presence of Christ a reality. Rushing mighty wind in the soul. Anchored on the promises. Sunbeams of love. Kept from falling. Walking in the way. Name of the way. Filled to overflowing. Surrounded by God's presence. Angel visit. Recapitulation of testimony.

CHAPTER XX.

Singularly effective labors. Church in the wilderness. Varied ministrations. Angel of mercy. How born into the kingdom of grace. Remains of the carnal mind. Wrestling with the angel of the covenant. Midnight devotions. Walking and talking with God. Witness lost, and how. Covenant with God. Coming to the Father through the Son. Fighting in Canaan. Witness of purity regained. Converse with Deity.

CHAPTER XXI.

College days. Converted. Theological studies. Enters the ministry. Smitten by a wise man. God uses the pruning knife. Civil duties. Preaching self, not Christ. Full consecration. Believing and knowing. Call to preach made plain. Not authorship or professorship, but the gospel. Conventionalism and sectarianism in one black bundle. Right text. Sinai of eternity. Ocean of love. Ark of faith. Scene in the church. Sealing of the Spirit. Keen battles. Stepping stones to glory.

PROMISE OF THE FATHER.

CHAPTER I.

"Stand up for Jesus! All who lead his host,
Crowned with the splendors of the Holy Ghost!
Shrink from no foe, to no temptations yield,
Urge on the triumphs of this glorious field —
Stand up for Jesus."

O not be startled, dear reader. We do not intend to discuss the question of "Women's Rights" or of "Women's Preaching," technically so called. We leave this for those whose ability and tastes may better fit them for discussions of this sort. We believe woman has her legitimate sphere of action, which differs in most cases materially from that of man; and in this legitimate sphere she is both happy and useful. Yet we do not doubt that some reforms contemplated in recent movements may, in various respects, be decidedly advantageous. But we have never conceived that it would be subservient to the happiness, usefulness, or true dignity of woman, were she permitted to occupy a prominent part in legislative halls, or take a leading position in the orderings of church conventions. Ordinarily, these are not the circumstances where woman can best serve her generation according to the will of God. Yet facts show that

1

it is in the order of God that woman may occasionally
be brought out of the ordinary sphere of action, and
occupy in either church or state positions of high responsibility ; and if, in the orderings of providence, it
so occur, the God of providence will enable her to meet
the emergency with becoming dignity, wisdom, and
womanly grace.

Examples of modern and ancient days might be
furnished of women who have been called to fill positions involving large responsibilities, both civil and
ecclesiastical.   It was thus that Deborah, a prophetess,
the wife of Lapidoth, was called to judge Israel — not
because there were no men in Israel who might fill the
position, but because God, in his wisdom, had so ordained ; and it was also by the direction of Providence
she was compelled to take the lead in the orderings of
the battle — not because there were not men in Israel
to do this, for she sent and called Barak, who might,
as captain of the host, have led forth the people to
conquest, but his faith and courage were insufficient
to lead out Israel.   Her disinterested, womanly heart
would have given Barak the honor of the conquest,
but he was faint-hearted ; and the holy zeal of this
mother in Israel nerved her for the conflict, and, with a
faith and courage outbraving every difficulty, she led
forth the armies of God to glorious conquest.   Yet who
talked of Deborah as overstepping the bounds of womanly propriety, in either judging Israel, or in leading
forth the armies of the living God to victory ?   Whisperers might have said that, in using this gift of proph-

ecy with which God had endued her, and in leading out Israel to conquest, she stepped beyond the sphere of woman, and weakened her influence ; and thus, perhaps, the Merozites were hindered from coming up to the help of the Lord against the mighty, and brought down the curse of the God of battles on themselves. But whether there were such whisperers is not recorded ; and if so, in fact, their names are written in the dust, while the name of this ancient prophetess, who led Israel forth to victory, stands recorded in the Book of eternal remembrance.

And when Josiah the King of Israel and his officers of state saw, from the reading of a book found in the house of the Lord, that great wrath was impending, they did not go to Huldah the prophetess for advice, because there was not a male prophet who might have been consulted ; for it was in the days of Jeremiah the prophet, that this official deputation went from the king to Huldah.   And when, in the order of God, woman has from time to time been called to sustain positions of momentous trust, involving the destinies of her country, facts show that she has not been wanting in ability to meet the demands of her station in such a manner, as to command the respect of her constituents or the homage of her subjects.   Look at Her Most Gracious Majesty Queen Victoria, the reigning sovereign of the most mighty, intelligent people of this or any other age.   Who questions her ability for her station, and talks of her as having transcended the bounds set by public opinion of the sphere of woman ?

And is it in religion alone that woman is prone to overstep the bounds of propriety, when the impellings of her Heaven-baptized soul would lead her to come out from the cloister, and take positions of usefulness for God ? Whence has the idea obtained that she may not even open her lips for God in the assembly of the pious, without being looked upon repulsively, as though she were unwomanly in her aims and predilections ?

And where is the beloved female disciple of any denomination, truly baptized of the Holy Ghost, but feels the Spirit's urgings to open her mouth for God ? We do not now speak of that cold, worldly conformed professor, who has never, in obedience to the command of the Saviour, tarried at Jerusalem, as did Mary and the other women, on the day of Pentecost. We speak of that consistently pious, earnest, Christian woman, whose every-day life is an ever-speaking testimony of an indwelling Saviour, and on whose head the tongue of fire has descended. And it is of the power of an ever-present Jesus that the Spirit would have her testify ; but the seal of silence has been placed on her lips. And who has placed the seal of silence on those Heaven-touched lips ? Who would restrain the lips of those whom God has endued with the gift of utterance, when those lips would fain abundantly utter the memory of God's great goodness ? Not worldly opinions or usages, for these reprove. Think of a refined social gathering of worldlings, to which invitations have been extended to ladies with the expectation that the seal of silence would be imposed ! No, it is not the world·

that forbids ; for due consideration will constrain us to acknowledge that in this regard " the children of this world are wiser in their generation than the children of light." Who is it then that forbids that woman should open her mouth in either prayer or speaking in the assemblies of the saints ?

And here we come to the point, and are forced to an answer to which in the name of the Head of the church we claim a rejoinder. Our answer is this : The Christian churches of the present day, with but few exceptions, have imposed silence on Christian woman, so that her voice may but seldom be heard in Christian assemblies. And why do the churches impose it ? The answer comes from a thousand lips, and from every point. The Head of the church forbids it, and the churches only join in the authoritative prohibition, " Let your women keep silence in the churches." And here we come fairly at the question. If the Head of the church forbids it, this settles the question beyond all controversy.

But if Paul's prohibition, " Let your women keep silence in the churches," is to be carried out to the letter in relation to the prophesying of women, — that is, her speaking " to edification, exhortation, and comfort," — regardless of explanatory connections and contradictory passages, why should it not be carried out to the letter in other respects ? If the apostle intended to enjoin silence in an absolute sense, then our Episcopalian friends trespass against this prohibition at every church service, in calling out the responses of women in com-

1 *

pany with the men in their beautiful Church Liturgy, and when they repeat our Lord's Prayer in concert with their brethren. And thus also do they trespass against this prohibition every time they break silence and unite in holy song in the church of God of any or every denomination. And in fact, we doubt not but it were less displeasing to the Head of the church that his female disciples were forbidden to open their lips in singing, or in church responses, than that they should be forbidden to open their lips in fulfilment of the " Promise of the Father," when the spirit of prophecy has been poured out upon them, moving them to well nigh irrepressible utterances of God's great goodness.

Under what circumstances was this prohibition given ? Was it not by way of reproving some unseemly practices which had been introduced into the Corinthian church, and which, in fact, seem to have been peculiar to that church, for it is in connection with this and kindred disorders which had been introduced among the Corinthian believers, in connection with the exercise of the gift of prophecy, that Paul says, " We have no such custom, *neither the churches of God ;* " that is, the other churches of God over which the Holy Ghost had made them overseers. Surely it is evident that the irregularities here complained of were peculiar to the church of Corinth, and in fact, we may presume, were not even applicable to other Christian churches of Paul's day, much less Christian churches of the present day, as no such disorders exist. The irregularity complained of was not the prophesying of women, for this the apostle admits, and directs how the women shall appear when engaged in the duty of praying or prophesying. But the prohibition was evidently in view of restraining women, from taking part in those disorderly debates, which were not unusual in the religious worship of those days. In the Jewish synagogues it was a matter of ordinary occurrence for persons to interrupt the speaker by introducing questionings, which frequently resulted in angry altercations. This practice had now, we have reason to infer, been introduced into the Corinthian Christian assemblies, and women — doubtless devoid of spirituality — were disposed to take part in these debates. This unseemly practice the apostle reproves, and says, " Let your women keep silence," &c. Any one who will carefully look at this subject, with its connections, will observe that it was in reference to this reprehensible practice, which had obtained in the Corinthian church, that Paul enjoins silence, and not in reference to the exercise of the gift of prophecy, which, in connection with this subject, he so plainly admits. Otherwise the apostle's teachings were obviously contradictory. But a careful review of the subject in connection with the well-known usages of that day, will relieve it of all difficulty, and show that Paul had these questionings in view and not the ordinary speaking of women in prophesying ; for says he, " If they will learn any thing, let them ask their husbands at home. "

But Paul also says, " I suffer not a woman to teach, nor usurp authority over the man." It will be found by an examination of this text with its connections, that the sort of teaching here alluded to, stands in necessary connection with usurping authority. As though the apostle had said, The gospel does not alter the relation of woman in view of priority. For Adam was first formed, then Eve. And though the condition of woman is improved, and her privileges enlarged, yet she is not raised to a position of superiority, where she may usurp authority, and teach dictatorially, for the law still remains as at the beginning. It is an unalterable law of nature. Adam was first formed, then Eve, and all the daughters of Adam must acknowledge man first in creation, long as time endures.

But the sort of teaching to which the apostle here alludes, in connection with usurping authority, cannot be of the sort to which he refers, 1 Cor. xiv. Here Paul admits the prophesying of women in public assemblies, and of course could have had no intention, in his Epistle to Timothy, to forbid that sort of teaching, which stood in connection with the exercise of the gift of prophecy, which arose from the immediate impulses of the Holy Ghost, and which is rendered abundantly plain by another passage in his Epistle to the Corinthians, in which he notices the public prophesying of females, and gives particular directions respecting their conduct and appearance, while engaged in that sacred duty. " Every man *praying* or *prophesying*, having his head covered, dishonoreth his head. But every woman that prayeth or prophesieth with her head uncovered, dishonoreth her head." That this passage, as well as the fourteenth chapter of the same Epistle, particularly relates to the conduct of the Corinthian Christians in their assemblies for worship, and can have no special bearing on the present day, is obvious, and is allowed by eminent commentators, and is indeed evident from the whole tenor of the advice which is here given. The apostle therefore recognizes the public prophesying of females.

With respect to the prophesying to which the apostle here alludes, as exercised by both men and women in the churches of the saints, he defines its nature. (See 1 Cor. xiv. 3.) The reader will see that it was directed to the " edification, exhortation, and comfort of believers," and the result anticipated was the conviction of unbelievers and unlearned persons. " Such," says the author of an excellent work, " were the public services of women which the apostle allowed, and such was the ministry of females predicted by the prophet Joel, and described as a *leading* feature under the gospel dispensation. Women who speak in assemblies for worship under the influence of the Holy Spirit assume thereby no *personal authority* over others. They are instruments through which divine instruction is communicated to the people."

It may be conceived by some that the devoted Christian female, who is willing thus to be led by the Spirit into paths of usefulness, may lose, in some degree, those lovely and becoming traits of character, which we admire in the female sex. As far as our observations have aided us, the effect has been diametrically opposite.

Religion does not despoil woman of her refined sensibilities, but only turns them into a finer mould, and brings out to the charmed beholder every thing that is pure, lovely, and of good report. Says the late Mr. Gurney, a minister in the Society of Friends, "We well know that there are no women among us more generally distinguished for modesty, gentleness, order, and a right submission to their brethren, than those who have been called by their divine Master. into the exercise of the Christian ministry." And who finds fault with the ministry of woman as practised among the society of Friends? We imagine few are so fastidious.

But says one, Is the proclamation of the gospel, as dispensed by women among the people called Friends, of such manifest utility as to warrant the belief of a divine call to this work? Says a theological writer, in treating on this subject, "There is, however, in some sections of the Christian church, a recognition of the full and free agency and operation of the Holy Spirit which divideth to every man severally as he will, and a thankful acceptance of that great gospel truth, 'There is neither Jew nor Greek, there is neither male nor female,' but 'they are all one in Christ Jesus.' Among such the preaching of women has been acknowledged to be a special gift from Christ, who only has a right to appoint, and who alone can qualify his ministers effectually to publish the glad tidings through him. And so effectually have these glad tidings been proclaimed by females that many have been through their instrumentality converted from the error of their way, and brought from darkness to light ; many hungry and thirsty souls have been refreshed and strengthened, and many living members of the church edified together. Can we believe that the Holy Spirit is *now* more limited in its manifestations and in its requirements than when by his inspirations Miriam prophesied and sang the praise of Jehovah ? "

Says the devoted philanthropist, Miss Bosanquet, afterwards the wife of the distinguished Vicar of Madely, Rev. J. Fletcher, who felt herself called to proclaim the power of saving grace to others, " Some think it inconsistent with that modesty the Christian religion requires in women professing godliness. Now, I do not apprehend Mary could in the least be accused of immodesty when she carried the joyful news of her Lord's resurrection, and in that sense taught the teachers of mankind. Neither was the woman of Samaria to be accused of immodesty when she invited the whole city to come to Christ. Neither do I think the woman mentioned in 2 Sam. xx. could be said to sin against modesty, though she called to the general of the opposing army to converse with her, and then went to all the people to give them her advice, and by it the city was saved. Neither do I suppose Deborah did wrong in publicly declaring the message of the Lord, and afterwards accompanying Barak to war because his hands hung down at going without her. But says the objector, All these were extraordinary calls ; sure you will not say yours is an extraordinary call ? If I did not believe so, I would not act in an extraordinary manner. I praise God, I feel him near, and prove his faithfulness every day."

That Christ was successfully preached to the Samaritans through the instrumentality of a woman is manifest, John iv. 39. "Many of the Samaritans believed on him for the saying of the woman." This woman was the first apostle for Christ in Samaria. She went and told her fellow-citizens that the Messiah was come, and gave for proof that he had told her the most secret things she had ever done.

But Providence, under ordinary circumstances, assigns woman a sphere of action both suited to her predilections and her physical and mental structure. Indeed, can we conceive of a work more important than that which in the general orderings of Providence falls to woman? "The future destiny of the child is always the work of the mother," said the sagacious Napoleon. The training of the human mind irrespective of sex, as it comes forth fresh from the hand of the Dispenser of life, is, for the most part, committed to woman. What a high and holy trust! It were difficult to give a just presentation of the magnitude of this work. Immortal minds are to be trained for immortality and eternal life; and all the minutiæ of future life, whether for good or evil, are to show the result of these early trainings. And to all eternity, as millions on millions of ages pass away, the result of those early motherly trainings will influence largely the destiny of that deathless spirit. Not only will the women of this age have to do with the women of the future age, but, as the men of the future age will have had their early training mostly from the women of the present age, how greatly have women to do with the destinies of the moral and religious world! Wonderful indeed is the work to which woman has been called in the social relation. Says Mrs. Hale, " But with the privileges we must take the position of women ; leave the work of the world and its reward, the government thereof, to men ; our task is to fit them for their office, and inspire them to perform it in righteousness."

It is not our aim in this work to suggest, in behalf of woman, a change in the social or domestic relation. We are not disposed to feel that she is burdened with wrong in this direction. But we feel that there is a wrong, a serious wrong, affectingly cruel in its influences, which has long been depressing the hearts of the most devotedly pious women. And this wrong is inflicted by pious men, many of whom, we presume, imagine that they are doing God service in putting a seal upon lips which God has commanded to speak.

It is not our intention to chide those who have thus kept the Christian female in bondage, as we believe in ignorance they have done it. But we feel that the time has now come when ignorance will involve guilt ; and the Head of the church imperatively demands a consideration of the question proposed in the following pages.

2

CHAPTER II.

WOMAN.

"Not she with traitorous kiss her Saviour stung;
Not she denied him with unholy tongue;
She, while apostles shrank, could danger brave,
Last at his cross, and earliest at his grave."

IMPORTANT QUESTION.

A QUESTION of grave interest is now demanding the attention of all Christians, irrespective of name or sect. Especially does it demand the attention of the Christian ministry, inasmuch as it is believed by many to stand in vital connection with the ultimate triumphs of the cross.

And ere we lay this question before you, Christian reader, let us ask, that you will present yourself, as in the more immediate presence of the Father of Lights, and implore the illumination of the all-gracious Spirit, resolved that you will yield your mind up to the convictions of truth, and in outspoken declaration defend its claims.

The question is this: Has not a gift of power, delegated to the church on the day of Pentecost, been neglected? Or, in other words, has not a marked speciality of the Christian dispensation been comparatively unrecognized and kept out of use?

When the Founder of our holy Christianity was about leaving his disciples, to ascend to his Father, he commanded them to tarry at Jerusalem until endued with power from on high. And of whom was this company of disciples composed? Please turn to the first chapter of the Acts of the Apostles. Here we see that the number assembled in that upper room were about one hundred and twenty. Here were Peter, James, John, Andrew, Philip, Thomas, Bartholomew, Matthew, James the son of Alpheus, and Simon Zelotes, and Judas the brother of James. "These all continued with one accord in prayer and supplication with the women, and Mary, the mother of Jesus, and with his brethren." Here, we see, were both male and female disciples, continuing with one accord in prayer and supplication, in obedience to the command of their risen Lord; they are all here, waiting for the promise of the Father.

And here let us ask, From whence has the doctrine obtained, that women may not open their mouth in supplication and prayer in the presence of their brethren? Surely, those who thus set forth, teach for doctrines the commandments of men. And if the usage of apostolic days reprove those who have thus *publicly* taught, is not a *public* refutation of the error called for? Has not an endowment of power thus been kept back in the church? and will not God require for this? Who that has heard the melting, subduing tones of the female voice, as it has fallen on the ear of man in prayer, but will be penetrated with the force of the fact, that a gift of power has been withheld from the social assemblies of the pious, of serious magnitude?

And who were these women who continued with one

accord in supplication with their brethren ? Were they
not those female disciples who followed the Man of Sorrows with unflinching faith and undaunted step, during
all his homeless journeyings, listening to his teachings,
and ministering to him of their substance ? Were not
these the women, who, after all the male disciples
forsook their suffering Master, followed him to the
cross, and, with agonized hearts, witnessed his last
sufferings, heard his expiring groan, and followed his
body to its burial, and, after the sepulchre had hidden
his form from their vision, sat over against the tomb to
mourn, till the curtain of night shrouded the place where
their Lord lay from their weeping eyes ? Yes, these
were the women, who early, ere the day had yet
dawned, were with their costly spices at the tomb of
their Lord, the strength of whose quenchless love knew
no barriers.   Neither the great stone, nor the governor's
seal, could debar them from the object of their love.

> " Not she with traitorous kiss her Saviour stung ;
>   Not she denied him with unholy tongue :
>   She, while apostles shrank, could danger brave,
>   Last at his cross, and earliest at his grave."

Reader, are you one of those who, with unhelping
hand and repulsive glance, have looked down on the
loving, self-sacrificing manifestations of woman's devotion to her Saviour ? How unlike are you in spirit to
the mighty angel at whose very presence the earth
quaked, when those hardy keepers of the grave became
as dead men ! That countenance which, as lightning,
struck terror to the hearts of the sturdy guards of the

grave, only beamed in love and gentleness on these devoted women. Had the world ever witnessed such unyielding love? — such unflinching constancy, amid scenes of ignominy, suffering, and terror? O reader, have you ever rejected a loving, persuasive testimony in honor of Jesus, because it fell from the affectionate lips of a woman? Behold these women, now about to receive from the lips of this mighty angel the first commission ever given to mortals, to proclaim a risen Christ. "Fear not," said the angel, "for I know that ye seek Jesus, who was crucified. He is not here, for he has risen, as he said. Come see the place where the Lord lay." How sweet the message, and how loving and sympathizing the tones of this mighty angel to the stricken hearts of these affectionate mourners! But he would not have them linger. And well did the mighty angel know that it was not in woman's heart to be selfish in her joy; and he bids them hasten quickly, and tell the disciples that their Lord had risen from the dead, and would go before them into Galilee, where they should see him. What a message! And from what a source was it received!

Think you that John, James, or Peter would have received that message with a repulsive look, because delivered by the angel to a woman, and first communicated to man by her? How strange and unwarrantable the infatuation of some who profess to be Christ's disciples of the present day, who contemptuously hear "the testimony of Jesus, which is the spirit of prophecy," because it falls from the lips of a woman!

2*

But though these women were by this mighty angel intrusted with the most glorious commission ever delivered to mortals, this was but a small honor, compared with that which awaited them. As they ran quickly, so true to the principle of their unselfish, womanly natures, to bring their sorrowing brethren word, Jesus, the Prince of life and glory, the blessed and only Potentate, Lord of lords and King of kings, met them. And what were a commission from the most mighty of angels, compared with a commisson from the Lord of angels? " All hail!" said He who spake as man never spake. They pause. Though no longer the man of sorrows, his sympathies are unchanged, and he greets these, his beloved courageous female disciples, with most inspiring words. " All hail!" exclaims the newly-risen Prince of life. Joyous salutation! Its inspirations speak more than friendship ; it is the voice of affection, and flows out from the heart of infinite love, inspiring blissful confidence, and moving them to holy adoration. Their risen Lord is still their Friend, and in untold transports they bow and worship before him, and cling to his feet. Does he chide them? No! Had a vestige of fear lingered about their stricken hearts, it were now forever banished. " Be not afraid : go tell my brethren, that they go into Galilee, and there shall they see me." Wonderful commission! Behold the first heralds of the gospel of a risen Saviour! The first commission ever given to mortals, direct from the newly-risen Head of the church, is now being given to these affectionate, unflinching female disciples, who, with undaunted step, had followed the Man of Sorrows through all his weary pilgrimage here on earth. Blessed daughters of the Lord Almighty! now is your constancy rewarded. The first proclamation that falls upon the ear of man, of a risen Jesus, is to burst from your lips. The first sight ever given to mortals of the glorified body of the world's Redeemer, is now being given to your entranced vision. O, amazing sight! Yet your glorified Lord is still your same compassionate friend as when he communed with you before passing through the portals of the grave!

He would not that your timid natures should be over-awed with the wondrous sight which is now being revealed to your astonished vision, nor with the magnitude of the amazing commission which ye are now to receive from his glorified lips. No, the tones falling from those lips are still, as ever, all gentleness and love : "Be not afraid. Go tell my brethren that they go into Galilee, and there shall they see me. Go to my brethren, and say unto them, I ascend unto my Father and your Father, and to my God and your God." What a message! Think you that those dear apostles, the brethren of our Lord, rejected this message from the Saviour, because it fell from the lips of a female disciple?

"Go tell my brethren," said the Son of God. Says an eminent commentator, in reviewing this text, "Behold what honor God puts upon those who persevere in his truth, and continue to honor him before men. Thus these faithful women proclaim the gospel of a risen Saviour to those who were afterward to be the teachers of the whole human race." We will not here speak of the assumptions of those who arrogate to themselves the sole privilege of preaching the gospel ; but we here see who received the first commission to proclaim a risen Saviour ; and we think the fact sufficiently suggestive to demand a consideration of the question, whether the endowment of power, promised as a *speciality* of the Christian dispensation, has not been singularly neglected.

And " Fear not ye " was gently said,
   For why do ye thus seek
The living here among the dead ?
   Did he not to ye speak
Of this his rising when he was with thee ?
Remember ye his words in Galilee ?

O, they his words remembered then,
   For memory's spell is broken,
And thought's deep fount is fathomed when
   The words of Christ are spoken :
And holy Joy, with its attendant train,
Brings to the greeting soul sweet bliss again.

Thus it was now with those ;
   But ah ! the very joy
Which from some sweet disclosure flows
   Will almost bliss alloy ;
For when they his remembered words received,
For very joy they scarcely yet believed.

CHAPTER III.

"Pride and self-sufficiency smile at the idea of a female prophet, a female judge, a female poet, a female warrior; and yet, in truth, women have filled all these offices with credit to themselves, and with satisfaction to the public. In the honored list of those who 'through faith subdued kingdoms, wrought righteousness, obtained promises, stopped the mouths of lions, quenched the violence of fire, escaped the edge of the sword, out of weakness were made strong, waxed valiant in fight, turned to flight the armies of the aliens,' female names, too, stand recorded with commendation and renown."

AUTHOR OF SACRED BIOGRAPHY.

DID the tongue of fire descend alike upon God's daughters as upon his sons, and was the effect similar in each?

And did all these waiting disciples, who thus, with one accord, continued in prayer, receive the grace for which they supplicated? It was, as we observe, the gift of the Holy Ghost that had been promised. And was this promise of the Father as truly made to the daughters of the Lord Almighty as to his sons? See Joel ii. 28, 29. "And it shall come to pass afterward, that I will pour out my Spirit upon all flesh; and your sons and your daughters shall prophesy, your old men shall dream dreams, your young men shall see visions. And also upon the servants and upon the handmaids in those days will I pour out my Spirit." When the Spirit was poured out in answer to the united prayers of God's sons and daughters, did the tongue of fire descend alike upon the women as upon the men? How emphatic is the answer to this question! "And there appeared unto them cloven

tongues, like as of fire, and it sat upon *each of them*."
Was the effect similar upon God's daughters as upon
his sons? Mark it, O ye who have restrained the
workings of this gift of power in the church. "And
they were *all* filled with the Holy Ghost, and began to
speak as the Spirit gave utterance." Doubtless it was
a well nigh impelling power, which was thus poured
out upon these sons and daughters of the Lord
Almighty, moving their lips to most earnest, persuasive, convincing utterances. Not alone only did Peter proclaim a crucified risen Saviour, but each one,
as the Spirit gave utterance, assisted in spreading the
good news; and the result of these united ministrations
of the Spirit, through human agency, was, that three
thousand were, in one day, pricked to the heart.
Unquestionably, the whole of this newly-baptized company of one hundred and twenty disciples, male and
female, hastened in every direction, under the mighty
constrainings of that perfect love that casteth out fear,
and great was the company of them that believed.

And now, in the name of the Head of the church,
let us ask, Was it designed that these demonstrations of
power should cease with the day of Pentecost? If the
Spirit of prophecy fell upon God's daughters, alike as
upon his sons in that day, and they spake in the midst
of that assembled multitude, as the Spirit gave utterance, on what authority do the angels of the churches
restrain the use of that gift now? Has the minister of
Christ, now reading these lines, never encouraged open
female testimony, in the charge which he represents?

Let us ask, What account will you render to the Head of the church, for restricting the use of this endowment of power? Who can tell how wonderful the achievements of the cross might have been, if this gift of prophecy, in woman, had continued in use, as in apostolic days? Who can tell but long since the gospel might have been preached to every creature? Evidently this was a *speciality* of the last days, as set forth by the prophecy of Joel. Under the old dispensation, though there was a Miriam, a Deborah, a Huldah, and an Anna, who were prophetesses, the special outpouring of the Spirit upon God's daughters as upon his sons, seems to have been reserved as a characteristic of the last days. This, says Peter, as the wondering multitude beheld these extraordinary endowments of the Spirit, falling alike on all the disciples, — this is that which was spoken by the prophet Joel, " And also upon my servants and upon my handmaidens will I pour out my Spirit."

And this gift of prophecy, bestowed upon all, was continued and recognized in all the early ages of Christianity. The ministry of the Word was not confined to the apostles. No, they had a laity for the times. When, by the cruel persecutions of Saul, all the infant church were driven away from Jerusalem, *except the apostles,* these scattered men and women of the laity " went every where *preaching the word,*" that is, proclaiming a crucified, risen Saviour. And the effect was, that the enemies of the cross, by scattering these men and women, who had been saved by its virtues,

were made subservient to the yet more extensive proclamation of saving grace.

Impelled by the indwelling power within, these
Spirit-baptized men and women, driven by the fury
of the enemy in cruel haste from place to place, made
all their scatterings the occasion of preaching the gospel
every where, and believers were every where multiplied, and *daily* were there added to the church such as
should be saved.

Says the Rev. Dr. Taft, " If the nature of society,
its good and prosperity, in which women are jointly
and equally concerned with men, if, in *many cases*,
their fitness and capacity for instructors being admitted to be equal to the other sex, be not reasons
sufficient to convince the candid reader of woman's
teaching and preaching, because of two texts in Paul's
Epistles, (1 Cor. xiv. 34 ; 1 Tim. ii. 12,) let him consult the paraphrase of Locke, where he has proved to a
demonstration that the apostle, in these texts, never
intended to prohibit women from praying and preaching in the church, provided they were dressed as became women professing godliness, and were qualified
for the sacred office.   Nor is it likely that he would, in
one part of his Epistle, give directions how a woman,
as well as a man, should pray and prophesy in public,
and presently after, in the very same Epistle, forbid
women, endowed with the gifts of prayer and prophecy, from speaking in the church, when, according to
his own explication of prophecy, it is ' speaking unto
others for edification, exhortation, and comfort.'   Be-

PROMISE OF THE FATHER.   25

Women make a part of all.   The wish of Moses.

sides, the apostle, in this Epistle to the church at
Corinth, says, ' Follow after charity, and desire spiritual gifts, but rather that ye may prophesy.' Again,
' I would ·that ye all spake with tongues, but rather
that ye prophesied.' Here the apostle speaks to the
church in general; and the word *all* must comprehend
every individual member; and since he had just before
given directions about a woman's praying and prophesying, we conclude that his desire extended to women
as well as to men. Certainly the word *all* includes
both men and women; otherwise the mind of Paul,
' who was made a minister of the Spirit,' would have
been more narrow than that of Moses, who was only a
minister of the *law;* for when Joshua came and told
Moses that Eldad and Medad prophesied in the camp,
and desired him to forbid them, Moses said unto him,
' Enviest thou for my sake? Would God that all the
Lord's people were prophets, and that he would put his
Spirit upon them.' Now, all the Lord's people must
certainly comprehend the Miriams and Deborahs in the
camp, as well as the Eldads and Medads."

Dr. Clarke says, (Rom. xvi. 12,) "' Salute Tryphena
and Tryphosa, who labored in the Lord. Salute the
beloved· Persis, who labored much in the Lord ' — two
holy women, who, it seems, were assistants to the
apostle in his work, probably by exhorting, visiting the
sick, &c. Persis was another woman, who, it seems,
excelled the preceding; for of her it is said, she *labored
much in the Lord.* We learn from this, that Christian
women, as well as *men,* labored in the ministry of the

3

word.   In those times of simplicity, all persons, whether men or women, who had received the knowledge of the truth, believed it to be their duty to propagate it to the utmost of their power.

" Many have spent much useless labor in endeavoring to prove that these women did not *preach.*   That there were some *prophetesses,* as well as *prophets,* in the Christian church, we learn ; and that *woman* might pray or prophesy, provided she had her head covered, we know ; and that whoever prophesied, spoke unto others to edification, exhortation, and comfort, St. Paul declares, 1 Cor. xiv. 3.   That no preacher can do more, every person must acknowledge ; because to edify, exhort, and comfort, are the prime ends of the gospel ministry.   If women thus prophesied, then women preached."

Chrysostom and Theophilact take great notice of Junia, mentioned in the apostle's salutations.   In our translation (Rom. xvi. 7) it is, " Salute Andronicus and Junia, my kinsmen, and my fellow-prisoners, who are of note among the apostles."   By the word *kinsmen* one would take Junia not to have been a woman, but a man.   But Chrysostom and Theophilact were both Greeks ; consequently, they knew their mother tongue better than our translators, and they say it was a woman ; it should, therefore, have been translated, " Salute Andronicus and Junia, my kinsfolk."   The apostle salutes other *women* who were of note among them, particularly Tryphena and Tryphosa, who labored in the Lord, and Persis, who labored much in the Lord.

Again, if we look into ecclesiastical history, we shall find women very eminent in the church long after the days of the apostles; I say women who were distinguished for their piety, their usefulness, and their sufferings. Witness the story of Perpetua and Felicitas, martyrs for the Christian faith, which contains traits that touch the most insensible, and cannot be read without a tear. Eusebius speaks of Potominia Ammias, a prophetess in Philadelphia, and others, who were equally distinguished by their zeal for the love which they bore to Jesus Christ.

Justin Martyr, who lived till about A. D. 150, says, in his Dialogue with Trypho, the Jew, "that both *women* and *men* were seen among them who had the gifts of the Spirit of God, according as Joel the prophet had foretold, by which he endeavored to convince the Jew that the *latter days* were come; for by that expression, Manassah Ben Israel tells us, all their wise men understood the times of Messias."

Dodwell, in his Dissertations on Irenæus, says, "that the extraordinary gift of the spirit of prophecy was given to others besides the apostles, and that not only in the *first* and *second*, but in the *third* century, even to the time of Constantine, men of all sorts and ranks had these gifts — yea, and *women* too." Therefore we may certainly conclude that the prophetic saying of the Psalmist, lxviii. 11, was verified: "The Lord gave the word, and great was the company of those that published it." In the original Hebrew it is, "Great was the company of women publishers, or women evangelists." Grotius explains Ps. lxviii. 11, "*Dominus dabat sermonem, id est, materiam loquendi uberem, nempe ut feminarum prædicantium (victorias) multum agmen diceret, scilicet, eaquæ sequuntur* "— "The Lord shall give the word, that is, plentiful matter of speaking; so that he would call those which follow the great army of preaching women, viz., victories, or female conquerors."

A SUPPOSITION.

Suppose one of the brethren who had received the baptism of fire on the day of Pentecost, now numbered among those who were scattered every where preaching the word, had met a female disciple who had also received the same endowment of power. He finds her proclaiming Jesus to an astonished company of male and female listeners. And now imagine he interferes and withstands her testimony by questioning whether women have a right to testify of Christ before a mixed assembly. Would not such an interference look worse than unmanly? And were her testimony, through this interference, restrained, or rendered less effectual, would it not, in the eye of the Head of the church, involve guilt? Yet we do not say but a person may err after the same similitude and be sincere, on the same principle that Saul was sincere when he withstood the proclamation of the gospel, and made such cruel havoc of the church. He verily thought he was doing God service. But when his mind was enlightened to see that, in persecuting these men and women, he was withstanding

God, and rejecting the divinely-ordained instrumentalities by which the world was to be saved, he could no
longer have been sincere unless he had taken every
possible pains to make his refutal of error as far reaching as had been his wrong. And how the heart of that
beloved disciple of the Saviour would have been grieved,
and her hands weakened, by one whom she would have
a right to look to for aid against the common enemy,
and for sympathy in her work !

A large proportion of the most intelligent, courageous, and self-sacrificing disciples of Christ are females.
" Many women followed the Saviour " when on earth ;
and, compared with the fewness of male disciples, many
women follow him still. Were the women who followed
the incarnate Saviour earnest, intelligently pious, and
intrepid, willing to sacrifice that which cost them something, in ministering to him of their substance ? In
like manner, there are many women in the present day,
earnest, intelligent, intrepid, and self-sacrificing, who,
were they permitted or encouraged to open their lips in
the assemblies of the pious in prayer, or speaking as
the Spirit gives utterance, might be instrumental in
winning many an erring one to Christ. We say, were
they permitted and encouraged ; yes, encouragement
may now be needful. So long has this endowment of
power been withheld from use by the dissuasive sentiments of the pulpit, press, and church officials, that it
will now need the combined aid of these to give the
public mind a proper direction, and undo a wrong
introduced by the man of sin centuries ago.

3 *

But more especially do we look to the ministry for the correction of this wrong. Few, perhaps, have really intended to do wrong ; but little do they know the embarrassment to which they have subjected a large portion of the church of Christ by their unscriptural position in relation to this matter. The Lord our God is one Lord. The same indwelling spirit of might which fell upon Mary and the other women on the glorious day that ushered in the present dispensation still falls upon God's daughters. Not a few of the daughters of the Lord Almighty have, in obedience to the command of the Saviour, tarried at Jerusalem; and, the endowment from on high having fallen upon them, the same impelling power which constrained Mary and the other women to speak as the Spirit gave utterance impels them to testify of Christ.

"The testimony of Jesus is the spirit of prophecy." And how do these divinely-baptized disciples stand ready to obey these impelling influences ? Answer, ye thousands of Heaven-touched lips, whose testimonies have so long been repressed in the assemblies of the pious ! Yes, answer, ye thousands of female disciples, of every Christian land, whose pent-up voices have so long, under the pressure of these man-made restraints, been uttered in groanings before God.

But let us conceive what would have been the effect, had either of the male disciples interfered with the utterances of the Spirit through Mary or any of those many women who received the baptism of fire on the day of Pentecost. Suppose Peter, James, or John had questioned their right to speak as the Spirit gave utterance before the assembly, asserting that it were unseemly, and out of the sphere of woman, to proclaim a risen Jesus, in view of the fact that there were *men* commingling in that multitude. How do you think that He who gave woman her commission on the morning of the resurrection, saying, " Go, tell my brethren," would have been pleased with an interference of this sort ?

But are there not doings singularly similar to these being transacted now? We know that it is even so. However unseemly on the part of brethren, and revolting to our finer sensibilities, such occurrences may appear, we have occasion to know that they are not at all unusual in religious circles. We will refer to a Christian lady of more than ordinary intellectual endowments, of refined sensibilities, and whose literary culture and tastes were calculated to constitute her a star in the galaxy of this world.

A LIFE PICTURE.

I have seen a lovely female turn her eye away from the things of time, and fix it on the world to come. Jesus, the altogether lovely, had revealed himself to her, and the vision of her mind was absorbingly entranced with his infinite loveliness, and she longed to reveal him to others. She went to the assembly of the pious. Out of the abundance of her heart she would fain have spoken, so greatly did her heart desire to win others over to love the object of her adoration. Had she been in a worldly assembly, and wished to attract others with an object of admiration, she would not have hesitated to have brought out the theme in conversation, and attracted listeners would have taken her more closely to their hearts, and been won with the object of her love. But she is now in the assembly of the pious. It is true many of them are her brothers and sisters, but cruel custom sealed her lips. Again and again she goes to the assembly for social prayer and the conference meeting, feeling the presence and power of an indwelling Saviour enthroned uppermost in her heart, and assured that he would have her testify of him. At last she ventures to obey God rather than man. And what is the result? A committee is appointed to wait on her, and assure her that she must do so no more. Whisperings are heard in every direction that she has lost her senses; and, instead of sympathizing looks of love, she meets averted glances and heart repulses. This is not a fancy sketch; no, it is a life picture. Ye who have aided in bringing about this state of things, how does this life picture strike you?

WHO WAS REJECTED?

Think of the feelings of the Christian lady, who has thrown herself in the bosom of your church community, in order that she may enjoy the sympathies of Christian love and fellowship. Has grace divested her of refined sensibilities? No! grace has only turned those refined sensibilities into a sanctified channel, and given her a yet more refined perception of every thing pure, and

lovely, and of good report.   What must be the sufferings of that richly-endowed, gentle, loving heart ?   But
was it not her loving, gentle, indwelling Saviour, that
would fain have had her testify for *him* ? and in rejecting her testimony for Jesus, did not Jesus, the Head of
the church, take it as done unto himself?

And what is TRUTH ? should be the word:
  And every human soul
Should feel his inmost being stirred,
  To know it as a whole.

Truth is divine, though it may flow
  From human lip or lyre ;
And he who touches it shall know
  God will for this require.

O, what are human agencies !
  Themselves, alas, how weak !
But God ordains as he doth please,
  And through them he doth speak.

And when TRUTH speaks, whoe'er may touch
  To turn aside the word,
God will reprove the act as much
  As though from Sinai heard.

Who toucheth truth, or blunts its force,
  May heedlessly pass by,
Unmarked in time ; but deep remorse
  Awaits him endlessly.

CHAPTER IV.

"The Saviour and his apostles bear such ample witness to the worth of woman's services in the true church, it would seem a marvel that men who profess to be Christians should ever have degraded her from the rank of visible helper, which Christ gave her."

MRS. HALE.

N what does the gift of prophecy consist? We have remarked that it was not our aim in this volume to set forth the expediency of woman's preaching, technically so called. But the scriptural idea of the terms *preach* and *prophesy* stands so inseparably connected as one and the same thing, that we should find it difficult to get aside from the fact that women did preach, or, in other words, prophesy, in the early ages of Christianity, and have continued to do so down to the present time, to just the degree that the spirit of the Christian dispensation has been recognized. And it is also a significant fact, that to the degree denominations, who have once favored the practice, lose the freshness of their zeal, and as a consequence their primitive simplicity, and, as ancient Israel, yield to a desire to be like surrounding communities, in a corresponding ratio are the labors of females discountenanced.

This is a most suggestive consideration, and if any one reading these pages is disposed to doubt the statement, let him take pains to inquire into the facts in the case. We might specify more than one denomination to which this is particularly applicable. We do not doubt but spiritual religion is now mainly on the rise in the Church of England. The Church of Rome has made her insidious approaches in the form of Puseyism, and not a few have been deluded by her sophistries, and proportionately as the deceptive principles of this fallen church prevail, will nunneries be multiplied. Yes, *nunneries*, which, though not confining their sad and worse than useless victims within walls,

> " By vows and grates confined,"

will debar them, by church dogmas, from yielding to the dictates of the Spirit, and engaging in the holy activities which Scriptural Christianity inculcates. But within the precincts of the Established Church of England, as with many other churches of the present day, as the pure flame of evangelical piety begins to revive, and the corruptions of the Church of Rome are being discountenanced, again we witness the recognition of the spirit of prophecy as poured forth in primitive days on the daughters of the Lord Almighty.

We took up a periodical a short time since, where we were pleased to see recordings by a Churchman in England, who states, as an indication, that the revival flame which had been spreading with such glorious rapidity through America, was now beginning to burst forth in Europe; and among the most prominent of his recordings corroborative of the fact, he mentions the labors of a highly esteemed Christian lady. The item reads thus : —

" A special work of grace has been going forward at

Beckenham, in connection with the readings and ex-
positions of Scripture, by a lady, who has for years em-
phatically been a female missionary.   A Christian
friend, who was present, not long since, at one of these
readings, was intensely interested in what he heard, as
well as in the crowded attendance of working men and
their families.   Miss Marsh, the daughter of the venerable Dr. Marsh, one of the oldest teetotallers of
Britain, is the lady in question.   She is well known as
the authoress of the ' Life of Captain Hedley Vicars,'
' English Hearts and Hands,' and a touching narrative
just published, entitled ' A Light for the Line,' detail-
ing the life and conversion, useful and dying experience
of a navvy."

But, in fact, the word *preach*, taken in connection with
its attendant paraphernalia, oratorical display, onerous
titles, and pulpits of pedestal eminence, means so much
more than we infer was signified by the word *preach*,
when used in connection with the ministrations of Christ
and his apostles, that we were disposed to withhold our
unreserved assent to women's preaching in the technical
sense.   But our desire is to stand up fairly with truth
on this point, and, fearful that we may be misunderstood,
we wish to state unequivocally, that in a scriptural sense
we believe all Christ's disciples, whether male or female,
should covet to be endued with the gift of prophecy ;
then will they proclaim, or, in other words, *preach*
Christ crucified, as far as in them lies, under all possible
circumstances ; and it is thus only that the command of
the Head of the church can be obeyed — " Preach the
gospel to every creature."

Says the learned Dr. Wayland, " I think the generic idea of preaching the gospel in the New Testament, is the proclamation to every creature of the love of God to men through Christ Jesus. This is the main idea. To this our Lord adds, according to the other evangelists, ' teaching them to observe all things whatsoever I have commanded you.' A discourse is not preaching because it is delivered by a minister, or spoken from the pulpit, or appended to a text. Nothing is, I think, properly preaching, except explaining the teachings, or enforcing the commands, of Christ and his apostles. The command was, Go abroad every where ; proclaim to every creature the news of redemption ; tell them of the love of God in Christ Jesus. All things are now ready ; bid them come and welcome to the marriage supper of the Lamb.

" When the Israelites were bitten by the fiery flying serpents, and the bite was inevitably fatal, Moses was directed to set up a brazen serpent, with the assurance that whosoever that had been bitten looked upon it, should be healed. You can imagine how the first man who felt its saving efficacy flew to communicate the news to his brethren, and urge them to avail themselves of the remedy which had delivered him from death. Every man who was healed became immediately a herald of the glad tidings to others. Every one who was saved became a publisher of the salvation, or, in other words, a preacher, until, in a few minutes, the news spread throughout the encampment, and, in this sense, every tribe was evangelized."

4

Now, imagine a female, with all the sympathies of her loving nature, to have been among these bitten and newly restored ones. Think you that she would have been less tardy than her newly recovered brethren, or less energetic, or less persuasive in her efforts in inducing other wounded ones to look and be healed?

The excellent author from whom we have just quoted again says, " Allow me to illustrate the meaning of the term *preach,* as used by our Lord, by an occurrence of which I was an eye witness. It so chanced that at the close of the last war with Great Britain, I was temporarily a resident of the city of New York. The prospects of the nation were shrouded in gloom. We had been for two or three years at war with the mightiest nation on earth, and, as she had now concluded a peace with the continent of Europe, we were obliged to cope with her single-handed. Our harbors were blockaded. Communication coastwise, between our ports, was cut off. Our ships were rotting in every creek and cove where they could find a place of security. Our immense annual products were moulding in our warehouses. The sources of profitable labor were dried up. Our currency was reduced to irredeemable paper. The extreme portions of our country were becoming hostile to each other, and the differences of political opinion were imbittering the peace of every household. The credit of the government was exhausted. No one could predict when the contest would terminate, or discover the means by which it could much longer be protracted.

" It happened that on Saturday afternoon, in February, a ship was discovered in the offing, which was supposed to be a cartel, bringing home our Commissioners at Ghent from their unsuccessful mission. The sun had set gloomily before any intelligence from the vessel had reached the city. Expectation became painfully intense, as the hours of darkness drew on. At length a boat reached the wharf, announcing the fact that a treaty of peace had been signed, and was waiting for nothing but the action of our government to become a law. The men on whose ears these words first fell, rushed in breathless haste into the city, to repeat them to their friends, shouting, as they ran through the streets, Peace! peace! peace! Every one who heard the sound repeated it. From house to house, from street to street, the news spread with electric rapidity. The whole city was in commotion. Men bearing lighted torches were flying to and fro, shouting, like madmen, Peace! peace! peace! When the rapture had partially subsided, one idea occupied every mind. But few men slept that night. In groups they were gathered in the streets and by the fireside, beguiling the hours of midnight by reminding each other that the agony of war was over, and that a worn-out and distracted country was about to enter again upon its wonted career of prosperity.

" Thus, every one becoming a herald, the news soon reached every man, woman, and child in the city, and, in this sense, the city was evangelized. All this, you see, was reasonable and proper. But when Jehovah has

offered to our world a treaty of peace, when men
doomed to hell may be raised to seats at the right hand
of God, why is not a similar zeal displayed in proclaiming the good news? Why are men perishing all
around us, and no one has ever personally offered to
them salvation through a crucified Redeemer?"

We have been informed, that the ladies were in no
wise less earnest in their activities on that memorable
night, than their more hardy friends of the other sex
in heralding the news of peace.

One of the most eminent Bible expositors who has
adorned this or any other age, in his comment on Joel,
ii. 26, says, " Your sons and daughters shall prophesy
— shall preach, exhort, pray, and instruct, so as to benefit the church." If the reader object to this interpretation, we will present the definition given by the Holy
Spirit through the apostle Paul, (1 Cor. xiv. 3 :) " He
that prophesieth speaketh unto men to edification, exhortation, and comfort." " That prophecy means, in
the New Testament, the gift of exhorting, preaching,
or expounding the Scriptures, is evident from many
places in the Gospels, Acts, and Paul's Epistles."

Rev. J. Benson, the commentator, says, " The gift of
prophecy was bestowed upon some women under the Old
Testament, as upon Miriam, (Exod. xv. 20,) upon Deborah, (Judges iv. 14,) and Huldah, (2 Kings xxii. 14.)
But this gift was more frequently conferred on the
female sex in the times of the New Testament. Thus
we read of the four daughters of Philip the evangelist
who prophesied. (Acts xxi. 9.) Rev. Dr. A. Clarke

says, "If Philip's daughters were prophetesses, why not teachers?" Says Barnes, in his Notes, (1 Cor. xi 15,) "But every woman that prayeth or prophesieth." In the Old Testament prophetesses are not unfrequently mentioned. So also in the New Testament Anna is mentioned as a prophetess. (Luke ii. 36.) That there were females in the early Christian church who corresponded to those known among the Jews, in some measure as endowed with the inspiration of the Holy Ghost, cannot be doubted. That they prayed is clear; and that they publicly expounded the will of God is apparent. Also see note on Acts ii. 17. It would seem, however, that females shared in the remarkable influences of the Holy Spirit. Philip the evangelist had four daughters which did prophesy. (Acts xxi.) It is probable also that the females of the church of Corinth partook of this gift.

Says the author of a work entitled "Scripture Doctrine," &c., (1 Cor. xi. 5,) "But every woman that prayeth or prophesieth with her head uncovered," &c. The apostle has joined praying and prophesying together; and as praying in a public assembly — for of such he was treating — is universally allowed to be a part, and, indeed, a very prominent part, of the ministerial office, and women did exercise this part of the ministerial function in being the mouth of the people to God, here we have a presumptive proof, that prophesying means preaching, and, we think, a demonstration that the speaking in the church, which the apostle reproves in women, must be wholly confined to asking ques-

4 *

tions, (whispering or chattering ;) otherwise it would
be a prohibition against their praying as well as preach‧
ing.   For how could women pray in public if it was a
shame for them to speak in the church, in the sense
wherein it is frequently understood?   The apostle,
when he uses the word " prophecy," precisely fixes
its meaning, (1 Cor. xiv. 3–5 :) " He that prophesieth
speaketh unto men to edification, exhortation, and comfort ; " (ver. 4,) " He that prophesieth edifieth the
church ; " (ver. 31,) " For ye may all prophesy, one
by one, (that is, all who were qualified for, and called
to the ministry,) that all may learn, and all may be
comforted."   All may learn from those who prophesied ; and women did prophesy ; therefore women
were teachers by whom the church was exhorted, edified, and comforted.

In this common acceptation we frequently find the word
prophesy in the Old and New Testament.   Thus, (Ne-
hemiah vi. 7,) it is said, " Thou hast appointed prophets to preach."   Hence prophets were preachers, and
to prophesy is to preach.   Gen. xx. 7, where the Lord
saith of Abraham to Abimelech, " He is a prophet, and
will pray for you."   Here it seems to signify a man
well acquainted with the Supreme Being, capable of
teaching others in divine things, and especially a man
of prayer.   Exod. vii. 1, 2, " Aaron thy brother shall
be thy prophet ; that is, shall speak unto Pharaoh."
Acts xv. 32, " Judas and Silas, being prophets, exhorted the brethren with many words."   Luke ii. 38,
" Anna, the prophetess, coming into the temple, gave

thanks unto the Lord, and spake of him [Christ] to *all* them who looked for redemption in Israel." Luke i. 67, " Zacharias prophesied, saying, Blessed be the Lord God of Israel, who hath visited and redeemed his people." Our blessed Lord styles John the Baptist a prophet, (Luke vii. 26 ;) and Zacharias, the father of John, speaking of him by the Spirit of the Lord, calls him a prophet of the highest, (Luke i. 76 ;) that is, a teacher, commissioned by the Lord himself, to instruct the inhabitants of Judea in the things which related to the manifestation of the Messiah and his kingdom ; (also 1 Cor. xiv. 25.) In most of these places prophesying has no other meaning than preaching ; and among the preachers we have a female.

Besides, should it be granted that prophesying means foretelling things to come, an insurmountable difficulty yet remains ; for if it was unlawful for women, who had that gift, to speak in the church, how were they to communicate what was revealed to them ?

The simple fact seems to be, that though prophesying sometimes means predicting, or foretelling future events, it means preaching in the common acceptation of the word ; and whenever it is used in the former sense, it includes the publishing these predictions to those concerned. Hence, under the law, such persons were styled *nabi*, (prophets,) from *ba*, which signifies to come and to go, because of their coming and going between God and the people. So under the gospel dispensation they are called prophets, from *pro* and *phemi*, *dico*, I speak or utter forth, because ministers are the

Lord's messengers, to publish his word of reconciliation
to the people.   But, whatever be the meaning of praying and prophesying as it respects the man, it has precisely the same meaning as it respects the woman.
Therefore some women, as well as some men, might
speak to others to edification, exhortation, and comfort.
This kind of prophesying or teaching was predicted by
Joel, ii. 28, and referred to by Peter, Acts ii. 17.   Had
there not been such gifts bestowed on women, the
prophecy could not have been fulfilled.   The only difference marked by the apostle was, the man had his head
uncovered because he was the representative of Christ ;
the woman had hers covered because she was placed by
the order of God in a state of subjection to the man.
It was also customary amongst the Greeks and Romans,
but amongst the Jews it was an express law, that no
woman should be seen abroad without a veil.   This was
and is a common custom through all the East.   A
modest woman never appeared in public without a veil.
Should she do so, she would dishonor her head, that is,
her husband ; for all who did not thus recognize the
custom of the time were regarded as disposed to be
faithless in the marriage covenant.

Says Rev. Joseph Sutcliff, in a letter to Miss Drury,
" I am fully persuaded that St. Paul's arguments against
the praying and prophesying of women in public are
founded on the custom of the Oriental nations — not
to admit mixed companies of men and women on any
occasion, excepting only among their own kindred ;
consequently, so far as European manners deviate from

the Oriental, the force of these arguments are inapplicable to us."

What would be thought of a Christian minister of the present day who would strenuously enforce as a scriptural requisition that every female member of his charge should adhere to the custom of coming to the house of the Lord veiled or muffled, as enjoined by the apostle Paul, 1 Cor. xi. 4–16 ? Yet there would be far more consistency in enforcing a scrupulous adherence to this custom, which has become obsolete except in Eastern heathen countries, than in enforcing the doctrine that women shall not pray or prophesy in religious assemblies. "Judge ye yourselves, is it comely that a woman pray unto God *uncovered ?* " — that is, unveiled. But it seems not to have entered into the apostle's conceptions that the daughters of the Lord would not obey the impellings of their Spirit-baptized souls, and pray and speak as the Spirit gave utterance. That they would do so he anticipates as a matter of course, and therefore suggests the manner in which they shall be attired in the performance of the duty.

But why do not ministers of the present day enforce as a scriptural doctrine this ancient practice of covering the head in public assemblies, as now practised in Eastern heathen countries? Because the dictates of common sense tell them that it was merely an enjoinment of temporary expediency suggested by the then prevailing custom, and can have no bearing on the present day. But, while justly no account whatever is made of the apostle's admonition in regard to the veiling of the head, another subject, standing in vital connection with the spiritual interest of thousands, is overlooked. Overlooked, did we say? Nay, far worse than this : by the identical passages where Paul so evidently infers that Christian women were expected to obey the constrainings of the divinity within them, and pray or prophesy as the Spirit gave utterance — by these same passages those who would restrain the Spirit's utterances justify their resistance.

Hundreds of ministers in the present day are standing in an attitude of open resistance to the use of the gift of prophecy in women. Let a female member of their charge attempt to open her lips in prayer or in speaking of the revelations of infinite grace to her soul, though all the former indices of her Christian life may have been as marked for pious consistency and eminent devotedness as that of the late Mrs. President Edwards, or the most eminent for piety of this or any other age, her character for religious propriety would be sacrificed. She would at once be branded as a fanatic, and regarded as a subject of public animadversion and church discipline.

Acts xviii. 26. "Whom when Aquila and Priscilla had heard, (Apollos,) they took him unto them, and expounded unto him the way of God more perfectly." "This eloquent man, and mighty in the Scriptures, who was a public teacher, was not ashamed to be indebted to the instructions of a Christian woman in matters that not only concerned his own salvation, but also the work of the ministry in which he was engaged." So says Dr. Adam Clarke.

1 Cor. xiv. 34. "Let your women keep silence," &c. The apostle had been treating of the gift of tongues, and of persons prophesying one after another. It is evident in these public assemblies there were people of different nations, as on the day of Pentecost, and that one minister had the gift of one tongue, and a second of another, in the same diversity as they had the other miraculous gifts. That they all had not a universal knowledge of all languages is clear from the apostle Paul's words, (1 Cor. xiv. 18,) "I speak with tongues more than ye all." How reasonable it is, then, to conclude that there were a few inquisitive women in the assembly, who, not understanding what was said, but prompted by curiosity, perhaps by a better motive, might ask questions, to the interruption of the speaker and the auditory! Therefore the apostle gives this admonition: "Let your women [*that is, wives*] keep silence, and, if they will learn any thing, let them ask their husbands at home;" which clearly shows that the prohibition was not a general one, and that it must be confined to asking questions; at least, the silence here enjoined was never intended to prohibit those pious females from instructing and comforting the Corinthian Church, to whom he had before given directions respecting their adorning while thus employed; for what has women prophesying to do with asking questions, wanting information, and asking husbands at home? There were at Corinth, it appears, some married women who were frequently asking bold, impertinent questions, occasioning debates, contention, and confusion. Let

such women keep silence, and ask their husbands at home ; for it is a shame for such women to speak in church.

1 Tim. ii. 12. " But I suffer not a woman to teach," &c. Rev. Dr. Taft says, " I think the passage ought to be read thus : ' I suffer not a woman to teach by usurping authority over the man.' Most persons opposed to the praying or prophesying of females understand from this passage that no woman is to teach, and that all teaching by women is usurping authority over the man. But this grants too much, inasmuch as it involves the following difficulties : No woman is to keep a school. No woman is to teach her children to sew, or cook, or read, or write, &c. No woman is to write books ; for this is one excellent method of teaching. No woman is to pray in public ; for praying is one method of conveying instruction upon doctrinal, experimental, and practical religion. No woman is to prophesy, even supposing the term applies only to foretelling future events. While that knowledge lies hid in their own mind, there is no teaching ; but, if God commands them to prophesy aloud, and they obey him, by this they teach to others that knowledge which before lay hid in their own breasts.

" If it be objected to this that the teaching here forbidden means only that they are not to teach the science of religion, still all the difficulties remain, except the two first ; for the things belonging to religion may be taught by the pen as well as by the mouth, on our knees as well as in any other position.

A female expounding the word to a teacher.   Wresting the Scriptures.

" But the teaching here forbidden only means face to face, — but I ask, Is not this taking too great liberties with the text ? — St. Paul does not say that this is the only kind of teaching which he forbids ; but, supposing it was, then the apostle contradicts himself. That he admits and encourages this kind of teaching is plain from 1 Cor. xi. 4 ; for, in whatever sense we understand prophecy, it must of necessity imply teaching. Again, the sense of the text, as objected, is contradicted in Acts xviii. 26." Priscilla, a female, expounded the word to Apollos. The doctor says, " I defy any man to split that hair, and prove that expounding is not teaching. But all these difficulties will be removed by understanding the passage thus : ' I suffer not a woman to teach by usurping authority over the man.' And pray, who does ? I have not heard of any such usurpation in the church."

What serious errors in faith and practice have resulted from taking isolated passages dissevered from their proper connections to sustain a favorite theory ! It is thus that the Universalist would have all men unconditionally saved, inasmuch as the Bible says, " Christ is the Saviour of all men," disconnected with the fact that Christ is only the *special* Saviour of them that believe. The Antinomian may gather his faith from the Bible, inasmuch as the Bible says that " men are saved by faith, and not by works." And the evil doer may take the Bible as a plea for his evil doings, inasmuch as it is said in the Bible, " Let us do evil that good may come." And on the same principle has

5

the passage, " Let your women keep silence in the churches," been wrested from its explanatory connections, and made subservient to the egregious and most harmful error of withstanding the utterances of the Holy Spirit from the lips of women, and thereby averting the attention of the Christian world from an endowment of power ordained by God as a speciality of the last days. And permit us here to say that we are constrained to believe that this is one among the more prominent innovations of the " man of sin " — yes, a relic of Popery, which, before the brightness of Christ's appearing, must be openly abrogated.

The scriptural way of arriving at right Bible conclusions is by comparing scripture with scripture. And had this scriptural mode of interpretation been observed in regard to this subject, a distinguishing characteristic of the last days had not been disregarded, and an endowment of power withheld from the church, which might have resulted in the salvation of thousands.

Yet that serious errors might occur from the misapprehension of the Scriptures, the apostle Peter foresaw ; and of this he forewarned the brethren in his General Epistle to the churches. Some had, even in that infant state of the church, wrested the writings of Paul to the destruction of right principles, and doubtless made his doctrines contradictory, as many have done in regard to the subject before us. It was therefor Peter, in referring to the writings of Paul, said to his brethren, " Even as our beloved brother Paul also, according to the wisdom given to him, hath written unto you ; as also in all his Epistles, speaking in them of these things, in which are some things hard to be understood, which they that are unlearned and unstable wrest, as they do the other scriptures, to their own destruction." (See 2 Peter iii. 15, 16.)

God has, in all ages of the church, called a few of his handmaids to eminent publicity and usefulness; and when the residue of the Spirit is poured out, and the millennium glory ushered in, the prophecy of Joel ii. 28, 29, being fully accomplished in all its glory, then probably there will be such a sweet blending into one spirit, the spirit of faith, of love, and of a sound mind, such a willingness to receive profit by any instrument, such a spirit of humility, in honor preferring one another, that the wonder will then be, that the exertions of pious females to bring souls to Christ should ever have been opposed or obstructed. May the Lord hasten the time!

> " But what is truth ? 'Twas Pilate's question, put
> To Truth itself, that deigned him no reply.
> And wherefore ? Will not God impart his light
> To them who ask it ? Freely ; — 'tis his joy,
> His glory, and his nature, to impart.
> But to the proud, uncandid, insincere,
> Or negligent inquirer, not a spark."

CHAPTER V.

"One of the results of God's great work which is now going on in the world will be to raise and perfect woman's position and character. The darkest page in human history is that of the treatment of woman. But when, in the progress of divine truth, it is understood that man cannot fulfil his own destiny, and is not the completion of himself without her, — in other words, when by being restored to God he is restored to himself, — he will also be restored to that which is a part of himself, and will thus perfect, in completed unity, what would otherwise remain in the imperfection of an undeveloped and partial nature."   REV. DR. UPHAM.

HAS not the exercise of the gift of prophecy been used to profit by women of every age?

We have already referred to many women, who in the apostolic age used this gift to the edification of the church. We might refer to others, particularly to Phebe, the *servant of the church*, or *deaconess*, as the Greek word signifies, of the *church at Cenchrea*. Deaconesses were ordained to the office by the imposition of the hands of the bishop. Theodoret says, "The fame of Phebe was spread throughout the world, and she was known, not only to the Greeks and Romans, but also to the Barbarians;" which implies that she had travelled much, and propagated the gospel in foreign countries. "It is reasonable to suppose, in view of her being a succorer of many," says Rev. Mr. Benson, "that this acknowledged servant of the church was a person of considerable wealth and influence, or we may suppose the appellation 'servant of the church' was given her on account of the offices she performed as a deaconess." Says another able divine in his comment on this subject, "There were deaconesses in the primitive church, and it is evident that they were ordained to this office by the imposition of the hands of the bishop, and the form of prayer used on the occasion is still extant in the apostolic constitution. And this order was continued for several centuries in the church, *until the reign of the man of sin* commenced."

Not only the community who, under God, took its rise from Wesley, but many of the earnestly pious of all denominations, seem now disposed to recognize Wesley as having been greatly instrumental, under God, in the revival of primitive Christianity. To those acquainted with the history of the church, at the time this great reformer was raised up, we need not say that the reception of the full baptism of the Holy Ghost was but faintly, if at all, recognized as the privilege of the believer. But as soon as this primitive flame again revived, just so soon was this gift of power, anciently promised as a speciality of the last days, newly recognized. What a host of "laborers together in the gospel" were quickly raised up. And who, that has read the correspondence and journal of this great and good man, but has marked his special recognition and appreciation of this endowment of power. Not more appreciatively did an ancient apostle regard "those women that labored with him in the gospel," than did this modern apostle and his coadjutors, especially the eminent and devoted Fletcher, the Vicar of Madeley.

It is true, that some of the respected denomination

5 *

that bear his name may not, in modern days, be fully, in this regard, answerable to the practices of the Founder, and fathers in the ministry. Yet there is still in the usages of this denomination much that demands consideration. In most places woman is encouraged to use the gift of prophecy intrusted to her, so far as to testify of the dealings of God with her soul. Various social meetings are held, in which the female disciple is expected to take a part, such as the love feast and the weekly class meeting. In the days of the Founder of Methodism, women were appointed to take the lead of female classes. The whole membership being divided into classes, and punctuality, as far as health and circumstances will admit, in attendance on class meeting being a test of membership, this devolves a large amount of most important labor upon the pious women of the church, peculiarly adapted to their sphere.

The wisdom of this ordainment in Methodism cannot but be strikingly obvious to all who have considered it; and that it should have grown so generally into disuse with this sect in America is regarded by many as a singular and unaccountable departure from their primitive simplicity. British Wesleyans, we understand, still abide by the old landmarks in this respect, and a large share of the spiritual culture of the female portion of the membership of this body devolve on females. What an auxiliary to the pastorate is this! And what faithful minister of any denomination but would be greatly relieved in his pastoral labors, if he might have nursing mothers, who may thus ever have a constant affectionate supervision over such a large portion of his flock! We have within our reach Mr. Wesley's correspondence and journal, and one would be surprised, in glancing over it, to observe the frequent and appreciatory allusions made to his female helpers.

A recognition of the full baptism of the Holy Ghost, as a grace to be experienced and enjoyed in the present life, was the distinguishing doctrine of Methodism. And who can doubt but it was this speciality that again brought out a host of Spirit-baptized laborers, as in the apostolic days? And the satisfaction with which this apostolic man recognized and encouraged the use of this endowment of power is every where observable throughout his writings. Says one, "Mr. Wesley pressed into the service of religion all the useful gifts he could influence." He well knew that in the ratio in which the devoted female, or any other instrumentalities, were calculated to be useful, to just that degree would the grand adversary raise up opposing agencies to withstand.

To his friend Miss Briggs he writes, "*Undoubtedly* both you and Philothea, and my dear Miss Perronet, are now more particularly called to speak for God. In so doing, you must expect to meet with many things which are not pleasing to flesh and blood. But all is well. So much more will you be conformed to the death of Christ. Go on in his name and in the power of his might. Suffer and conquer all things." (See Wesley's Works, vol. vii. p. 103.) Again, "I am glad that sister Crosby has been at Beverly, and that you

56 PROMISE OF THE FATHER.

Wesley's helpers in the gospel. Secret of success. Dr. Chalmers's opinion.

had an opportunity of hearing her. She is useful wherever she goes, particularly in exciting believers to go on to holiness," (vol. vii. p. 46.) Mr. Wesley expressed great joy on hearing of her success in various places, and constantly encouraged her efforts. Vol. iv. pp. 448, 449, he says, " No society in the country grows so fast as this, either in grace or numbers. The chief instrument in this glorious work is Miss Perronet, a burning and shining light." In vol. iv. p. 653, he gives his views of his much esteemed friend, Mrs. Fletcher, an eminently holy and useful woman, who had been largely endued with the gift of prophecy, and whose praise was in all the churches, as one richly blessed with the gift of utterance, to proclaim the saving power of Christ to others. Here he also speaks of another pious female, whom he sets forth as one of the most useful class leaders he had ever known. One who had not been favored with advantages for extemporaneous speaking as some others, he still encourages to labor, as the necessities of the case might require: he says, " You may read to them the notes on any chapter before you speak a few words, or read them one of the most awakening sermons, as other women have done long ago." To some of these female laborers we may refer more particularly in the subsequent pages of our work. It was said by the late Dr. Chalmers, as illustrative of the great success of the early members of this denomination, that " they were all at it, and always at it." And may we not conclude, that the enlistment of this gift of power had something to do with the extraordinary influence which attended the early ministrations of this people?

Mr. Wesley, who, as it is well known, was a minister of the Church of England, was at first disposed, as most ministers of the Established Church, to oppose any thing that might seem like an innovation on the ordinary usages of that church. But he had himself diligently sought for and obtained the baptism of the Holy Ghost. Through the fervor of his ministrations, the Pentecostal flame began to diffuse, and as men and women of the laity caught the flame, they also began to speak, as the Spirit gave utterance, as in apostolic days. Mr. W. was absent from London when these ministrations of the laity commenced; but the thing being new and unlooked for, he immediately, on hearing of it, hastened up to London, with a resolve to put a stop to what he considered to be a glaring irregularity. He conversed with his mother on the subject, who was herself a distinguished member of the Established Church, as were her ancestors, and told her his intention. The name of a layman, who was among the first to transgress in prophesying, as did Eldad and Medad in the camp of Israel, was then brought forward. Said Mrs. Wesley, "You know what my sentiments have been. You cannot suspect me of favoring readily any thing of this kind. But take care what you do with respect to that young man, for he is as surely called of God to preach as you are." This kept him from a hasty execution of his purpose; and it being found, upon inquiry, that good was done, the practice was suffered to continue.

The conversion of sinners by the preaching of any person, whether male or female, was a strong proof, in Mr. Wesley's judgment, of a divine call to the great and important work; this will appear from his most excellent sermon on Mark ix. 38, 39. It was, no doubt, from a conviction of the success attending the efforts of his mother, Mrs. S. Wesley, to promote the spiritual advantage of the inhabitants of Epworth, that caused him to say, " that even she, as well as her father and grandfather, her husband and three sons, had been, in her measure, a preacher of righteousness."

The fact was this : When Mr. Wesley's father was from home, Mrs. W. used to read sermons and pray with the people, in the vicarage house at Epworth, on the Sunday evenings, to as many as the room would contain ; sometimes there were two hundred present on these occasions, and much good was done. Of this admirable lady the learned Dr. Adam Clarke says, " She had a strong and vigorous mind, and an undaunted courage. She feared no difficulty, and, in search of truth, at once looked the most formidable objections full in the face ; and never hesitated to give an enemy all the vantage ground he could gain, when she rose up to defend either the doctrine or precepts of the religion of the Bible. She was not only graceful, but beautiful in person. As a Christian she was modest, humble, and pious. Her religion was as rational as it was scriptural and profound. In forming her creed she dug deep, and laid her foundation upon a rock, and the storms and adversities of life never

shook it. Her faith carried her through life, and it
was unimpaired in death. She was a tender mother, a
wise and invaluable friend. If it were not unusual to
apply such an epithet to a woman, I should not hesitate
to say, she *was an able divine.*"

Over a century has rolled away, and still we may
thankfully record that this ancient flame, though not
cherished as it might have been, has not died out, either
among the people called Wesleyans, who began to date
their rise, as a denomination, from about this point, or
from the Established Church of England, from whose
altar, under God, Wesley first caught the living flame.
We have already given an item illustrative of the fact
that this ancient flame is yet alive in the Church of
England ; and still not only her sons, but her daughters of the laity, are disposed, as in the days of Wesley,
and as the mother of Wesley, to act upon the principle, that " there is neither Jew nor Greek, there is
neither bond nor free, there is neither male nor female ;
for ye are all one in Christ Jesus." We have referred
to Mrs. Wesley's endeavors to promote the spiritual
advantage of the inhabitants of Epworth, and, though
a century has intervened, how similar are the efforts of
a Christian lady of the Church of England, to whom
we have referred in a former chapter, at the present day
residing at Beckenham, England.

And how does this lady, who, a talented reviewer
of her own denomination tells us, is a lady of great
dignity and modesty of character, and one who, in fact,
is shrinking from all that is ultra and well-grounded

by her sense of propriety against trespassing beyond the bounds which define the lady and place woman in her true position, how do we see this Christian lady fulfilling the duties of her position?

Why, much, doubtless, as either one of the affectionate Marys would have done, had they, after being baptized with the Spirit, been placed in similar circumstances with herself. Hundreds of common working men, such as heard the Saviour gladly, came to reside in the neighborhood. She says, " I felt anxious to meet these men for the purpose of imparting instruction on Sabbath evenings, and twice in the week, especially as I found, on inquiry, that few, if any of them, at that time, ever seemed to think of entering any place of worship."

And how did she carry out her truly Christian purpose? We are told cottage readings were thus established, and have been the means of much good. The meetings held on Sunday, Monday, and Friday evenings, conducted by this lady, are opened with singing, then extempore prayer, then a chapter of the Bible is read, then an extempore address from a verse or a passage of Scripture, then singing and prayer. Testaments are distributed to new-comers who have none, and tracts and cards, containing short and appropriate prayers, are ready for circulation ; kind and encouraging words are spoken to each of those who come forward after the meeting, or linger at the door or on the roadside, to converse with their friend and benefactress.

How well it is for this lady, and the cause which she represents, that there is no one to rise in the midst and betray their circumscribed knowledge of Scripture truth by the exclamation, " What does Paul say about women's preaching?" or that she is not being called before a church inquisition to answer for her temerity in presuming to open her lips before men. Yet a case somewhat similar to this we have ourselves witnessed.

Says her reviewer, " Her efforts to make Bible Christians of those who come under her instruction are much to be admired. If first impressions upon the minds of inquirers after truth influence their whole subsequent life and fix their eternal destiny, how important is it to take them directly to the fountain head, and not stop at any of the broken cisterns of human invention so often met with, and around which so many gather! There are, alas! two ways of reading the sacred volume. One is to study it in a prayerful, teachable spirit, with a desire to learn what God would have us do ; the other is to take it up in self-righteousness, and so distort it as to make it suit our prejudiced, and, very often, most unscriptural views ; hence the various and diversified opinions regarding its teachings."

Some Christian friends have remarked Miss M. " must be a wonderful woman." Wonderful, because consistent! Is it not melancholy that consistency in professing Christians is so unusual as to be a wonder? She makes no more nor louder professions, nor are her vows different from those of professing Christians generally. All are alike under the same obligations and pledges, and she has not gone one jot or one tittle beyond hers. At what a *fearful* distance, then, many followers of the Saviour must be from their God, if they be " followers " at all! She but lives " as one should live who has been washed in the blood of Jesus Christ ; " and all professors deny their profession in proportion as their lives differ from hers.

Says the reviewer of Miss M., " In prayer we have the secret of her success." And under what circumstances do we see this all-powerful gift of prayer brought into exercise ? Not only in the closet and in the social circle, with the physically and spiritually diseased, but she also lifts up her voice in extemporary prayer in the presence of her congregation, numbering, as we have been informed occasionally, from three to four hundred. Now, is it not sad to think that there are hundreds of Christian ministers, who, if they could speak out, would withstand not only this Christian lady, but any and every other lady who would thus assume the responsibility of opening her mouth in prayer in the presence of men.

Not only has the gift of prophecy, as poured out upon woman in fulfilment of the promise of the Father been withstood, but with equal tenacity has the right to open her lips in prayer been contested. We have sometimes thought if one gift of usefulness above another had been intrusted to woman, it is her gift in prayer. Added to the winning tenderness of her nature, when in union with the heart of Infinite Love, how melting and subduing are the tones of her voice in its influences as it falls upon the ear of hardy men!

We were well acquainted with an infidel lawyer, who, for literary ability, and in his profession, had distinguished himself as one among a thousand of his professional brethren. This gentleman was first aroused to a consideration of his eternal interests by incidentally hearing the affecting tones of a female voice upraised to God in prayer. That voice proceeded from the midst of a religious assembly. His predilections were such as not to dispose him to enter the place of prayer; but those tones fell upon his spirit's ear as he stood a listener without. It was here that his heart was softened by the subduing power of grace; and the arrow of the Almighty rankled in his bosom until that arrow was extracted by the hand of the heavenly Healer, and his spirit made whole.

But are there not scores of church assemblies all over the land, where, if the voice of woman should occasionally be heard with one accord, in supplication with her brethren, as on the day of Pentecost, would fain hush that voice, as though it were wrong that the lips of a female should be opened in giving utterance to the constrainings of the Spirit in the presence of her brethren? Surely this thing, if wrong, is *fearfully* wrong. Has not a gift of power delegated to the church been kept out of use? And if the neglect of this gift has been through the *traditions* of men, rather than the oracles of God, is it not greatly important that ministers of the sanctuary should hasten to rectify

the wrong, and on this important subject give the
trumpet a certain sound? We do not wonder that
the reviewer of Miss M. should say, " In prayer we
have the secret of her success. She took every soul
with her to the throne of grace." To use her own
words, " The shortest way to any heart is round by
heaven ; so I went to God to open the door."

Do we not see, in this consistent Christian lady, only
about what we might infer would be far more general,
if the gift of prophecy, as bestowed upon the daughters of the Lord Almighty, had not been neglected.
Has not the Christian church the world over, in all the
scattered and various divisions, neglected a speciality of
the last days, which, if properly recognized and brought
into use, might have resulted in the salvation of tens
of thousands of unsaved sinners ?

We copy some of the above dottings from an article
in the Young Men's Magazine. The reviewer is a
member of the Protestant Episcopal Church, and, to
be consistent with himself as such, cannot be disposed
to favor unauthorized innovations or unseemly manifestations of religious zeal. In closing his review of
" English Hearts and English Hands " he says, " No
lady can read this book attentively without being convinced that her sex exercises an *influence far greater
than ours.*"

Corroborative of the preceding views in relation to
the far-reaching influence of woman, is the testimony
of Sir Richard Otley. This gentleman was chairman
of a missionary meeting held at Colombo, March 26,

1824. The name of Mrs. M. Smith, of the Cape of Good Hope, being brought before the meeting, the distinguished chairman said, "The name of Mrs. Smith has been justly celebrated by the religious world, and in the colony of the Cape of Good Hope. I heard a missionary of talents state, that wherever he went in that colony, at six hundred or a thousand miles from the principal seat of government among the natives of Africa, and wherever he saw persons converted to Christianity, the name of Mrs. Smith was always hailed as the person from whom they received their religious impressions. And although no less than ten missionaries, all men of piety and industry, were stationed in that settlement, the exertions of Mrs. Smith alone were more efficacious, and had been attended with greater success, than the labors of those missionaries combined together. . . . After such an example in heroism and magnanimity," says Sir Richard, "what may we not expect from affording women an enlightened education, and *calling into action* the virtues which they are capable of displaying when justice is done them, and when they are made to support that station in society which they are capable of adorning!" The Rev. I. Campbell, missionary to Africa, in a letter to the editor of the Evangelical Magazine, says, "For many years past Mrs. Smith took the lead in most of the plans for doing good in that country; for she possessed the happy art of setting all her friends to work in one way or other. Her fluency, the seriousness of her address, and the earnestness of her manner, when recommending plans of usefulness, generally prevailed. So extensive were the good effects of her pious exhortations that on my first visit to the colony, wherever I met with persons of evangelical piety, I generally found that their first impressions of religion were ascribed to Mrs. Smith."

In the Society of Friends, the gift of prophecy, as dispensed to women, is openly recognized. Many among their most acceptable ministers are women. Says Mr. J. J. Gurney, widely known in Europe and America as one of their most devoted and learned ministers, in behalf of his people, " We believe that we must not limit the Holy One of Israel, or oppose to the counsels of infinite wisdom our own fallible determinations. We dare not say to the pious, modest female, 'Thou shalt not declare the word of the Lord,' when we believe that from an infinitely higher authority there is issued a directly opposite injunction — 'Thou shalt go to all that I shall send thee, and whatsoever I command thee thou shalt speak.' Now that women are often led to proclaim the word of the Lord among us ; that it is laid upon them as an indispensable duty ; that they are from time to time constrained, under the influence of the Holy Spirit, to rise up in our meetings for worship, in order to instruct, exhort, convince, and console, or to kneel down and address the Most High, as the organs of the assembly ; and further, that their services of this description are frequently accompanied with life and power, and greatly tend to the edification of their hearers, — are facts, the truth of which long experience

PROMISE OF THE FATHER. 67

Nothing astonishing or novel in the ministry of women.   Isaiah's wife.

has taught us, and which no persons who are acquainted intimately with our society will be disposed to deny. Nor is there any thing astonishing or novel in this particular direction of the Holy Spirit. Nothing astonishing, because there is no respect of persons with God. The soul of the woman, in his sight, is as the soul of the man ; and both are alike susceptible of the extraordinary as well as the general influences of the Spirit. Nothing novel, because in the sacred records of antiquity there are found numerous examples of women, as well as of men, who were impelled to speak to others on matters of religion, by the direct and immediate visitations of the Holy Ghost.

"It was doubtless under such an influence that Miriam responded to the songs of Moses; that Deborah uttered her psalm of triumph; that Hannah poured forth in the temple her acceptable thanksgivings ; that Huldah prophesied to King Josiah and his officers ; that the aged Anna spake of Christ to all them that looked for redemption in Israel ; that Elisabeth addressed the mother of our Lord, and that Mary sang praises to her God and Saviour. Of the individuals here mentioned, Miriam, Deborah, and Huldah are expressly called prophetesses. The wife of Isaiah was a prophetess. We read also of *false* prophetesses — a circumstance which clearly indicates that there were *true* prophetesses, who were the objects of their imitation, and from whom they were distinguished." (Ezek. xiii. 17.)

If we might judge of the prevailing sentiments and usages of most Christian denominations at the present

day, it might be inferred that the manifestations of the
Spirit were more limited now than before the ushering
in of the last days, of which Joel spoke, which was to
be signalized by the pouring out of the Spirit alike
upon God's daughters as upon his sons.   Surely there
must be some mistake somewhere.

Christian ministers, of every name and order, we ask
you, in the name of thousands of your Christian sisters,
upon whom God has poured out his Spirit, and who, in
the social, prayer, and conference circle, would fain
open their lips for God, will you not take this matter
with you, as you enter into the inner sanctuary of the
divine presence ?   Will you not, in prayerful waiting
before the Head of the church, and in the light of the
Holy Scriptures, investigate the subject, in view of
bringing out a speedy answer, which may bear the light
of eternity, and which, when reviewed in the day of
reckoning, will meet your responsibilities ?   Have you
trained the male and female members of your flock to
right views on this subject, befitting the dispensation of
power under which they live ?   Do you urge not only
your male members to the indispensable duty of looking for the full baptism of the Holy Ghost, but also
your female members to look for this present endowment of power, resolved that when, in answer to their
united supplication, the Spirit is poured out upon the
sons and daughters of the Lord Almighty, you will not
restrain the utterances of the Spirit, though its manifestations may contradict all your former sentiments on
this subject ?

CHAPTER VI.

"But I venture to assert that, in the moral progress of mankind, woman has been God's most efficient agent, the co-worker with his providence in those remarkable events which have changed the fate of nations, brought light out of darkness, and given impulse and direction to the souls of men, when these sought to advance the cause of righteousness." AUTHOR OF DISTINGUISHED WOMEN.

E cannot resist the conviction that the restraining of the gift of prophecy, as given to woman in fulfilment of the promise of the Father, involves far greater responsibilities than has been, or perhaps may be, apprehended. We should wonder if restive influences, whose tendencies would be to dissuade the mind from an avowed recognition of the doctrines of this work, should not come pressing upon the reader; but, if so, let the source from whence these restive feelings emanate be carefully noted. The subject of which we treat stands in vital connection with the salvation of thousands; and, if so, may we not anticipate, that he whose ceaseless aim it is to withstand the work of human salvation in every variety of form, will, as an angel of light, withstand the reception of truth on this subject?

Again we repeat that it is our most solemn conviction that the use of a gift of power, delegated to the church as a speciality of the last days has been neglected.— a gift which, if properly recognized, would have hastened the latter-day glory. We believe that tens of thousands more of the redeemed family, would

have been won over to the world's Redeemer, if it had
not been for the tardiness of the church in acknowledging this gift. We believe it is through the workings
of the Man of Sin, whose aim it is to withstand the
upbuilding of Christ's kingdom on earth, that this
deception has been accomplished. We believe that he
who quoted Scripture to our Saviour has in all deceiva-
bleness quoted Scripture to pious men — men who
would not wickedly wrest the Scriptures to their own
destruction, but who, from a failure in not regarding the
scriptural mode of interpretation, by comparing scripture
with scripture, have unwittingly followed the traditions
of men, and have thereby been guilty of the egregious
error of making the inspired teachings appear contradictory, and of withstanding the workings of the Holy
Spirit in accordance with those teachings, in the hearts
of thousands of the daughters of the Lord Almighty.

We believe that the attitude of the church in relation
to this matter is most grievous in the sight of her Lord,
who has purchased the whole human family unto himself, and would fain have every possible agency employed
in preaching the gospel to every creature. That He
whose name is Faithful and True has fulfilled his ancient promise, and poured out his Spirit as truly upon
his daughters as upon his sons, has been demonstrated
in a manner so extraordinary that we have actually hesitated in giving many of the facts which we have on
hand. But why hesitate? Cannot God take care of
his own work? So we conclude. Surely it was not
necessary for Uzzah to steady the ark. We shall there-

fore proceed to lay before the reader instances in confirmation of the fact that God as truly pours out the spirit of prophecy on his daughters now as on the day of Pentecost.

We will introduce to the reader Mrs. Mary Taft, formerly Miss Mary Barritt, the talented lady of the Rev. Dr. Taft, author of Memoirs of Eminently Holy Women. We have before us the Diary of this extraordinary woman. If the criterion by which we may judge of a divine call to proclaim salvation be by the proportion of fruit gathered, then to the commission of Mrs. Taft is appended the divine signature, to a degree preëminently unmistakable. In reviewing her Diary, we are constrained to believe that not one minister in five hundred could produce so many seals to their ministry. And not only from her own recordings do we learn of her eminent success, but from various other sources. We were in company, since we commenced the preparation of this volume, with an eminent minister, formerly a resident of England, who was well acquainted with this extraordinary servant of the church ; and he informs us that, of those who had been brought to Christ through her ministrations, over two hundred entered the ministry.

From her journal we find, in her visits from place to place, that many hundreds were won over from the ranks of sin to the service of the Saviour through the persuasive power of the Spirit's utterances as they fell from her lips. She seldom opened her mouth in public assemblies, either in prayer or speaking, but the Holy

Spirit accompanied her words as they fell upon the ears of the people, in such a wonderful manner that sinners were convicted, and, as in apostolic times, were constrained to cry out, from the disquietude of their souls, " Men and brethren, what must we do to be saved ? " Some may be disposed to question, and speak of the scenes we may portray as unwarrantably exciting ; and in like manner, or somewhat similar, may we conceive, will guilty sinners again be alarmed, or, in other words, excited, when the light of the Spirit, unhindered by human interventions, shall dart upon the mind, and all in whose hands God has put a two-edged sword, shall be permitted to wield it under the Spirit's dictation.

We will give some passages from the Memoirs of Mrs. T. And let the reader mark these recordings closely, and ask himself whether we might not hope for a return of the success of apostolic days if there might be a return to the simplicity of the principles of Christianity as in the days of its infancy, when every possible agency was earnestly recognized and employed which might be subservient towards meeting the spirit of the command, " Preach the gospel to every creature."

Mrs. T. was powerfully converted to God when about thirteen years of age. Speaking of several weeks' painful conviction previous to her conversion, she observes, " My sorrow was so great that it drank up my spirits, and my mother remarked to many that during this period she never saw a smile on my countenance." After her translation from the kingdom of darkness into the kingdom of God's dear Son, her joy was great ;

and she longed to spread far and near the fame of Jesus' saving power. At this early age, she says, " I felt much concern for the happiness of my neighbors, and took every opportunity of talking to and praying with them. I saw clearly that poor sinners were exposed to the most tremendous danger through sin, and felt particularly desirous of preventing their ruin ; hence I took every opportunity of inviting them to hear the word of God preached, and felt very thankful when the preacher spoke to the consciences of the people, and faithfully warned them of their danger, while he directed the mourners in Zion to the wounds of a crucified Saviour, and pointed them to ' the Lamb of God that taketh away the sin of the world,' and endeavored to build up believers ' in their most holy faith.'

" Wherever these were wanting, I conceived the end of preaching to be lost, and felt much pain to sit under such discourses, however fine or eloquent, insomuch that I frequently wept, when under the word, to see the people careless, inattentive, and unconcerned, or to hear the preacher use expressions, or speak in a style, which I knew the people could not understand. I kept wishing and praying, as I went to hear sermons, that God would come with his servant, that he would give him purity of intention, a single eye to his glory, and enable him to preach a present and free salvation ; that he might preach ' repentance towards God, faith in our Lord Jesus Christ, and also holiness, without which no man shall see the Lord ;' and that he would do it in plain Scripture language, that the people might all understand. I wished the way to heaven to be made as plain from the pulpit as it was in the Scriptures, that a wayfaring man, though a fool as touching human knowledge or scholastic learning, might not err therein.

"I not only attended all the means of grace, and began to exhort the people from house to house, and many times with tears told them the danger they were in, and exhorted them to flee from the wrath to come, but I began to pray in the prayer meetings. The first time was one Sabbath evening. After several had sung and prayed, one of the class leaders called upon me to pray. I did so ; and the Spirit of the Lord came upon me in an extraordinary manner, so that I entered upon the spirit of my duty, not of praying merely, but of exhortation. I faithfully warned sinners of their danger, and exhorted penitents to come to God through Christ. I continued from this time to assist in the prayer meetings, and very frequently gave a word of exhortation from a verse of a hymn, from any providential occurrence in the neighborhood, or from what came immediately from above, just as the Spirit of the Lord led me.

"Several persons came to me at my father's house, to inform me of the good they had received in the meetings I had attended ; and numbers came to invite me to different places to pray with the sick, to talk with others about their souls, and to hold public meetings, so that I had frequently to go two, three, or four miles, with a few friends, in the evening, to attend to these requests.

"About this time I suffered from a quarter I did not

expect. The superintendent preacher, Mr. C., told some friends that, unless I immediately gave over exhorting and praying in meetings, the next time he came he would put me out of the society. The cause of his speaking thus was as follows : Christopher Lister, a local preacher, was appointed to preach at Gisborn, a village in the Colne circuit ; and I had to hold a meeting at Rimmington, two miles distant, at the same time. The day following Mr. Lister went to Mr. Collins, and told him he went to Gisborn, but had no congregation, except some old women and children, all having gone after the female preacher, adding, ' If you don't stop her, I shall give up my place.' Mr. C. replied, ' I will stop her the next time I am in Colne.' But to the honor of this good man, Mr. Lister, be it spoken, that, when he saw the arm of the Lord made bare, and sinners brought to God in every direction, he declared to some friends that he should ever think it an honor to sit behind me when speaking, in order to snuff the candles for me ; and he continued in this mind to the day of his death.

" When I heard that I was to be turned out of the society for praying, and exhorting sinners to turn to Christ, I felt it exceedingly. I counted the cost, but concluded to obey God rather than man. I valued the having my name among God's people, but I thought more highly of its being enrolled in the book of life ; and I believed, if I did not occupy the talent God had given me, he would blot it out of his book. Therefore I durst not desist, and with a degree of painful anxiety

76   PROMISE OF THE FATHER.

Providential interposition.   Mr. H.'s prejudice against woman's speaking.

waited my expulsion ; but before the preacher came in
his regular turn, he was ordered from his circuit for
immorality of conduct, and he has since come to an
untimely end.   Here I saw the providential interposition of my heavenly Father, and I fully believed he
would stand by me through life.

" Soon after this another preacher came to my father's
to desire I would give over speaking and praying in public, to which I replied, ' I will, if you will answer for
me at the day of judgment for the one talent God hath
given me ; ' but he went away saying, ' That I cannot do.'

" Some time before this, when reading the Scriptures,
I have seen such light in them as I had never done
before.   While the Lord, by his Spirit, hath immediately said, ' You must speak from that,' I have risen
up, thrown down the book, and have thought, ' I will
not look at it again for a month.'   O, the astonishing
.mercy and long forbearance of God, to bear with my
unfaithfulness !   I did not now, nor ever have since, wondered much at the conduct of Jonah.   Notwithstanding, I was still much prejudiced against women's speaking, not understanding the Scriptures, or the custom of
the Oriental nations in not admitting of mixed companies ; yet I durst not forbear altogether, though I
many times attempted to run from the presence of the
Lord, or to shun the work he had assigned me.

" When Mr. L. Harrison first came into the Colne
circuit, his prejudice against women's speaking was very
strong, and he spoke quite freely against it at several

places. My mother thought it best to have a little friendly conversation with him. For this purpose she went to the chapel house where he lived, and, among other things, asked him how he understood that passage of Scripture, 'Help those women that labored with me in the gospel.' He replied, 'My wife helps me when she sweeps the house, makes the bed, mends my clothes, &c.' She replied, 'Mr. H., is that the gospel? Then I have done with you, if that be your gospel.'

" Soon after this we had a love-feast at Colne, in which I spoke at large my religious experience, and my whole mind relative to what I had suffered on account of my call to speak and act for God. Such an unction rested upon me, and such a divine influence accompanied what was said, that nearly the whole congregation were in tears. Mr. W. Sagar went to Mr. H., and said, ' It is at the peril of your soul that you meddle with Mary Barritt. God is with her ; fruit is appearing wherever she goes.' From this time Mr. H. became my firm friend and advocate ; and afterwards, when he travelled in the Bradford and Redford circuits, he sent for me, and prepared my way to the utmost of his ability.

" After this, that dear woman, Ann Cutler, now in glory, came to our house, and asked me if I thought I had any business at home ; to which I abruptly said, ' I think I have none any where else, excepting on Sabbath days.' The reason of this was, the Sabbath day preceding I had walked to Ackrington, a distance of ten or twelve miles, and arrived there about nine o'clock, and found a large congregation waiting for me, to whom I spoke with much freedom and power, after which Ann Cutler broke out in prayer. We had a day never to be forgotten. The people assembled again at one. I spoke, and afterwards Ann Cutler spoke : we continued till five. Several were liberated, and others went away in distress. We began again at seven, and continued till midnight. The arm of the Lord was made bare, numbers were wounded and healed. The glory of God was in the midst.

"Rev. Mr. Thomas Shaw accompanied me to Garragill, a place in my brother's circuit. On our way we had many blessed seasons at several places, where we stopped and held meetings : Barnard Castle was one of them, where much good was done. He delivered me to the care of John Walton, a very pious man and useful local preacher. We had several powerful meetings before we left Garragill : many were awakened, and several saved, especially on the Sabbath day. On Monday we arrived at Hexham, where my brother received us gladly, and the more because he would have Mr. Walton to preach for him that night, who said he had no objection, provided he would let his sister go with him into the desk to speak after he had done. My brother hesitated, for he had never heard me himself : he said I might go into the singing pew, and speak and pray there. Mr. W. preached in a most powerful manner, after which he requested me to address the people, which I did. While I was engaged, the Holy Ghost descended in an extraordinary manner, insomuch that the whole congregation were in tears. He gave out for me to speak at five in the morning, when we had a large congregation, and much good was done.

"At Hexham, and in the circuit, the Lord was with me : many souls were brought into liberty. We had a good time at Braistywood; but a more glorious work broke out in Dallogill : in one night, thirty-six souls found peace with God. It was very late when I went to rest, and had not retired more than one hour before I was called up to pray with the distressed, who had gone part of the way home, but had returned, their agony of soul being so great that they could not proceed.

"After speaking at Greenhow Hill one Sunday morning, many cried out for mercy, during which I was suddenly moved by the Spirit of the Lord to look up, when upon the hay loft I saw several young men leaning upon the beam, particularly one who was laughing. Immediately I was powerfully moved by God to pray aloud, in the following words, three times : 'O God, bring down that laughing sinner!' when, suddenly, his face gathered paleness, and in an instant he fell down among the people, cried aloud for mercy, and continued in such distress that he could neither eat, drink, work, nor sleep, till Tuesday morning, when he followed us to Pately Bridge Chapel, where the Lord graciously spoke peace to his soul, and soon after called him to preach the gospel.

" Went to Whitby on Thursday, where I labored at night: we had a good season. A young woman cried out for mercy. The people seemed affrighted ; but the Lord vindicated his own cause. Four or five obtained pardon that night, eight or ten the next night, still more the following evening, and on the Sabbath very many more. On Tuesday we had a very powerful time. It was estimated that over one hundred were liberated in one week. After this, the Lord abundantly blessed the labors of good Messrs. Brown and Vasey, insomuch that there were three hundred added the first quarter, and in the next quarter two hundred more."

About this time she received a letter from the Rev. Mr. Fenwick, from which we will give an extract.

"God himself has sent you, like the great Wesley and the great Whitefield, namely, as a blessing to the nation. Nevertheless, you will have great need of the faith of Abraham, the resolution of a Joshua, the meekness of a Moses, the strength of a Samson, the patience of a Job, the head of a Solomon, the zeal of King David, the love of St. John, the determination of St. Paul. My prayer is, that God may put on you his whole armor, causing you to comprehend, with all saints, what is the length, breadth, depth, and height of the love of Christ, which passeth knowledge, and to be filled with all the fulness of God. Remember not a few eyes are upon you, some for good, but not all. Let Christ be your all and in all ; and in one word, let him be your finished example. I remain your everlasting friend, brother, and servant to command, in the peaceable gospel of the Son of God."

" Felbeck, near Pately. Here I spoke twice. There were many who cried for mercy, and afterwards found liberty through the blood of the Lamb. While here, about four o'clock in the morning, our room door was suddenly opened, and Mrs. Weatherhead and Mrs. Malthouse, and, soon after, several others, came in, crying aloud for mercy. Mrs. James Rydal, a most pious and useful woman, and very active in our prayer meetings, was with me. We continued praying with the penitents till six o'clock, when several of them found peace with God, and rejoiced exceedingly.

" From thence, in company with a number of friends, we went to Minskip. We spent a very profitable afternoon in conversation and prayer. At intervals I prayed much that the Lord would show me what he would have me speak from that evening. Mr. Malthouse had sent through the village and to Borough Bridge to inform the inhabitants that I would speak that night at seven. The evening was fine and clear — scarce a cloud could be seen on the sky. A large concourse of people had assembled. We began with singing and prayer. I then read the hymn commencing, —

> ' He comes! he comes! the Judge severe;
> The seventh trumpet speaks him near.'

On coming to the lines, —

> ' His lightnings flash, his thunders roll —
> How welcome to the faithful soul!' —

instantly a flash of lightning blazed through the place, and then followed a peal of thunder that shook the whole building. Immediately numbers cried out for mercy, as if the last day was come. The vivid lightning and thunder continued the whole night. Numbers were awakened that evening, and many found peace with God.

"My next journey was to York. I travelled round the circuit more than once, and God was with us of a truth. At Wighill the Lord wrought a glorious work: a large number of souls were saved, both old and young, rich and poor. On the Sabbath a magistrate, together with a clergyman of the Church of England, came to hear me, purposing to put a stop to our proceedings, in case they found it to be true, what they had heard about disorderly meetings. What they thought and felt while I was speaking I know not; but in the midst of the service, a mob being outside of the door, making a noise, the magistrate sent a message to this effect — that if they did not quietly disperse, or cease from disturbing the congregation, he would have them taken up, and committed to prison.

"A letter received about this time from the eminently devoted Bramwell says, 'Your way is open. Numbers receive the power. O, go on as your strength will permit, and the Lord Jesus be with you. I have some serious reflections that your time will be short, and I think shorter than mine. You do more work in less time, consequently will sooner fulfil your task. If I did more for God, I might go with you. Amen. I am still convinced that the Lord would have us feel and labor like Paul, and leave all *annoyances* in his hands.

Numbers will never be saved without great efforts in the instruments. But, O, how mysterious is this! notwithstanding, let us pluck them as brands from the burning, to draw to God the next generation.'

"Some time after this, I went to Leeds, at the earnest request of the Rev. Mr. Mather, now in glory. The Lord was with us; many were awakened and brought to God. One forenoon the power of God came down among us of a truth; souls were crying out for mercy in eight or ten different places in the chapel. The friends believed there might be fifteen or twenty brought into liberty. Mr. Mather was filled with the power of God, and said he would vindicate such a meeting as that, at the Market Cross, if he was called to it. Glory be to God. Several that were brought to the Lord at this time have since been useful laborers in the vineyard of Christ.

"My brother brought his family to Colne, and I supplied his place on the Whitehaven circuit. The arm of the Lord was made bare in a wonderful manner, so that when he came back there were one hundred and eleven added to the society, and several more afterwards. At one village in the circuit, there were three clergymen of the Church of England came to hear, the eldest of whom sat in the chair before me while I spoke, and said Amen heartily. Another of them had been a persecutor of the Methodists in that part, but said afterwards to one of our friends, that if what he heard was the Methodists' doctrine he was sorry for what he had said, and hoped no one should hear him speak against them for the future.   My brother met me at Brampton. I had a most glorious time at Cockermouth; many were awakened and brought to God, especially a young man, who is now in the travelling ministry.

"At Stockton much good was done; five, if not more, were brought into the liberty of the children of God, three of whom became preachers of the gospel.   I then accompanied Rev. Mr. Vasey to Whitby, and the Lord was with us; we saw souls saved every night for a considerable time, and for several mornings in succession some obtained the blessing of entire sanctification.   God was with us of a truth.   One night one of our friends was going through Church Street, between ten and eleven o'clock, and heard the people at prayer in almost every house.   On Sabbath evening two found the Lord to save from the guilt of sin; but on Monday night the power of God came down like unto a mighty rushing wind; eight or ten found the love of God, and some backsliders were healed.

"Soon after this I rode to Buxton, and spoke from Daniel v. 27, 'Thou art weighed in the balances, and found wanting.'   The chapel was crowded to excess; both rich and poor, all appeared eager to hear the word.   Among the number was a Peer of the realm, who had a star on his breast.   He was very attentive, and the cries and distress of the people were very great: we continued till near midnight.   This season I can never forget; my soul was filled with the fulness of God; there was indeed a shaking among the dry bones; several were saved; and some time after, I received a letter, informing me that more than twenty had joined the society, who had received good at that time. All glory to God and the Lamb!

"At Mansfield I labored in the Calvinistic Chapel, with liberty and power. The reason of my speaking in this chapel was, it was much larger than ours, but it was far too small to contain all the people. The dissenting minister freely gave me his pulpit, expressing his satisfaction afterwards to our friends. The Lord reward him. Many wept, and some were blessed. Glory be to God, souls are turning to him in this place.

"Went to Macclesfield, having been invited by the Rev. Mr. Marsden, Mr. Heywood, and others. We had some gracious times in the country villages, especially at Lower Ease Chapel. I could speak from no passage but this — 'Come and see.' The chapel was crowded, and as I spoke, the power of God descended, so that many wept much, and in the prayer meeting many cried out for the disquietude of their souls. As I was describing the human heart, a course of sin, and the burning lake, many attended to the invitation, and were enabled to 'come and see' a sight they never saw before, namely, their own sinful and wicked hearts; others were enabled to believe in Jesus as exhibited upon the pole of the gospel, and were set at glorious liberty."

Of the Rev. Mr. Pawson, who was about that time President of the Wesleyan Conference, she says, "We arrived at Mr. Wade's, of Sturton. Here, for the first time, I met that venerable man of God, Mr. John Paw-

8

son.   On my entering the room he rose up, and turning to Mr. Wade, said, 'Now, sir, you can dispense with my labors, since Miss B. has come; I will return to Leeds.'   Mr. W. stopped him short, saying, 'Miss Barritt is come, and I am glad to see her; but it is your appointment, and I insist upon your keeping your place;' upon which he sat down.   Soon after Mr. W. began to make inquiries relative to the great work in Nottingham.   I related some particulars which had come under my own notice.   Mr. Pawson listened, and soon tears began to steal down his venerable face.

"After tea prayer was proposed, and Mr. Pawson said, 'Miss B. will pray with us.'   I did so, and felt my heart much enlarged and blessed.   Mr. P. prayed afterwards, and we had a good season.   His prejudice against woman's speaking melted away as snow before the midday sun, and from this time he became my firm advocate and friend.   He preached to us that evening with the Holy Ghost sent down from heaven.   Next morning he took Mr. W. aside, and insisted upon a promise that he would bring me to Thorner, to meet him in a month's time, to which arrangement I consented.   According to appointment, I met this aged and venerable servant of God, and spoke for him; he being present, we had a good time.   In the afternoon several souls were savingly brought to God; in the evening meeting, also, some received good to their souls, and were enabled to rejoice in God their Saviour.

"On Sabbath morning I spoke at South Kelseÿ, and the power of God was present of a truth; it was a time of general conviction; the most hardened were led to tremble with Felix, under the mighty power of God, and several cried aloud for mercy, yea, roared out by reason of the disquietude of their souls; some obtained pardon, and several a sense of sanctification by faith in that blood which cleanseth from all sin. I never was witness to a more glorious work, considering the number of people."

And here we must close our review of the labors of this daughter of the Lord Almighty. What we have given from her journals present but a limited view of a long life spent in labors abundant. These recordings, of nearly two hundred pages, are every where interspersed with such amazing scenes of pentecostal power, so similar to those we have here condensed and presented to the reader, that we have found it difficult to make our selections. And as our eye has glanced over the account of hundreds saved, we have wondered at the slowness of men's hearts in believing the things that are written, and in observing the signs of the times, and our hearts have in holy anticipation said, O that there were some noble, unflinching spirit of the present time, as in the age of Justin Martyr, who, in contending for the truth with Trypho the Jew, maintained that the latter days were indeed come, specifying as his argument "that both women and men were seen among them who had the gifts of the Spirit of God, according as Joel the prophet had foretold; for by this expression, Manassah Ben Israel tells us, all their wise men understood the times of Messias."

Though Mrs. T., in the prosecution of her work, had so many glorious conquests, she had also many crucifying conflicts. It is enough for the disciple that he be as his Master, and the servant as his Lord; but every one that is perfect shall be as his Master. If it was for envy that the Master was delivered, it is not surprising that one who, by her usefulness, through the power of the Spirit which rested upon her in such an eminent degree, should have brought multitudes together, and thus attracted the attention of the populace, to the neglect of some public teachers, who perhaps were less intent on securing the agency of the Spirit to give efficiency to their labors.

But though Mrs. T. was not left to pursue her victorious course without feeling that she was withstood, and too often were these restive influences from sources where she would fain have looked for sympathy, yet there were not a few of the more noble minded both among the ministry and laity who were rejoiced to witness the honor that the Lord had conferred on this daughter of heaven, in that she had been made so abundantly successful in winning souls to Christ. It is thus we see an eminent minister, who had been called to the highest post of honor within the gift of the church to which Mrs. T. belonged, earnest in enlisting her services. We see occasionally, among her auditory, a Peer of the realm, magistrates, and other persons of rank. We see clergymen of various denominations, and one of these, (of the Established Church of England, with his clerk,) who, though despoiled of his congregation by the engrossing desire of the people to hear the gospel proclaimed from the persuasive lips of this modern Mary, leaving his deserted church, not to warn his people against this infringement on ordinary church usage, but to hear for himself, and encourage, by his presence, any instrumentality which God might employ in winning men from sin to holiness. We see also that her correspondents were from among the most useful and honored ministers in the denomination to which she was attached.

But it is not unusual for sons in the gospel to grow far wiser than the more eminent fathers upon whose labors they have entered. It was thus in the days of the devoted Pawson, Mather, Blackborne, Vasey, Marsden, Bramwell, &c. And it is only thus that it may be apologized for, that the devoted Mrs. T. was not on one occasion recognized as a fellow-helper with her husband, the Rev. Dr. Taft. By way of advising or reproving some gainsayers under circumstances of this description, the Rev. Mr. Pawson writes, —

"It is but too well known that religion has been for some considerable time at a very low ebb in Dover. I therefore could not help thinking that it was a kind providence that Mrs. Taft was stationed among you, and that by the blessing of God she might be the instrument of reviving the blessed work of God among you. Perhaps there never was a time when the Lord so greatly condescended to the curiosity of mankind, in order to do them good, as at the present. He has been pleased to raise up and send forth all sorts of instruments. Men almost of all descriptions — poor men, rich men, learned and unlearned; and if he is pleased to send by a woman also, who shall say unto him, ' What doest thou?'

" As to myself, I have long thought it more difficult to prove that women ought not to preach than many imagine. Let any one seriously consider, (1 Cor. xi. 5,) ' prophesieth with her head covered.' Now, prophesying there has generally been understood to mean preaching. If, then, the women never did preach at all, why did the Lord, by the apostle, give these instructions respecting their heads being covered or uncovered? I seriously believe Mrs. Taft to be a deeply pious, prudent, modest woman. I believe the Lord hath owned and blessed her labors very much, and many, yea, very many souls have been brought to the saving knowledge of God by her preaching. Many have come to hear her out of curiosity, who would not have come to hear a man, and have been awakened and converted to God. I do assure you there is much fruit of her labors in many parts of our connection. I would, therefore, advise you by no means to oppose her preaching; but let her have full liberty, and try whether the Lord will not make her an instrument of reviving his work among you. I am an old man, and have been long in the work; and I do most seriously believe, that if you do not yourselves hinder it, God will make Mrs. T. the instrument of great good to you. Take care you do not fight against God. Many will come to hear her every where, who will not come to hear your preachers. Let these poor souls have a chance for their lives ; do not you hinder them."

To this letter of advice is added a short note from another minister of honored memory — the Rev. J. S. Pipe. It reads thus : —

" From a long acquaintance with Mrs. Taft, I most heartily unite with our honored father, Mr. Pawson, in beseeching you not to hinder her exercising her talents among you ; for I most assuredly believe that God has called her to declare the glad tidings of salvation to the world, and that he has already honored her in the conversion of *multitudes*."

The estimation in which the labors of Mrs. T. was held by ministers of other denominations than her own, may be gathered from notes similar to the subjoined, which we find interspersed throughout her journal. " Mr. Child, the Calvinist minister, would have me speak in his chapel. He is a most precious man of God. This venerable servant of Christ, as soon as I had done speaking, said, ' The Lord has certainly stepped out of his common way this night, in order to do you good. The truths you have heard, if not properly improved, will surely rise up against you in the last day.' He then begged, in the most tender and affectionate manner, that they would all begin to seek the Lord. This was one of the best seasons of my life. The Lord was very present to many ; some felt his healing influence, and others experienced his cleansing grace."

From the review we have given of Mrs. Taft's labors, we presume none will question but she had received a commission from the Head of the church for the great work in which she had been so abundantly successful. Of many honored ministers of her day, who were her correspondents, and who gratefully availed themselves of her labors, and whose letters to her have been published, we see the names of the Rev. Messrs. Mather, Pawson, Hearnshaw, Blackborne, Marsden, Longden, Vasey, Bramwell, with many more well known as among the more eminent ministers of her time.

As we trace the onward and upward pathway of this devoted daughter of the Lord Almighty, it is inspiring to see her evident increase in holy faith and courage. No faltering marks her career, no misgivings in regard to the divinity of her call, but the yet more confirming assurances of the Holy Spirit that she had been divinely aided and directed in her labors.

In some closing remarks, on one occasion, she says, "In Yorkshire Dales, extending from Ripon to Bainbridge, Reeth, and Richmond, the Lord enabled me to gather the harvest in handfuls, and every where he gave me fruit. I might add many things also with respect to my convictions, views and feelings, and conduct, relative to my public work. Suffice it to say, that the Almighty, in a most extraordinary manner, removed my scruples, answered my objections, and thrust me out into his vineyard. Indeed, nothing but a powerful conviction that God required it at my hand, and that I should lose my *own soul* if I did not endeavor to save the souls of others, could have supported me in it. Added to this, the Lord gave me souls in almost every place, whenever I stood up in his name before the people.   And more especially did he thus encourage me on occasions when almost overwhelmed with the magnitude of the work.   This wonderful condescension and stupendous love of Christ to me, deeply humbles my soul before him.

> ' And shall I slight my Father's love,
>   Or basely fear his gifts to own ?
> Unmindful of his favors prove ?
>   Shall I, the hallowed cross to shun,
> Refuse his righteousness t' impart,
> By hiding it within my heart ?
>
> ' No ; though the ancient dragon rage,
>   And call forth all his hosts to war,
> Though earth's self-righteous sons engage,
>   Them and their god alike I dare ;
> Jesus, the sinner's friend proclaim —
> Jesus, to sinners still the same.' "

And again, as she was about to leave a people among whom she had labored, she says, " I can take this people to record that I am clear of their blood.   I trust I shall ever endeavor, by the grace of God, to keep this in view.   It was not man, nor the praise of man, which induced me to call sinners to repentance.   I never did, and I hope I never shall, pay much regard to their praise or dispraise, to the smiles or frowns of breathing worms, so that God's name may be glorified, sinners saved, and I be clear when God judgeth the world, having finished the work he called me to do."

Though abundant in labors, Mrs. T. was a most devoted wife and affectionate mother.   Few seemed to enjoy the sweet satisfaction of these social relations more than she.   The heart of her husband safely trusted in her; and he was prone to say, "Many daughters have done virtuously, but thou excellest them all." He was ever in perfect sympathy with her in her work, and of this the affectionate heart of Mrs. T. had a most grateful appreciation. From among the last records of her pen before us, we will transcribe an interesting memento corroborative of this. Her husband, with herself, having been invited to the charge of a people in the place of her nativity, she says, "Some of us wept for joy at our first interview, and a few of us agreed to meet statedly at the throne of grace, for God's special blessing upon our appointment and labors. My soul is truly alive to God; blessed be his holy name. My earnest desire and prayer is, that souls may be saved. Truly can I say that this is more to me than any thing else. Were it not for this, none would hear my voice in the house of God. It is not, and never was, because I was willing to be seen and heard that sinners have been called to listen to my voice. It is because I love and pity them, and long that they should be saved. And in trying to save souls, my own soul is watered, and my joy much increased, and, best of all, I feel the approbation of God the Holy Spirit in this. I travail in birth for souls. Lord, give me many souls in every place on this circuit.

> 'I cannot willing be
>   Thy bounty to conceal
> From others, who, like me,
>   Their wants and hunger feel.
> I'll tell them of thy mercy's store,
> And try to send a thousand more.'

Church of England minister and his wife.

"I know my conduct herein has been rendered *vile* in the esteem of some ; this I must leave to the Judge of all : let it be my business to guard against prejudice. Thank God, I feel free now. What a mercy my husband is of the same mind with me, as touching my public work, and he encourages me in it! So was Mr. Fletcher, though a clergyman of the Church of England, with respect to the labors of his good wife ; he never hindered her, or laid any stone of stumbling in her way, but, contrariwise, encouraged her.

"In the midst of all, God hath given me his approving smile, and a blessed consciousness that I was acting under his divine sanction and influence, and, with purity of intention, designing only to promote his glory among men, and the real good of my fellow-creatures. These have been my constant support under powerful temptation, fierce persecution, and severe affliction.

"In addition to this, the Lord has graciously raised me up friends, the remembrance of whose kindness and attention is engraven on my heart in indelible characters ; and he has given me very many living epistles of evangelical truth, 'seen, and read, and known of all men.' Many of these God hath appointed to occupy very important offices in his church, several of whom are travelling preachers, while others are laboring for God, in a more limited sphere, as local preachers. These are my letters of recommendation, written as by the finger of God. These I expect to be my crown of rejoicing in the day of the Lord Jesus."

CHAPTER VII.

"I would the precious time redeem,
And longer live for this alone,
To spend, and to be spent, for them
Who have not yet my Saviour known;
Fully on these my mission prove,
And only breathe, to breathe thy love."

SAYS the Rev. G. Coles, who has recently introduced to the Christian world many veritable
"Heroines," not of those who have distinguished themselves, as Joan of Arc, in the san-
guinary scenes of the battle field, but such as have
shown themselves singularly brave in withstanding sin,
and in fruitful endeavors to establish the peaceful kingdom of Christ on earth, —

"That woman, in her first creation, was inferior to
man in physical strength, is cheerfully admitted; and
in this sense, perhaps, more than in any other, is she to
be regarded as the 'weaker vessel.' But is she inferior
in mental endowment and moral courage, in spiritual
attainment and in holy enterprise? No, indeed; far
from it. What saith the Scripture? What saith reason? Reason would say that that which by universal
consent is esteemed the *better half* cannot be the *worse*.
That which was twice modelled and fashioned by the
Creator, and of course doubly refined, cannot be inferior.
The Holy Book seems to intimate that in those cases
where the trial was a fair one the weaker vessel was

the stronger reasoner. Witness the case of Deborah and Barak, Manoah and his wife, Abigail and David, Huldah and Josiah, the wise woman and Joab.

"Are they, then, inferior in literary capabilities and attainments? Never, where they have had equal opportunities with men. Witness the instances — Hannah More, a Mrs. Somerville, a Mrs. Sigourney, and others, whose works are read, if not with everlasting wonder, yet with perpetual delight. Neither are they inferior in spiritual gifts. Experience shows that many women are equally gifted and more acceptable in their religious exercises in social meetings than their brethren. They may not be as fierce in controversy, but their improvements are often far more edifying whenever they pray or speak in the name of the Lord.

"The supposition that, under the gospel dispensation, women are prohibited from exercising their spiritual gifts, is purely gratuitous, and is completely set aside by the plain declarations of the New Testament. The author of the Acts of the Apostles informs us, (Acts i. 14,) that all the apostles continued with one accord in prayer and supplication with the women. To suppose that the men prayed in the presence of the women, and not the women in the presence of the men, seems to be a far-fetched and overstrained interpretation of the text."

Says another writer, the Rev. H. Woodruff, "Christian women can talk; and it is generally thought that they are more eloquent, winning, and persuasive, in proportion to their educational advantages, than the other sex. But they have not only the gift of utterance ; they have influence to give force to their teaching, and weight to their example.   Dr. Adam Clarke calculates the influence of one woman to be equal to seven men and a half.   If this be true, her responsibilities must be great, and her means of doing good of the most effective and delightful character.   Let it be brought to bear upon the interests of the church, and where it can serve for the *world's salvation.*

"Christian women have souls to save, and their growth in grace is affected by the exercise of their gifts, and in bearing the cross.   Personal interest, and the interest of the church, and the interest of the general cause, all combine, and seem to urge upon our female friends the importance of immediate and efficient action. When the Spirit of God is received into the heart, God will be honored, known, and confessed, in their private and public devotions.   The Spirit of God is 'like fire pent up in the bones; it must accomplish the end whereunto it was sent.'   'In the last days, I will pour out my Spirit upon all flesh; your sons and your daughters shall prophesy.'   They shall teach by example and precept ; their mouth shall be opened ; words of angelic eloquence shall fall from their lips.

• "Our brethren are frequently so entangled with the world, such alliances are formed, and business transactions subject their reputations to censure, and their motives are impugned in such a way, that their means of doing good are often curtailed, and their influence disparaged.   In this respect the female part of the church have the advantage.   Retired from the turmoil

PROMISE OF THE FATHER. 99

How men injure their influence.   Why women love Jesus.

and perplexities of business life, the mind is, or may be, free from the anxiety and distraction of debts, or business competitions, with a reputation and religious influence that have not been scathed and trammelled by exposure to the storms and combative elements of business or political life, they are free to throw their whole souls most effectively into the work of God."

Dr. T. E. Bond, Jr., observes, " that women should love Jesus of Nazareth, and devote themselves to sustain and spread the doctrines of the cross, was a natural consequence of the fact, that, of all the religions of the earth, Christianity was the only one that placed women upon an equality with men. The thing was unheard of; even the Jews had never conceived the true relation of the sexes. Husbands, love your wives as your own flesh. Your obligations to them are as strong and wide reaching as theirs to you. Marriage is a mutual conveyance of right, a mutual abnegation of sovereignty, a mysterious coalescence and intermerging of being. All this was strange, and to most men utterly absurd teaching; to women it was music from heaven, and they responded to it from every faculty of their nature. They were the strength of the early church, as they are the strength of the church to-day. They did more to extend it, to hallow it, and adorn it, and immeasurably less to mutilate and disgrace it, than men did; and to this day the love of Christ glows in their hearts with a steadier and purer power than the harder and coarser nature of man can exhibit."

" I hold it to be a great error," says Rev. Mr. Jobson, " to maintain that woman has no veritable mission in the church. No class of persons has contributed more largely to the Christian ministry, and to the Christian church, than Christian females. Not only Timothy Cecil, John Newton, and the Wesleys, but thousands more, who have been eminent for their usefulness, have acknowledged this. Women were also associated with the apostles with the first scenes of Christianity at Jerusalem ; and we learn from St. Paul's tender salutations and greetings at the end of his Epistles how they continued to be valued for their labors among the saints."

That Christian women have indeed a veritable mission in the church it is our aim to establish. While we would not have it inferred that their mission has been utterly disregarded in some portions of the Christian church, yet in others it has been treated with neglect or contempt, and in not a few wholly withstood. In the future pages of our work, we shall refer to a few of the many instances of this sort which have come under our observation. We shall now proceed to adduce still further testimony that the God of the Scriptures has not forgotten his ancient promise, but that the spirit of prophecy is still being poured out upon the daughters of the Lord. In the mouth of two or three witnesses every word shall be established. We shall therefore continue, throughout the process of our work, to bring forth our witnesses from among those accredited Christian females upon whose head the tongue of fire has fallen. Says Burder, in his History of Pious Women, of the late lamented Mrs. Fletcher, formerly Miss Bosanquet, —

" She was altogether an extraordinary person, endowed with strong understanding, great decision of character and simplicity of mind, heroic zeal, and unbounded benevolence. In the apostolic age she would have been a Priscilla, and have taken her rank among the presbyteresses or female confessors of the primitive church. She had all the spirit of a martyr. Had she been born within the Romish communion, she would probably have been enrolled among the saints of the calendar. The community to which she attached herself alone afforded a sphere suited to the energies of her character, which might otherwise have remained dormant, because, under ordinary circumstances, zeal such as hers is apt to be regarded as the worst of heresies."

This eminent Christian lady was born at Laytonstone, in the county of Essex, England, September, 1739. At five years of age she was powerfully wrought upon by the Holy Spirit, and much concerned to find out the way to heaven. About that time a Methodist servant maid came to live in the family, who knew something about experimental religion, and, finding the sister of Miss Bosanquet under a concern for her soul, talked with her on the subject. The sister related the conversation to Miss Mary. This was made the occasion of a deep and uneffaceable impression on the mind of Mary. How little did this pious servant maid know what she was doing, when she threw this little germ into the impressible soil of lovely childhood ! Could she have imagined that this little germ of grace was destined to grow up to such a plant of renown, whose fragrance and sheltering foliage was destined to be so blessed to the poor and the rich, and whose fruit was to be so precious to the taste of unborn thousands ?

When Miss Bosanquet was between seven and eight years old, according to her own account, she experienced the pardoning love of God. In a letter to Mrs. Taft she says, " When about twelve years old, I used to read and pray with some poor neighbors (before my parents were up) in one of the little cottages near our garden."

When about the age of sixteen, she had a heavy cross to take up. Having been brought up in the gayeties and amusements of fashionable life, when she saw the sinfulness of following and being led by them, she was determined to renounce them altogether ; and, when requested by her father to go to the play, she begged to be left at home, and laid open her whole mind to him on the subject. The result was finally, as may be seen in her Memoirs, written by herself, that she had to leave her father's house, and take lodgings in an obscure street and in unfurnished rooms in the city of London. Before she took that step, she says, " A particular person used to upbraid me with the reflection, ' You will soon find the difference between your father's house and such poking holes as you will live in. There you will not have one inch but the common street ; whereas you have been used to large and fine gardens, in which you much delighted. And how tired you will be of such trash as you will provide, instead of the plentiful provision of his table ! Before you have lived so for six months, I will engage you will wish yourself back again, and your religion out of the way.'" But was it so? Ah, no! Once indeed she was sick, and thought, "If I had some spice boiled in water, and port wine with it, it would help me." But she was unwilling to break in upon that rigid system of economy which she had adopted, and made it a matter of prayer, and was answered almost as by miracle; "for at that very time," she says, "a relation called, and brought me a quantity of spice as a present; and the very next day my father called in his chariot, and brought me a hamper of port wine; neither of them knowing any thing of my wants."

In the years 1761 and 1762, a great revival of religion took place in the Methodist society in London of which she was a member. A *wonderful* outpouring of the Spirit of God was experienced, both by the preachers and the people. At that time "the people of Laytonstone," she says, "were much on my mind. I had both my birth and maintenance from that place, and I could not help thinking I owed something to their souls." The particulars of her removal to that place are related in her Memoirs. There she opened, in her own house, an asylum for the poor and the orphan. To these she devoted her time, her heart, and her fortune. Mr. Wesley often visited her establishment, and speaks of it with admiration. It appeared to him the only perfect specimen of a Christian family he ever saw. Here she spent the prime of her life in acts of heavenly charity. Here she began to exhort, to read and expound the Scriptures.

In 1768 she removed from Laytonstone, and settled in Yorkshire, where she remained till November 12, 1781, when she was married to that eminently holy and useful minister of the gospel, Mr. Fletcher. "A happier union has seldom, if ever, occurred. Two spirits more congenial never met in the pathway of life. Their union was a source of ineffable happiness to themselves, and a blessing to the people among whom they lived." But it was of short duration. By a most inscrutable providence, one of the happiest, holiest, most gifted, and most devoted of Wesley's sons in the gospel, was taken to his final reward in heaven, in the fifty-sixth year of his age, and fourth of his married life. And his widow, one of the holiest and best of women, was left to supply his lack of service in the parish of Madely for thirty years. Perhaps there never was a widow, since the days of St. Paul, more worthy of " double honor" than Mrs. Fletcher ; " well reported of for good works ;" having " brought up children," having " lodged strangers," having " relieved the afflicted," having " followed every good work." Did " Tryphena and Tryphosa labor in the Lord" ? so did Mrs. Fletcher. Did " the beloved Persis labor much in the Lord" ? so did she. " Favor is deceitful, and beauty is vain ; but a woman that feareth the Lord, she shall be praised."

" In her spirit and conduct she manifested much of the power of religion ; unfeigned sincerity, humility, and cheerfulness were conspicuous in her at all times. She had the happy art of adapting her conversation to both rich and poor, and by sound reason, and her winning manners and conduct, she was the blessed instrument of bringing *many* to Jesus Christ.

"Mr. Fletcher, and after his death Mrs. Fletcher, were the principal instruments in building and fitting up several rooms, or small chapels, in the parish of Madely; and in addition of the pulpit in each of those chapels, Mrs. Fletcher had a seat elevated a step or two above the level of the floor. In those enclosed and elevated seats, she exercised her talents in publishing salvation in the name of Christ. In expounding the Scriptures she manifested great wisdom; and what is much better, faithfulness and truth; giving her readers a clear and comprehensive view of the whole counsel of God. Some of her discourses were remarkable for ingenuity and originality. Had she been a woman of feeble mind, or a mere formal professor, she could not have retained her influence and popularity for so many years in the same place; for her congregations were full as large after thirty years' labor as when she first opened her commission among them.

"As a public speaker, Mrs. Fletcher was not only luminous, but truly eloquent; and although her discourses were not strewed with many flowers, they displayed much good sense, and were fraught with the riches of the gospel. Sometimes her style was rather vehement, though she did not overstep the modesty of her nature. At other times it was pathetic, soft, and flowing. She excelled in that property of an orator which can alone supply the place of all the rest — that eloquence which goes directly to the heart.

'Truth from *her* lips prevailed with double sway,
  And they who came to *mock* remained to pray.'

In a word, she was the honored instrument of doing much good ; and the fruit of her labors is now manifest in the lives and tempers of many, who will be the crown of her rejoicing in the day of the Lord Jesus." — *Hodson's Funeral Sermon.*

Says the Rev. Henry Moore, editor of her Memoirs, " In truth, her preaching was but an enlargement of her daily and hourly conversation. Her family, her visitors, might be said to be her congregation. And as she never, in her more public efforts, meddled with the government of the church, usurped authority over the man, or made any display of a regular authoritative commission, but merely strove to win souls by pureness, by knowledge, by long suffering, by kindness, by the Holy Ghost, by love unfeigned, by the word of truth, by the power of God, while she was herself the servant of all, may not every pious Churchman and Methodist say, ' Would to God all the Lord's people were such prophets and prophetesses' ? "

To those of the Wesleyan faith, who are disposed not to sympathize with the exercise of this gift of prophecy in woman, permit us to say, that an unwillingness to recognize, or to call into use, this endowment from on high, should certainly be unlooked for from this portion of the sacramental host of God's elect. Mr. Wesley, as a minister of the Established Church of England, was slow to admit any thing, however specious, that might seem to be a departure from the usages of that honored church. It was therefore that he would at once have put a stop to the preaching of *laymen,* and he regarded all as laymen who had not received *Episcopal ordination.*

He was not in London when his first lay preacher began to extemporize, and on hearing it, in his zeal for his church, he hastened home, and would quickly have put a stop to it, had not his mother, who was also a strong Church woman, interfered. With true motherly and Christian dignity she bids her son beware, and said, "I charge you before God, take care what you do, for that man is as truly called of God to preach the gospel as ever you were." He was thus kept from a hasty execution of his purpose; and if he had not been thus withheld, what may we conjecture would have been the state of the great Wesleyan body to-day? May we not rather ask, Would there have been any distinct body bearing the Wesleyan name? and thousands among the most successful preachers, who have ever proclaimed the everlasting gospel of the Son of God, would never have been permitted to enter the field?

It was on the same principle that Mr. Wesley at first hesitated in recognizing female laborers; but when he saw that the divine unction attending their ministrations proved the divinity of their mission, he was satisfied that God had not only called laymen, but laywomen, to proclaim salvation through Christ. It was thus that this apostle of modern days was led to acknowledge that the Lord had indeed, in fulfilment of his ancient promise, poured out his Spirit upon his daughters alike as upon his sons.

His views on this point may be found in his correspondence with several of his female helpers who labored much in the Lord.   Mr. Wesley was free to acknowledge that the whole work of God denominated Methodism was something out of the common order. In writing to his friend, the devoted Mrs. Fletcher, he says, " It is plain to me that the work of God termed Methodism, is an extraordinary dispensation of his providence.   Therefore I do not wonder if several things occur therein which do not fall under the ordinary rules of discipline."

Mrs. Fletcher, as we observe in the preceding pages, felt that the pentecostal flame had fallen on her head, and its consuming influence she felt absorbing her whole being, and constraining her lips to holy utterances.   She felt, doubtless, as divinely assured that He whose name is Faithful and True had, in remembrance of his promise, poured out his spirit of prophecy upon her, as on either of the Marys, or other women, on the day of Pentecost.   She had tarried at Jerusalem, in obedience to the command of her risen Saviour, in order that she might receive the baptism of fire; and now that it had fallen upon her, she felt moved to irrepressible utterances, and in obedience to these impellings of the Spirit, she had opened her lips for God, by way of expounding the Scriptures, in all the things concerning Christ and his glorious kingdom.

And now this heaven-baptized daughter of the Lord writes to this modern apostle concerning this her extraordinary call.   In recognition of this call, Mr. Wesley, in reply, says, " My dear sister, I think the strength of the cause rests here — in *your* having an extraordinary call ; so, I am persuaded, has *every* one of our lay preachers ; otherwise I could not countenance their preaching at all." Thus we see that he who, under God, was the founder of the Wesleyan Church, regarded the divine commission of this daughter of the Lord as *unquestionable* as the call of any one minister in his connection. And it was in accordance with these convictions that this truly apostolic man did not hesitate in giving the right hand of fellowship ; as did the Apostle Paul, to a goodly number of women who labored with him in the gospel. And if Mr. Wesley's sons in the gospel are not affectionately mindful in regarding the validity of the claim of their sisters in Christ, when they would open their lips for God, in obedience to the constrainings of the Spirit, which still continues to be poured out upon the daughters of the Lord, we can only say, to the degree they resist this claim, they refuse to be answerable to the principles of their founder. And in so doing, they also reject the united voice of many of those fathers who have been accounted among the strongest pillars in the great fabric of Methodism.

Says the Rev. Alexander Mather, an honored minister of the Wesleyan Church, in writing to a female disciple, on whose head the tongue of fire had fallen, " Your call is of God ; I would have you go in at every open door, but do not wait till the door is thrown wide open ; go in if it be on the jar."

The Rev. Mr. Bradburn, another of the more eminent ministers of his day, in writing on this subject says, " For my own part, I *durst* not hinder a woman herein, when I clearly discover nothing contrary to genuine piety ; when I discover far greater abilities than I do in very many travelling preachers ; when thousands of good and wise people are for woman's preaching ; and when there is much good done by it wherever they go."

Rev. Dr. Taft says, " The fruit which has followed women's preaching, if not a positive, it is at least a presumptive proof, that those highly useful and laboriour instruments are called of God to publish salvation by Jesus Christ. And that there have been, and now are, such instruments, I assert in the name and fear of God ; and if required, can produce a cloud of signatures and witnesses ; and some of the seals to female ministry are now among the Methodist itinerant ministry, and very many more are acting as local preachers, and others as class leaders among us."   Writing to one of these female laborers, Dr. Taft says, " Multitudes of seals have been given you, and not a few in this place ; your life of public labor is nearly over ; and yet I trust it will still be said of you, as it was of another of your sex, ' that she hath done what she could.'   The encouragement you have had in your work from many eminent ministers of the gospel, must be to you a source of high gratification.   What Messrs. Pawson, Mather, Blackburn, Fenwick, Bramwell, Bradburn, Crook, Shaw, &c., thought of your call, and the manner in which it was fulfilled, their letters do abundantly testify."

CHAPTER VIII.

" And I entreat thee also, true yoke-fellow, help those women which labored with me in the gospel, with Clement also, and with other my fellow-laborers, whose names are in the book of life."

PAUL.

ERHAPS some well-meaning friends will wonder that we should be willing to jeopardize
the reputation of our work by presenting before the fastidious critic facts so extraordinary
and so likely to be repulsed. To such we will say,
that we have not reckoned without our host. We did
not set out to write a popular book : had we commenced our volume in anticipation of this, we should
not have chosen a theme which we so well knew would
be reproving to the formal professor, whether of the
ministry or laity.

Through the grace of our Lord Jesus Christ, we
have long since counted the cost of standing up with
truth, however disreputable its form in the eyes of the
multitude. He who was infinite in perfection, and was
from eternity the adoration of angels, was to the eye
of mortals, when on earth, " a root out of dry ground,
having no form nor comeliness." Though he declared
himself to be the Way, the Truth, and the Life, few
were disposed to follow him as the *Way,* and fewer still
were disposed to identify themselves with him as the
Truth, and in outspoken declaration make the precious
doctrines he taught their own. And though he assured them that the words he spake to them were

spirit and *life*, yet not a few were ashamed of his words. And many are ashamed of them still. The true doctrines of the cross will never be popular.

We are, therefore, aware that we have chosen an unpopular subject — unpopular, because it stands linked with the throne of the Eternal, and which, if rightly apprehended and acknowledged, will result in the mighty overturnings of the kingdom of darkness, and in bringing about the speedy enthronement of Him whose right it is to reign. Can we imagine that a subject which, by an eye of faith, and in the light of Scripture, and reason, promises such achievements for Zion, will be popular with the children of this world, or with world-loving ministers and church members?

It is only with those whose aim it is to elicit truth, and whose unyielding purpose, with the dying Dudley A. Tyng, is to " stand up for Jesus," to whom we can hope to commend successfully the doctrines of this work. We have concluded, though at the risk of not publishing a popular work, to stand up with truth ; and in so doing we have endeavored to ponder well the path of our feet ; and in coming up to our present standpoint, we feel, through grace, that we tread firmly. We trust that we have arrived at Bible conclusions on a subject which we presume will never be popular with an unsanctified ministry or people. The true doctrines of the cross never were, nor will be, popular with world-loving professors.

In presenting before the Christian public, in this the nineteenth century, the remarkable incidents by which a daughter of the Lord, who, in fulfilment of the promise of the Father, had been endued with the spirit of prophecy, was constrained to yield obedience to the impelling power within, we record nothing more wonderful than may every where be met with in the Old and New Testament Scriptures. The God of the Bible still lives. In his holy fear, and in his name, it is our purpose to exhibit, in this volume, his faithfulness in pouring out his Spirit on his daughters and handmaidens. And we think, also, he would have us bring out facts before the members of his household, and more especially before his sons and servants, illustrative of the exceeding wrong of having thus long withstood the gift of prophecy in woman.

And if the Lord of the household, in the wisdom of his councils, has seen fit thus to discipline a daughter of the household, whose restiveness was not so much from an unwillingness on her own part to open her lips in the proclamation of the gospel as from the known restraints she would meet with from others, it is more than reasonable that the wherefore of his councils should appear. Too well did she know the tone of feeling which would prevail on the part of her brethren if she should speak of her convictions of duty in regard to a work in the prosecution of which she knew that most of her brethren of the same household would withstand her. If it was from an enemy that she was to meet these anticipated repulses, it were comparatively a light matter ; but brethren belonging to the same household of faith with herself, she too well knew,

10 *

would be unwilling that she should enter the same field with themselves, and would contest the point of her right so to do.

She well knew that other daughters of the same household had been thus seriously withstood in their work ; that they had been constrained to withdraw themselves from those with whom they would have labored, and had gone to cultivate other portions of the field, and been compelled to estrange themselves from all their early associations in the household of faith.   Can we wonder, then, that the act of committing herself to such a work should be worse than death ?

But it is a *living* sacrifice that God requires.   Death, even though it were, as in the case of one whom we shall introduce, the death of a martyr, will not answer the requirements of the Lord our Redeemer, who would have the entire living being presented a ceaseless sacrifice on his altar.   But how pitiful, before God and man, that a state of things should exist in the Christian church that would make a duty, so evidently ordained of God, as a characteristic of the last days, so crucifying to the female members of the household of faith.   We feel verily ashamed before God and man in contemplation of the state of the Christian church in relation to this singularly important characteristic of the last days.   And we do not wonder that through the exceeding subtlety of the adversary, even good-meaning men should have suffered themselves to assume an attitude which, though not in all cases utterly dissuasive, is far from being helpful in bringing about such a state of sentiment as may consist with the *will* of the Father in behalf of the claims of his daughters.

Mr. Wesley, in his journal, thus introduces the name of one of his female helpers, Miss Sarah Mallet, afterwards Mrs. Boyce : —

" I was strongly importuned by our friends at Long Stratton to give them a sermon. I had heard of a young woman there who had uncommon fits, and of one that lately preached ; but I did not know that it was one and the same person. I found her in the house to which I went, and talked with her at large. I was surprised. *Sarah Mallet*, two or three and twenty years old, is, I think, full as much devoted as *Jane Cooper* was, and of as strong an understanding. Of the following relation, which she gave me, there are numberless witnesses. Some years since it was strongly impressed upon her mind that she ought to call sinners to repentance. This impression she vehemently resisted, believing herself quite unqualified, both by her sin and ignorance, till it was suggested, ' If you do it not willingly, you shall do it, whether you will or no.' She fell into a fit, and, while utterly senseless, thought she was in the preaching house at *Lowestoffe*, where she prayed and preached for nearly an hour to a numerous congregation. She then opened her eyes, and recovered her senses. In a year or two she had eighteen of these fits ; in every one of which she imagined herself to be in one or another congregation. She then cried out, ' Lord, I will obey thee ; I will call sinners to repentance.' She has done so occasionally from that time, and her fits returned no more.

" Perhaps this was intended to satisfy her own mind that God had called her to publish salvation, in the name of Jesus, to perishing sinners, and to incline her to take up that cross which appears to have been more painful to her than death itself ; but also to convince others that *even now* God hath poured out his Spirit upon his handmaids, and upon his daughters, that they may prophesy or preach, in his name, the unsearchable riches of Christ."

The author of Heroines of Methodism, in referring to this case, says, " Probably the experience of this young woman, and the wonderful dealings of the Lord with her, greatly helped to enlarge the views of that great man, Mr. John Wesley, upon the subject of female preaching. It is very evident, from his letters and conduct towards her, that he believed her, as a preacher, to be doing what the Lord required at her hands."

Says Miss M., " At thirteen, I became a member of the Methodist society, and the Lord made known to me what he would have me do. But O, how unfit did I see myself to be ! From that time the word of God was an unsealed book ; it was my companion day and night. My love to God and souls increased. I have been often led to cry out, in the bitterness of my soul, ' O Lord, I am but a child ; I cannot preach thy word.' But the more deeply was it impressed on my mind, ' Woe is me if I preach not the gospel,' till my distress of soul destroyed my body.

" In my twentieth year, the Lord answered my prayer

in a great affliction, and made known to others, as well
as to myself, the work he would have me do, and fitted
me in the furnace for his use. From that time I began
my public work. Mr. Wesley was to me a father and
a faithful friend. The same Lord that opened my
mouth, endued me with power, and gave me courage to
speak his word, has, through his grace, enabled me to
continue to the present day. The Lord has been, and
is now, the comfort and support of my soul in all troubles and trials. I have not, nor do I seek, either ease,
or wealth, or honor, but the glory of God and the good
of souls. And, thank God, I have not run in vain, nor
labored in vain. There are some witnesses in heaven,
and some on earth. When I first began to travel, I
followed Mr. Wesley's counsel, which was, to let the
voice of the people be to me the voice of God, and
where I was sent for to go. To this counsel I have
attended to this day. But the voice of the people was
not the voice of some of the preachers. Mr. Wesley,
however, soon made this easy, by sending me a note
from the conference held at Manchester, 1787, by Mr.
Joseph Harper, who was that year appointed for Nor-
wich. The note was as follows : * ' We give the right
hand of fellowship to Sarah Mallet, and have no objection to her being a preacher in our connection, so long
as she preaches the Methodist doctrine, and attends to
our discipline.' After I was married, I was with my
husband in the preachers' plan for many years. He

* "I have," says Dr. Taft, " the original document in my possession."

was a local preacher thirty-two years, and finished his work and his life well."

Mr. Wesley's letters to Miss Mallet are very characteristic of the good old patriarch of Methodism, brief, terse, pungent, kind. And at the age of eighty-five he writes thus to this extraordinary young woman : —

"I do not wonder you should have trials ; you may expect them from every quarter. You tread daily on dangers, snares, and death ; but they cannot hurt you while your heart cleaves to God. Beware of pride ! Beware of flatterers ! Beware of dejections ! But above all, beware of inordinate affection ! Those who profit by you will be apt to love you more than enough ; and will not this naturally lead you into the same temptation ? Nay, Sally, is not this the case already ? Is your heart filled wholly with God ? Is it clear of idols ? Is he still the sole object of your desire, the treasure and joy of your heart ? Considering your age, sex, and situation, what but omnipotence can keep you in the midst of fire ? You will not take it amiss if I ask you another question : I know that neither your father nor uncle is rich, and in travelling up and down, you will want a little money. Are you not sometimes sraitened ? Only let me know, and you shall not want any thing that is in the power of yours affectionately,

J. WESLEY."

And in this connection we will bring before the reader yet another Spirit-baptized female disciple, who was richly endowed with the spirit of prophecy. She was an honored friend and correspondent of the apostolic Wesley ; and not with a greater zest or with more affectionate entreaty would Paul have said, " Help those women which labored with me in the gospel," than this modern apostle would have enlisted the helpful sympathies of his brethren or sons in the gospel, for the sustainment of his female laborers, such as the devoted and eminently useful Mrs. Crosby, and others of like spirit, introduced in these pages. We will present to the reader a condensed view of the manner in which she was called to engage openly in the work of ministering to the saints, and calling sinners to repentance, and leave the reader to judge whether she had not received a commission from the Head of the church. She says, —

" Once, when I was kneeling down to pray, it was suggested to my soul with much power, ' Ask what thou wilt, and I will do it for thee.' My soul was amazed, and replied, ' Lord, I ask nothing in earth or heaven but perfect holiness ; ' and this I was assured I should receive. Not long after this, as I was praying, my soul was overwhelmed with the power of God ; I seemed to see the Lord Jesus before me, and said, ' Lord, I am ready to follow thee, not only to prison, but to death, if thou wilt give me strength ; ' and he spake these words to my heart : ' *Feed my sheep.*' "

Dr. Taft, in his Biographical Sketches of Eminently Holy Women, says that Mrs. Crosby, of Leeds, was an *itinerant,* yea, a *field preacher ;* that she generally held in the evening, and very frequently in the week days, a public meeting every morning at five o'clock, and also both in the forenoon and afternoon. On the Sabbath she generally went to the parish church, wherever she was, and held her meetings early in the morning, at one o'clock, and in the evening. The venerable Wesley, whom she always calls her father in the gospel, highly approved of her conduct, believing that she was one of those females to whom the Lord had given a dispensation to publish the glad tidings of salvation by Jesus Christ.

When Miss Bosanquet (afterwards Mrs. Fletcher) established a kind of orphan asylum at Laytonstone, in Essex, Mrs. Ryan, Miss Tripp, and Mrs. Crosby were her assistants in this great work of Christian benevolence. These pious females began more fully to enter into the work of the Lord, by holding public meetings for reading, exhortation, and prayer. Many attended, and much good was done. At their first public meeting the Lord was eminently present, and two souls were set at liberty from the guilt and bondage of sin.

After Miss Bosanquet was married to Mr. Fletcher, and she was settled at Madely, Mrs. Crosby continued to exercise her gifts in public, travelling from place to place. She kept a journal at intervals from 1761 to 1802. After her death her manuscripts fell into the hands of her friend Miss Tripp, thence into the possession of Mrs. Mortimer, (formerly Miss Ritchie,) and finally into the custody of Dr. Taft, by whom a considerable portion of them was published.

From an account of her awakening, conversion, and experience, given to Mr. Wesley, we make the following extract : " When I was about fourteen years of age, I began seriously to think I must not live as I had done. Accordingly, I went to church on week days, learned forms of prayer, and did many things for a time, but was always subject to bondage through fear of death, saying in my heart, ' O that I might never die, or that I knew God loved me.' Nevertheless, I found a strong propensity to delight in singing, dancing, playing at cards, and all kinds of diversions ; but this I endeavored to check from the beginning, not because I thought it sinful, but because I found the more I gave way to these things, the more unhappy I became.

" About the age of seventeen, while I was sitting alone, I was struck, as I thought, with *death*, being seized with a cold trembling from head to foot, which increasing, I directly fell on my knees, and prayed the Lord to forgive my sins, and save my soul. All that I knew to be sin was then placed before me, so that I had but little hope of mercy. But, while I laid myself down to die, my strength came to me again, for which I was very thankful, and made great promises to live to God.

" I was near twenty years old when God revealed his Son in my heart ; and now I thought all my sufferings were at an end. I feared neither earth nor hell ; and as to temptation, I scarce knew what it meant. I labored to persuade all with whom I had converse to come to Christ, telling them that there was love, joy, peace, for all that came to him. My soul was happy, and I desired only to live and die for Him who had revealed himself in my heart.

"I often painfully felt the sins of all mankind, as well as my own. For the more conscious I was of the depravity of my own soul, the more was I constrained to say, 'Lord, what havoc have sin and Satan made in the world!' From the love I felt to those I knew to be equally fallen from original righteousness with myself, I often desired to be instrumental in turning them to God, and never had a moment's peace any longer than I endeavored to aim at this wherever I went. One day, while I was sitting at work, the Lord Jesus appeared to the eye of my mind surrounded with glory, while his love overwhelmed me. I said, 'This is the power I have waited for,' and I was

> 'Constrained to cry, by love divine,
> "My God, thou art forever mine!"'

My soul seemed all love, and I desired nothing so much as to lay down my life for others, that they might feel the same. This was about three years and a half after I was justified. I now began to meet with trials from an unexpected quarter; but God had taught me, by this time, to be amazed at nothing but his goodness."

From her journal we give the following extracts: —

"In the evening (at Derby) I expected to meet about thirty persons in class; but, to my great surprise, there came near two hundred. I found an awful, loving sense of the Lord's presence, and was much affected, both in body and mind. I was not sure whether it was right for me to exhort in so public a manner, and yet I saw it impracticable to meet all these people by way of speaking particularly to each individual. I therefore gave out a hymn, and prayed, and told them part of what the Lord had done for myself, persuading them to flee from all sin.

" We had a lively prayer meeting at five, a good band meeting at ten, and another at two ; at five Mrs. C. walked with me to Beeston ; at seven the house was full of people, and they obliged me to get into their little desk. I had great liberty in speaking, and felt my Lord exceedingly precious.

" Sunday, Aug. 28. I had a good time at five. We met again at eight. I was blessed in hearing the first lesson (2 Kings xix.) read at church ; so I read it again at one to a house full of people, and found it spirit and life to my soul, and have cause to believe it was so to many. After tea I met the select band. Some young men had come six, some ten, and some twenty miles. The Lord was present at every meeting."

" Glory be unto thee, O Lord ! Thou hast enabled me this year to ride nine hundred and sixty miles, to hold two hundred and twenty public meetings, about six hundred select meetings, and to write one hundred and sixteen letters, many of them long ones ; besides many conversations in private with individuals who wished to consult me on the concerns of their souls, the effect of which, I trust, will be as ' bread cast upon the waters.' "

124   PROMISE OF THE FATHER.

Nearing her heavenly home.   On the wing for glory.

Mrs. Crosby, after writing a short narrative of the Lord's gracious dealings with her, adds, " I have neglected to record many of my journeys and labors, and also the blessed manifestations of his love and divine communion, both night and day, which I have often been favored with during these last twenty years or more. I am now nearly seventy, have lived nearly six years in this house (at Leeds,) and have found and still find it to be ' a peaceful habitation and a quiet resting place,' both of soul and body. My soul in general dwells in peace and love. I live by faith in Jesus, my precious Saviour, and find my last days are my best days. I am surrounded with mercies."

Such a life, it might be anticipated, would end in triumph. The sting of death is sin. But sin had been washed away. The sting of death being destroyed, she joyously awaited the moment when she

> " Might clap the glad wing, and soar away, -
> And mingle with the blaze of day."

Her ever-constant friend, Mrs. Tripp, gives the subjoined account of her entrance into the joys of her Lord : — " All the week preceding her death she was indisposed, but did not abate any thing of her usual exercises. Her spirit often seemed on the wing for glory, for she frequently sung more than she had done for some months ; so that I said, ' I think, my dear, you have tuned your harp afresh.' On Saturday she wrote two letters, went to the select band in the evening, and bore a blessed testimony for her Lord. On Sunday, though poorly, she attended preaching forenoon and evening, but returned, after the evening meeting, very ill and in much pain. During the night she prayed for her classes, bands, friends, and the church of God, that they might all meet above. A little before she expired, she said to one that was present, ' If I had strength, how I would praise the Lord ! ' But at eight o'clock, having closed her own eyes and mouth, she sweetly fell asleep in Jesus, October 24, 1804, in the seventy-fifth year of her age. So composed was her countenance, that when dead not the least trace of death was discernible."

> " Out of great distress they came ;
>   Washed their robes by faith below
> In the blood of yonder Lamb, —
>   Blood that washes white as snow ; —
> Therefore are they next the throne,
>   Serve their Maker day and night :
> God resides among his own,
>   God doth in his saints delight.
>
> " More than conquerors at last,
>   Here they find their trials o'er ;
> They have all their sufferings past,
>   Hunger now and thirst no more :
> No excessive heat they feel
>   From the sun's directer ray ;
> In a milder clime they dwell, —
>   Region of eternal day."

11 *

CHAPTER IX.

"Who are these array'd in white—
    Brighter than the noonday sun?
Foremost of the sons of light,
    Nearest the eternal throne?
These are they that bore the cros
    Nobly for their Master stood;
Sufferers in his righteous cause,
    Followers of the dying God."

IT is our aim in this humble volume to present what we believe to be *truth*. What is truth should be the one great question with every professed Christian, whether of the ministry or laity. But on the ministry truth has special demands. Every minister truly called of God is a legally authorized expositor of the word. He receives his commission direct from the court of Heaven; and, if faithful to his trust, great will be his reward in heaven. It has been divinely ordained that "the priest's lips should keep knowledge, and they "— that is, the people — " should seek the law at his mouth, for he is the messenger of the Lord of Hosts."

But in case the priest's lips fail to keep knowledge, and the people inquire at his mouth, and receive for doctrines the commandments of men, how momentous the responsibility! Is the minister now reading these lines asking himself, " What is truth in relation to the doctrines of this work? Has the promise of the Father been fulfilled? Am I now living in the last days of which the prophet Joel spake when he said, ' It shall come to pass afterwards that I will pour out my Spirit upon all flesh, and your sons and daughters shall prophesy, your old men shall dream dreams, your young men shall see visions ; and also upon the servants and upon the handmaids in those days will I pour out my Spirit.' "

Of this no room for doubt remains. The Scriptures of truth settle the question. The *last* days have been ushered in. Corroborative of this, the apostle Peter, after having himself been filled with the Holy Ghost, in token of the fulfilment of the promise of the Father, says, " It shall come to pass in the last days, saith God, I will pour out of my Spirit upon all flesh ; and your sons and your daughters shall prophesy, and your young men shall see visions, and your old men shall dream dreams ; and on my servants, and on my handmaidens, I will pour out in those days of my Spirit ; and they shall prophesy."

And if God, in his eternal faithfulness, thus remembered his promise to his sons, was he unmindful of his daughters ? No : truly as the word of the promise-keeping Jehovah was fulfilled in the pouring out of his Spirit upon his sons, in like manner was it fulfilled to his daughters. Did the sons prophesy, so also did the daughters. They *all* spake as the Spirit gave utterance. Was this outpouring of the Spirit on the daughters of the Lord to cease with the day of Pentecost, or was it destined to continue through the entire period of the last days ? No ! "The promise is unto you and your children, and all that are afar off." And that it

has continued to be poured out upon the daughters of
the Lord down through all succeeding ages, and to the
present day is being poured out, is what we have set
forth by most significant facts, and is what we shall still
bring forth testimony to prove in the succeeding pages
of this work.

But by whom has the exercise of the gift of prophecy in woman been most seriously resisted? Has not
the use of this endowment of power been withstood
mainly by those whose lips should keep knowledge?
Has not the people who have sought to know the law on
this important topic been met with dissuasive teachings,
as though God's ancient promise had not been fulfilled?
And if the gift has been received, and the spirit of
prophecy is now being poured out upon the daughters
and handmaids of the Lord, why should ministers,
whose lips, above all others, should keep knowledge,
and at whose mouth the people are seeking to know the
law on this subject, — why should these, above all others,
labor to restrain this gift of prophecy? Why do a
large portion of those whom the people are disposed to
look upon as able ministers of the New Testament
assume an attitude so repulsive on this subject? so
repulsive that it were, indeed, most crucifying to the
heart of the devoted sensitive Christian female to give
vent to the Holy Spirit's urgings on this point. The
question with every minister in relation to this momentous subject should be, *What is truth?* Surely sin
lieth at the door somewhere.

These reflections have been induced by reviewing the

experience of a lovely and beloved daughter of the
Lord, who, yielding to the impellings of her heaven-
baptized spirit, began to speak to the people as the
Spirit gave utterance. That she had received a divine
commission, who could doubt? The remarkable fruit-
fulness of her efforts proved, to saint and sinner, that
she spake as the Spirit gave utterance. She was naturally talented ; but she was also exceedingly sensitive.
Added to the refinements of nature were the more
lovely refinements of grace.

And here let me pause, and ask the minister who
may be reading these lines, Have you not observed
that it is only upon those female members of your
flock, who have known most of the refinements of
grace, having been numbered with those who follow
the Saviour most closely, that these constrainings of
the Spirit are felt? It is not from that heartless,
fashionable professor that you hear, as though she
would fain open her mouth for God. No ! it is that
lovely, affectionate Mary, who is more than willing to
sacrifice her earthly all for the privilege of breaking
the alabaster box of very costly ointment, and pouring
it on the head of her Saviour, and of washing his feet
with her tears. It is these only that take time to tarry
at Jerusalem until endued with power from on high,
that feel these constraining influences to open their
lips in the assembly in honor of their Lord.

And thus refined by both grace and nature was the
lovely Christian female we will now introduce to your
attentions, in testimony of the fact, that not only is the

Spirit still being poured out upon God's daughters, but that that Spirit may be *withstood by human agencies,* and thorns planted in the dying pillow of those who yield to these restraining influences.

Miss Elizabeth Hurrell was one of those whom Mr. Wesley honored with his correspondence and personal encouragement. Under the ministry of the Rev. Mr. Berridge, of Everton, she was awakened from the sleep of sin, and was soon after brought to an experimental knowledge of the truth as it is in Jesus.

Having given herself to the Lord, she endeavored, from the overflowings of benevolence, to bring others to him. She travelled through many counties in England, preaching the unsearchable riches of Christ; and many, very many, were, through her instrumentality, brought to the knowledge of the truth, not a few of whom were afterwards called to fill very honorable stations in the Methodist connection. Some were useful class leaders, others local preachers, and several travelling preachers. Mr. William Warrener, who was the first missionary appointed by Mr. Wesley to labor in the West Indies, and Mr. Henry Foster, who travelled several years in England, and died in the work, were brought to God through her instrumentality. Mr. John Lancaster, a very useful preacher at Pickering, and afterwards at Burlington, Yorkshire, was also converted under her ministry.

"It is very much to be lamented," says Dr. Taft, "that she ever relaxed, or in any measure buried that extraordinary talent which God had committed to her ;

but such was the fact. It has been supposed that she sunk beneath the *heavy cross* connected with the public ministrations of *females*, especially a female of such tender and delicate feelings as she possessed.

" But whether she turned aside from the path of duty to avoid suffering, or through the power of temptation, or from whatever cause, she deeply lamented the course she had taken, when death and eternity appeared in view. Indeed, for some considerable time, she seemed to be on the borders of despair. 'I am going to die,' said she. 'I am entering the eternal world; but all is dark before me: neither sun, moon, nor stars appear. O that I had my time to live again! I would not bury my talent as I have done.' It pleased the Lord, however, before she departed hence, to lift upon her the light of his countenance. He saw the genuineness of her repentance; he healed all her backslidings, and enabled her to bear ample testimony to his almighty power to save to the uttermost."

Miss Hurrell was of a delicate frame of body — a woman of great simplicity and integrity of mind. She possessed a wonderful facility of conveying her ideas and feelings with scriptural accuracy, and often manifested such strength of thought and felicity of expression as were irresistibly impressive. Her public labors were abundantly owned of God; and many will be the stars in the crown of her rejoicing in the day of the Lord Jesus.

Miss Sarah Lawrence was another handmaid of the Lord, who was also made a blessed recipient of the out-

pouring of the Spirit, and whose remarkable usefulness
proved that her mission was divine. When but a little
child, she saw herself a sinner in need of a Saviour,
and sought the Lord in the use of the means of grace,
and in importunate prayer. When about eighteen years
of age, she was confirmed in the Old Leeds Church.
She felt most deeply the solemnity of the obligations
she had thus taken upon herself, and, as she was returning home five miles distant, entreated the Lord that
she might ever be mindful of the holy responsibilities
she had that day assumed. While she was thus wrestling with the angel of the covenant by the way, ere
she had reached her home the Holy Comforter said
with great power to her heart, " I will keep thee as the
apple of mine eye." This filled her soul with consolation and strength.

In early childhood, he who hath said, " Leave your
fatherless children to me," consigned this lovely lamb
of the fold to the care of Miss Bosanquet, afterwards
Mrs. Fletcher. Providence is God in motion. Of
Miss Lawrence Mrs. F. says, " Providence cast her
into our hands when a little child. As she increased
in years we observed a remarkably upright and obedient
spirit in her, and a great attachment to us. When
very young, she would often cry to the Lord that she
might never be separated from me. Before she was
eight years old, she was often under strong conviction
for sin ; and from the time she was ten, she manifested
an earnest desire to be devoted to God. When she
heard us read in the family of the sufferings of our

Lord, or of the martyrs, it would kindle in her breast an intense desire to do something for Him who had borne so much for her."

But it was not until in the eighteenth year of her age, when on her return from the Old Leeds Church, after her confirmation, that she seems to have had the abiding assurance that her sins were forgiven, and her name written in the Lamb's book of life. She had now confessed Christ openly before men, and from this hour a new song was put in her mouth, and she was divinely assured that she had been brought out of spiritual bondage, and her feet set in the way cast up for the ransomed of the Lord to walk in. But though she enjoyed much peace and blessedness in the way upon which she had entered, she felt that there was still a higher elevation in Christian experience, which she longed to attain.

She saw it was the privilege of the believer to be constantly and consciously filled with the Spirit. And with unutterable longings she sought for the full baptism of the Holy Ghost. Though so young in years and just budding into womanhood, she counted all things loss for the excellency of the knowledge of Jesus Christ her Lord. And for this she was willing to be crucified to the world, and that the world should be crucified to her.

In regard to this stage of her experience, says Mrs. Fletcher, " Soon after she obtained a clear sense of the forgiveness of her sins, she saw it her privilege to be cleansed from all unrighteousness. The way she obtained this blessing shall be given in her own words.

12

' One Wednesday night, in that blessed meeting we used to have once a fortnight in Cross Hall, where so many were blessed, while I was waiting on the Lord, and saw myself as lying at the pool longing for the Lord to say, "*Be clean*," my soul was engaged in fervent prayer that I might that night be brought into clear liberty; and while my dear mistress (Miss Bosanquet) was praying, several promises were applied to my mind, such as " *Thou art clean through the word I have spoken unto thee*," &c. I now felt unbelief give way, and was enabled to cast my soul on the perfect atonement, and felt the divine efficacy of that blood which cleanseth from all sin.' "

After the inmates of Miss Bosanquet's orphan home were scattered, the God of providence having provided, through the agency of Miss B., favorable situations for those who had so long enjoyed the bounties of her hospitable roof, Miss Lawrence, who had now arrived at young womanhood, was permitted to have the prayer of her childhood answered. Miss B. having now become the wife of the devoted Vicar of Madely, Miss L. was still the humble yet chosen friend of Mrs. Fletcher, and remained with her till she passed from earth to heaven. The career of Miss Lawrence was comparatively short, but beautifully luminous. We will give it in Mrs. Fletcher's words.

" Some time after my dear Mr. Fletcher's death, as I was one day pleading with the Lord to raise up more helpers in the work, the word came to me, ' *The spirit of Elijah shall rest on Elisha.*' I thought it meant

Miss Lawrence; and soon after a visible concern arose in her mind, more forcible than ever, for the souls of the people, and in particular for those of the rising generation. And such a gift was then given her for children as I have hardly seen in any one, and a love that of a parent. Next, the sick were laid on her heart, and she ran far and near, to seek and to relieve them, both in soul and body, insomuch it greatly broke her little strength, which was always but small.

"One night she dreamed (see Acts x. 10–17) she was looking out at our chamber window on a parcel of fowls of all sorts and sizes in the yard, when she saw a very little bird flying to and fro over them, and as each put up his head, the little bird put a bit into his mouth. And after looking on them for some time, she thought she called me, and said, 'Only look how that little creature feeds those great fowls.' She then saw a most beautiful pillar in the sky; it appeared like gold, exceeding bright. She was solemnly affected at the sight, and awoke with the application of these words to her heart: 'I have made thee as this little bird; follow me, and I will make thee a pillar.' This brought to her mind a promise given her many years back: 'I will make thee a pillar in my house, to go out no more.'

"I have been humbled to the dust," continues Mrs. Fletcher, "at the ardent zeal and diligent application wherewith she sought after the good of her fellow-creatures. For reproving sin, and inviting to the means of grace few could equal her. Here I did indeed see the spirit of my dear Mr. Fletcher seem to rest on her; and, like him, she began a meeting in a very hardened part of the parish, with a bell in her hand.

" The town of Madely is a hardened spot.   I do not know that I ever found more discouragement in speaking any where than there ; and she was brought to shed tears over them many times, when, going from door to door, she entreated them to come, and in return, met with only reproach and rudeness.   But that was nothing to her, who sought no honor but from God.   Sometimes Satan would represent how ridiculous she appeared in their eyes, and when strangers passed by in carriages they would think her mad.   But, as the means she used had been instrumental in calling some, and had been blessed to many, as well as prevented much sin, she rejoiced to have the honor of being thought a fool for Christ.   And such an intense love did she feel towards them, at the very time they were ridiculing her, that she has told me, it seemed she could with pleasure submit to be bound to a stake and burned, if it might draw these souls to choose the way of life.

" One night, passing by a house where some young persons were dancing, she looked to the Lord for power, and, going in among them, she began to plead with them, and, in a very moving and tender manner, to express the love and concern she felt for their souls ; and, glory be to God, we have some in heaven who dated their first conviction from that hour.   Indeed, her whole soul seemed to be drawn out after the salvation of all around her.   She began meetings in different places, at

which numbers attended. Her method was, after singing and prayer, to read some life or experience, or some
awakening author, stopping now and then to explain
and apply it as the Lord gave her utterance ; and several, who are now lively members in our connection,
were brought in through that means. But in every step
she took she inquired of the Lord, fearing much to take
one out of his order.

"When the work commenced in Coalport, and the
inhabitants began to increase, she was strongly importuned to go and hold a meeting there. She complied
with the invitation, and continued to attend every other
Sunday night for four years. Sinners would scoff, but
the power of God was felt. Her word was gladly received by numbers, and deeply did they lament when
she could no longer meet with them as usual, and many
an earnest prayer did they put up that she might be restored to them again. I could never discern in her any
spirit but that of the most perfect deadness to the world,
and such a submission to crosses of every kind as au-
gured to me that her will was entirely lost in that
of God.

"She was for many years weak and infirm ; but her ardent desire for the salvation of souls carried her frequently beyond her strength, and many times, when
she was speaking to sinners with a view to bring them
to repentance, her poor body was fitter for the bed than
any other place.

"When in much pain from continual coughing, with
spasms all over her body, she sometimes cried out, —

12 *

'Corruption, earth, and worms
Shall but refine this flesh,
Till my triumphant spirit comes
To put it on afresh.'

About two weeks before she died, after suffering much
one night from her cough and other complaints, she
observed, ' What a sweet night I have had in the love
of God ! Such nearness to Jesus, such willingness to
suffer with him, did I feel, that I praised the Lord for
every fit of coughing. Continually I am pointed to
look at the dying Saviour in these words : —

"See, from his head, his hands, his feet,
Sorrow and love flow mingled down !
Did e'er such love and sorrow meet,
Or thorns compose so rich a crown ? " '

On Wednesday, Dec. 3, 1800, her happy spirit took
its flight to feast with Jesus' priests and kings."

Paul speaks in his journeyings of honorable women
not a few. It is our privilege to introduce yet another
daughter of the Lord, of honorable memory, who, from
among those of the generation just passing away, tarried
at Jerusalem, and was enabled to witness a good confession to the faithfulness of her promise-keeping Lord,
before a gainsaying world. That she had received the
baptism of the Holy Ghost, her every day life was an
outspoken testimony. Dr. Taft thus speaks of this
devoted disciple : —

"Mrs. B. Hall, of the city of York, was one of
the most eminent women of her time. She sought the
truth, doing the will of her heavenly Father, and soon

became far known for her piety.   Possessed of a small fortune, she could devote much of her time to religion, which was the delight of her soul.   Being thus devoted to God, and constantly attending the church, she became acquainted with Mr. Nelson, prebendary of Ripon, who had received much evangelical light from reading John Arndt's True Christianity.   When Mr. Wesley came to York, she presently embraced Methodism; but *before* that time, she had commenced the work of prayer, and expounding the Holy Scriptures to her neighbors twice a week, which practice she continued after she became a Methodist.   She was often visited by Quaker ladies, and had good ministers of the church to take breakfast with her.   She often corresponded with Mr. Wesley, and some of her letters are given in the earlier volumes of the Methodist Magazine."

Miss Newman is also another whose heaven-baptized soul led her out beyond the paths of ordinary useful-ness.   She began ·her Christian course with marked decision.   Previous to her conversion she kept a book store at Cheltenham, in Gloucestershire, England.   But on setting out in the way to heaven, she resolved that every obstruction that stood in the way of her own sal-vation, or the salvation of others, should be removed. As the Jews and Greeks at Ephesus, whose minds, through the teachings of Paul, were enlightened in relation to the evil tendencies of their books, burned them, though at the cost of fifty thousand pieces of silver, so the excellent Miss Newman resolved at once on sacrificing every thing which might be inimical to

the interests of her own soul, or in any way militate
against the spiritual interests of others.

In remembrance of the infinite price paid for the
redemption of the human family, she, with prompt and
true dignity of purpose, began at the commencement of
her heavenward course to act on the principle that the
Christian religion requires that which may cost its possessor something. She had on her shelves novels, plays,
and romances. But she could not now sell these to
poison the minds of others, any more than she could
injure her own soul by reading them herself. She
therefore, at the sacrifice of worldly gain, refused to
sell that which would poison the immortal mind, on the
same principle that she would refuse to sell that which
would poison the body. But in counting all things lost
for Christ, she gained all. " Every one that hath forsaken houses, or brethren, or sisters, or father, or mother,
or wife, or children, or lands, for my name's sake, shall
receive a hundred fold, and shall inherit everlasting
life." But not only was Miss N. willing to sacrifice
her earthly goods, — she also sacrificed her entire physical and spiritual being on Heaven's altar ; and her whole
subsequent life was a development of power, and
proved that she had received the baptism of fire. Dr.
Taft says, " She united with the Methodists, and became a very active and useful member of their society,
and soon began to exhort in prayer meetings. She
afterwards manifested her love for souls, by making
occasional visits to Tewkesbury and the adjacent places.
Her religious experience was clear, and included an

acquaintance with the deep things of God. She was a woman of strong understanding and amiable temper; prudence and modesty were leading traits in her character. Mr. Wesley had a high opinion of her qualifications and usefulness, and encouraged her in all her pious endeavors. She used to exhort and preach occasionally; and the Lord owned her labors in the salvation of many souls. Among those who were brought to God through her instrumentality were her own mother, and Mr. Cousins, who afterwards became her husband. After her marriage, Mrs. Cousins did not exercise much in public, for her health began to decline; and her husband also was considerably afflicted. He was called away in the midst of his usefulness; and she soon left this vale of tears to meet him in the skies.

From among the many Heaven-baptized women who, from time to time, have come up before us, is yet another of superior excellence — Mrs. Anne Gilbert. She was born of the Spirit in her youthful days. She soon found that, in order to retain a state of adoption, she must go on from grace to grace, and thus, in obedience to the teachings of the Spirit, walk in Christ as she had received him. She was not placed in circumstances to enjoy other helpful influences than those of the Scriptures, in regard to the doctrine of the full baptism of the Holy Ghost. But she felt that she needed a gift of power which she consciously did not possess, and in obedience to the Spirit's teachings through the written word, she resolved to tarry at Jerusalem until endued with power from on high.

And whoever resolved in the name and strength of the Lord Jehovah to have the purchased grace, and to have it *now*, but has quickly heard the Saviour say, " Be it done unto thee even as thou wilt." She had been living in the enjoyment of this precious grace some time before she had heard a single sermon on the doctrine of Christian perfection. Mr. Taft, in his Memoirs of Holy Women, thus speaks of her : —

" In the year 1771, going one day to the preaching in an adjoining village, the preacher happened not to come ; she therefore gave out a hymn and prayed. She told the people they need not be disappointed, for the Lord was present to bless them. Immediately she received such a manifestation of the love and power of God that she was constrained to entreat and beseech them to repent and turn to the Lord."

Thus began the public labors of this distinguished woman, which she continued for many years. She had a most persuasive and engaging address, and many were the seals that were added to her ministry. One of the preachers, in a letter to Miss Barritt, says, " I had the pleasure of hearing Mrs. Anne Gilbert preach in the chapel at Redruth, Cornwall, to about *fourteen hundred* people. She had a torrent of softening elo-quence, which occasioned a general weeping through the whole congregation. She was almost blind at the time, and had been so for many years." Mrs. Gilbert died at an advanced age, and in full assurance of faith and hope.

CHAPTER X.

"Let her honor the Lord's body, his church, by preparing the spices of grace for its embalmment when it seems cold and dead, and watch with weeping prayers for its revival by the power of God. When female piety is awake, watchful and zealous, the morning of gracious joy is not far distant, nay, has already dawned. It was not the sex, but the Christian virtues of these women of the cross, that triumphed in this awful extremity If they were more faithful, it was because they loved more. Love is the fulfilling of the law ; so also it is the perfection of Christianity."

REV. DR. BETHUNE.

REJECTED MESSAGE.

IMAGINE, after our Lord had commissioned Mary to proclaim the gospel of a risen Christ to her brethren, that these brethren had turned away contemptuously, refusing to accept the message, because it fell from the lips of a woman.

We know of a church with whom the signs of spiritual life were well nigh extinct. Judging from the nature of the difficulties under which this church was laboring, we may with certainty infer that the brethren composing the official board had not deemed it needful to tarry at Jerusalem until endued with power from on high. Imagine what an official board those disciples would have formed, who, a few weeks previous to the day of Pentecost, were contending which should be the greatest. Where the old leaven is not purged out by the purifying fires of love, what danger of fermentings, leading to those grievous dissensions which produce spiritual death, by quenching the Spirit of the living God ! And in this dangerous state, we fear, was the church to which we now allude. It had been for some time without a pastor, and its altar fires were well nigh extinguished.

About the time that this church was thus rapidly approximating towards spiritual death, God raised up an instrumentality by which he would have saved it. A female member of that church, the wife of one of the leading members, a lady of excellent reputation and intelligent piety, had fallen in with a book in which she saw the Bible view of Christian holiness illustrated with simplicity and force. She saw that this was the gift of power which that church must have in order to make it efficient in the evangelization of the world, — the baptism of fire, — by which alone the old leaven might be purged out, and its dissensions healed.

Church communities are made up of individuals, and as an individual, she resolved she would do her part towards bringing that ingredient of power into the church, by which alone it could be preserved from utter spiritual death. Perhaps with not greater earnestness and absorption did those women disciples wait with their brethren to be endued with power from on high, than did this disciple wait for the promised baptism.

But she saw that it was a baptism of fire, and before the vision of her mind deep and most penetrating tests were presented. She saw, if she would attain the image of the Saviour, that she must consent to searching trials, similar to those endured by her incarnate Lord, by which process might be brought out before the world whether she had really attained the image of the heavenly. O, it were indeed easier for the disciple to follow the Saviour up to the Mount of Transfiguration, and build tabernacles there, than to follow the Man of Sorrows in his homeless journeyings, amid the contradictions and scoffs of sinners, and amid the yet more painful trial of being rejected by his own, and reviled and crucified by his professed people, who before the world proclaimed themselves to be doing God service in thus dealing out ignominy, pain, and death.

We have thought that few things could have been more painful to the incarnate Deity, who in verity took upon himself our nature, than the fact which stands briefly recorded thus : " For neither did his brethren believe on him." O, when the members of the same household of faith, with whom, by ties of consanguinity, our very being seems blended, who know the sincerity of our motives, and on whom our very hearts have been accustomed to lean for sympathy amid the storms of this unloving, cold world — when this refuge fails us, and when these hearts on whom we have leaned pierce us through — O, indeed it is then that the disciple proves what it is to know the fellowship of Christ's sufferings.   Yet not till he counts the cost, and consents that he will thus endure, does he come to the point where he can be made conformable unto Christ's death.

Few are willing to have the grace at so great a cost ; but unless made conformable to Christ's death, we can never know the power of his resurrection, and prove

13

the excellency of a living, indwelling Christ within the heart. "Are ye able to drink of the cup that I shall drink of, and to be baptized with the baptism that I am baptized with?" This is the question which the Head of the church proposes to all who would be raised to entire newness of life, and bear the image of the heavenly.

And it was to this crucifying process that our friend saw that she must submit if she would have her petition answered for the full baptism of the Holy Ghost. But the cost was fairly counted, and the decision made. This done, and she found there was no need of *waiting* for the day of Pentecost to come. It had already come. "Not with observation." No rushing, mighty wind was heard. But self being dethroned, and every sin renounced, she was now ready to be filled with the Holy Ghost. Not that these àcts were sufficient to constitute her a meet residence for the Holy Trinity. The blood of Christ alone can do this. But in these acts the Holy Spirit had aided her. Every holy resolve that had been formed, every weight that had been laid aside, and every right-hand or right-eye sin, which, at such a painful sacrifice had been surrendered, — all had been accomplished through the agency of the Holy Spirit, with whom, as a *worker-together*, she had wrought in fitting herself for the abode of an indwelling Trinity.

And now the temple of her heart being prepared, she presented it in faith, through the blood of the everlasting covenant. First emptied, then cleansed and filled, — this is the divine order. But how rapid are the

PROMISE OF THE FATHER. 147

Habitation of God through the Spirit.   Irresistible impulse.

processes of the Spirit when grace finds a willing subject! It is not the order of Him who fills infinite
space that the soul should remain a vacuum. The design of infinite Love, in the redemption of the body, is,
that it should become a habitation of God, through the
Spirit. But every idol, whether it be reputation, estate,
family, friends, or life itself, all must be dethroned before
the full baptism of the Holy Ghost can be received ; for
" What agreement hath the temple of God with idols ? "
And the moment the last idol is surrendered, and the
whole being given up *through Christ*, that moment God
claims, and, through the blood of the covenant, puri-
fies the temple, and the Holy Ghost inly says to the
inmost soul, " Ye are the temple of the living God," as
God hath said, " I will dwell in them and walk in
them."

And now that our friend had presented herself as a
whole burnt sacrifice, and she began to feel the consuming fires of the Spirit absorbing her whole being,
such were her sympathies with Christ in behalf of the
dying church of which she was a member, that she
could not refrain her lips. As a daughter of the Lord
Almighty, she had obediently complied with the conditions upon which the promise of the Father is founded ;
and now the Spirit was being poured out upon her, and
the tongue of fire was given, she felt an irresistible impulse to speak, as the Spirit gave utterance. But the
testimony of Jesus is not only the Spirit of prophecy,
but Christ is of God made unto us wisdom. And by
this we may discern between the Spirit of truth and

the spirit of error. The Spirit of truth will never lead us into any unscriptural or unintelligible modes of usefulness. It will not lead us to unseemly or untimely utterances, or to any course which will not betoken soundness of mind. But it may lead us to a course which may occasionally be extraordinary.

This is an important point, and it should be duly considered. Says an eminent divine, " If Satan cannot succeed in getting us to go too slow, he will turn charioteer, and endeavor to get us to go too fast." But the full baptism of the Holy Ghost also implies entire sanctification ; that is, the sanctification of the *intellect*, with every other redeemed power, to God. And surely we may expect from those who possess this grace such a manifestation of wisdom as will commend itself to all who are spiritually wise. Yes, surely such will be wise, understanding what the will of the Lord is. Yet we do not doubt that those who are filled with the Spirit will often be led to the adoption of a course which the worldly wise may not approve. But though called to be singular for Christ's sake amid the chidings of the prudent of this world, wisdom is known of her children ; and thus it was in the case of our friend.

So deeply was her heart burdened for the church of her choice, and such perceptions did her indwelling Saviour give her of its responsibilities, in view of the blood of souls, which were being found upon its skirts, that, as before said, she could not refrain her lips. She *could* not, because she knew that her Saviour would have her speak. And when she sought unto God for wisdom in regard to the manner in which she might do this, so as to be heard by the church, the plan was so singularly novel, that she would never have consented to it, had she not first been crucified to the world, and the world to her. As it was, such were the shrinkings of her nature, that she saw she was in danger of losing the grace by not complying with the conditions on which she had received it, and on which alone she could retain it.

She had received it by presenting herself as a whole burnt sacrifice on the altar of God, and now she saw that it was only to be retained by *keeping* all upon the altar. And to be answerable to the conditions of the covenant, she saw but one path ; and that one path was by the way of a duty clearly discoverable on the heavenly chart. Her experimental apprehension of the indwelling of a risen Saviour in her heart was an endowment of power which every member of that church community needed, and she now saw that He who is no respecter of persons would have her, as his witness, confess the gift she had received to all, in order that all might be constrained to seek the same baptism of fire.

At this time there was no ministering servant of Christ to serve at the altar of this church, and, as before observed, its altar fires were fast waning. But He who purchased the church with his blood would not that its spiritual life should become extinct. He would fain have had the things that remained, and were ready to die, strengthened. He therefore moved this beloved,

13 *

newly-baptized female disciple to use means by which this church community were largely called together. A notice was read, one Sabbath morning, from the pulpit of a neighboring church, that in the Congregational church in that place a testimony would be given in for God. The thing was enacted in wisdom. No one in that community, save the one timid, shrinking disciple, who had prepared the notice, knew from whence it emanated. Much interest was excited, and inquiries quickly passed from one to another, who the witnessing stranger could be. Many crowded to the place, and in solemn silence sat down awaiting the presence of the anticipated stranger. Though the questionings had passed from one to another, and amazement had been expressed in regard to the wherefore of this gathering, yet now that the company were convened, and the doors were shut, a holy quiet prevailed, as though God were about to speak.

It was in reliance on infinite wisdom, and through the Holy Spirit's dictation, that that waiting company had been gathered; and now the Master of assemblies took the matter into his own hand, and seemed to set the tranquillizing seal of his presence on the assembly, so that the solemn quiet of the place appeared to say, God is here; and verily the God of the temple was there. He was there in the power of his Spirit; his grieved, insulted Spirit was there to plead that the expiring fires of that altar might be resuscitated. He had spoken in judgment. His holy name had been dishonored by that people; they had not been able to go

out before their enemies and win them over to Israel's
God, but, contrariwise, had been, by their dissensions,
scattered and smitten before their enemies; and now
the dishonored God of that temple had convened them
once more, to plead for the honor of his own cause,
that those altar fires might again be rekindled, and his
Israel endued with power from on high to win souls to
Christ.

Not more truly did the Saviour deliver a message,
through the lips of a devoted female, to those erring
disciples who forsook the Saviour, in the hour of his
greatest extremity, and fled, than he would now have
delivered a message to the brethren of this church community, through the lips of this devoted, intelligent
female disciple. Such had been her evident manifestations of devotedness and supreme love of Christ, that
we presume no one doubted she was a beloved disciple,
as was the devoted Mary of Magdalene. And in view
of the fact that the secret of the Lord is with them that
fear him, none would have doubted but the constancy
and nearness of her communion with Christ might have
resulted in her receiving a message from Jesus. And
such was the well-known character of her social and
domestic surroundings as might have insured an affectionate, thankful reception, if the theme had been on
some matter of worldly interest.

But now that this beloved, newly-baptized disciple
spake as the Spirit gave utterance, did her brethren receive this testimony for Jesus as it fell from her lips?
No! not because the message did not come clothed

with heart-thrilling pathos and divine power.   No! many felt this.   Perhaps there were few hearts so hardy but were deeply moved, and felt that she spake as the Spirit gave utterance.   And why did they reject this message, if coming thus from a known disciple of Christ, who had the confidence of the religious public, and whose wondrous message came clothed with divine authority, and the reception of which might, doubtless, have been the salvation of that church community? They rejected it because the church had imposed the cruel seal of silence on the lips of woman.   The message was manifestly important; and who was not ready to acknowledge this?   All knew that the fires of the Spirit were fast dying out in that church — that her spiritual power was well nigh, if not wholly, gone.

And now one of their own number had, in obedience to the command of the Saviour, tarried at Jerusalem until, endued with power and filled with the Holy Ghost, she would fain have all seek the same needful grace, and, with the same power impelling her that impelled those women on the day of Pentecost to speak as the Spirit gave utterance, she utters before the multitude the great things God has done for her, and her testimony is contemptuously rejected because it falls from the lips of a woman.   We say contemptuously — yes; for though the Spirit that empowered her was evidently more than human, and many wondered and wept, yet the Spirit resisted; and man, left to pursue the wrong, treads with yet more rapid pace the path of error, and the last state is far worse than the first.

It is sad to remember how this beloved disciple was reviled and rejected; how those who stood in high places in the church ridiculed, as a religious farce, these holy solemnities, and endeavored to incite even her nearest kindred to restraining and repulsive acts, till every earthly refuge failed her, and she was left, indeed, to drink of the cup of which her Saviour drank — to know a fellowship with his sufferings. We love and venerate the ministry, and, through grace, are ever disposed to keep in affectionate remembrance the prohibition, "Touch not mine anointed, and do my prophets no harm." But the voice of duty admonishes us to say, that the deepest wounds inflicted on the heart of this lovely female disciple were inflicted by the instigation of a minister of the same denomination, of a neighboring town. Not that he did not regard the utterances of the Spirit through her, as most needful and timely, but because she, being a woman, had dared to open her mouth in the presence of her brethren.

Had this minister obeyed the command of the Head of the church, and tarried at Jerusalem until endued with power from on high, he would himself have learned the wisdom that the Holy Ghost teacheth, and not have restrained its utterances. Had the cloven tongue of fire descended upon his own head, he would not have been such a stranger to its inspirations, as they fell from the lips of this Christian sister, and he might have been saved from blood-guiltiness, in view of the spiritual death which ensued from the fact that this message, which might have resulted in the spiritual life of that church through his means, was not received.

We need not ask the question whether God will not take this rejection as done unto himself: "He that rejecteth you rejecteth me." What an account will such ministers, who have thus kept female talent out of use, be called to render when God comes to require his own with *usury*, and the account of unused female talent is adjusted! Who can doubt but a speciality of the last days has been neglected?

> But where that lonely few
>   Who were with Christ below?
> Those who the Man of Sorrows knew,
>   And sometimes shared his woe?
> Ah! are they quite forsaken, quite forgot,
> And by the ascended Lord remembered not?
>
> O, no! that angel band
>   That rolled away the stone,
> With them he left the high command
>   That they should make him known
> As their now risen Lord — their Brother, Friend;
> Those loved on earth are loved, world without end.

CHAPTER XI

"And when they were come in, they went up into an upper room, where abode both Peter, and James, and John, and Andrew, Philip and Thomas, Bartholomew and Matthew, James the son of Alpheus, and Simon Zelotes, and Judas, the brother of James. These all continued with one accord in prayer and supplication, with the *women*, and Mary, the mother of Jesus, and with his brethren." ACTS i. 13, 14.

THE UNION MEETING.

OT long since the writer paused at a place where a union meeting was in progress. The meetings were being held daily in accordance with the then prevailing custom. A blessed Anna was there, now past her threescore years and ten, who from infancy had been nursed in the lap of fervent piety, and whose lips had long since been touched with hallowed fire, and whose life, for about half a century, had eminently adorned the doctrine of God her Saviour. She was a descendant of the late President Edwards, and the indices of grace with her were of a strong, vigorous character, and marked her as worthy the name of her eminent grandsire. Perhaps not more truly did the tongue of fire descend on the women who were assembled with their brethren on the pentecostal morning which ushered in the latter day glory, than it had now in the evening of the last days descended on this aged Anna, and other of the female disciples of this place. If we had judged from the number of earnest and intelligently pious females attendant on that union meeting, we should have anticipated blessed outpourings of the Spirit on the people of this community.

But though the meeting was punctually and largely attended, and many prayers were offered, yet no outpouring of the Spirit came, and there seemed to be such a want of power felt, that over and again did we hear the exclamation, "What can be the matter? Something seems to be wanting." A careful spiritual observer, acquainted with the history of that people, might have inferred what that something was.

Many years previous, when that church was first formed, so few were the male disciples, that it was actually difficult to hold a prayer or conference meeting without bringing in the aid of female laborers. In fact, that church was well nigh commenced, and in its infancy sustained, by these zealous women. But as years passed away, and the number of male disciples slowly increased, the voice of women was gradually hushed, and was in the end wholly silenced, in the presence of the brethren in all church assemblies. Yet the word of the Lord was as fire shut up in their bones. With intense longings, and pent-up consuming fervors, they mingled in these union prayer meetings. Fain would they have given vent to these consuming ardors, and in burning words mingled their voices with one accord in prayer, as did the women with their brethren on the day of Pentecost.

Though this was a union prayer meeting, and Christians of all denominations were invited, yet the fact seemed to be lost sight of, that in Christ Jesus there was neither male nor female; but these Christian women were not permitted to open their lips. We think few would be disposed to contest the point with us should we say that the tone of piety with the men in the church was seemingly far from being as elevated as with the women. The subject of tarrying at Jerusalem until endued with power from on high had, with several of these women been a theme of intensely absorbing interest and all-prevailing prayer, while with the most of the brethren, the agitation of the doctrine of the full baptism of the Holy Ghost as a blessing to be received now, and received by faith, would have been regarded as heretical.

As characteristic of the tone of piety in not a few of the brethren who took a leading part in the meetings, we might instance the manner of some of these prayers. We will refer to one not very unlike some others to which we listened, and leave the reader to judge. It was worded about thus : " Lord, grant that if the question were asked here this morning, as was asked in the days of thine incarnation, Who shall betray the Master ? that each brother may feel like saying, ' Lord, it is I, it is I ! ' " How much more was this like Peter, when following the Saviour afar off, or in fact like Judas, than like Peter *after* the day of Pentecost.

Is it not to be feared that in this, as in many other churches, prayers coming from the lips of a Judas might be less offensive than from the lips of a Heaven-baptized Mary ? But these utterances of a Mary, as our further recordings will show, were peremptorily silenced. And when we heard the exclamation, " What can be the matter ? " we could not but feel that the Spirit of the Lord was grieved, and God would have these lips, which he had touched with holy fire, opened in that assembly.

14

A lady of that community, of fine mental and literary endowments, the wife of a minister of well-known repute, and who had, within a few days previous, received the tongue of fire, felt so irresistibly constrained to open her mouth in prayer, and in speaking, that she could not refrain. About this time we were again passing through this place, and were delayed a few hours, when this lady called on us. The "union meetings" had now been held daily, several weeks in succession. But on inquiry, we were informed that few conversions had occurred in the church where the meeting was held. This and the contiguous church were the two most prominent in the sustainment of this union meeting; and these churches were the most marked in their resistance of the gift of utterance intrusted to women.

Neither had there been any special outpouring of the Spirit on the brethren, favoring the hope that their many prayers were about to result in the ingathering of many sinners. Was not the Holy Spirit grieved by the steady persistence of those churches in not authorizing that gift of power which God had long since put into that church to be brought into use? Still that ancient flame, through whose enkindlings mainly those churches had been brought into existence, was there. But its early fires were not now permitted to blaze out in that more enlarged Christian community, because a sufficient number of male disciples had been added, whose utterances were sufficient to fill up the time. The question was not whether these male disciples had received a more enlarged measure of grace by having received the

Holy Ghost since they believed, to encourage the belief that their utterances would be more in accordance with the mind of the Spirit, and accompanied with that unction which the Spirit alone can give. No; this seemed not to have been the question contemplated.

Sentiments emanating from the ministry had made it a law in those church communities that the voice of woman should not be heard in the presence of the brethren. And yet that ancient fire was there; and had it not been peremptorily restrained, doubtless scores, if not hundreds, had caught the flame. The lady who had now called on us, and on whose head, we do not doubt, the tongue of fire had descended as truly as on the head of Mary on the day of Pentecost, and who felt that she could no longer refrain her lips without *consciously* resisting the Holy Ghost, came to ask our advice on the subject. And in what a responsible position were we now placed! It is a serious matter to enact rules which withstand the operations of the Holy Spirit.

We sincerely believe that there was not one of the women on whose head the tongue of fire rested, who more intelligently and consciously felt the constrainings of the Spirit to open her lips in the presence of her brethren on the day of Pentecost, than this Christian sister felt that the Spirit was now urging her to speak. And yet she knew, notwithstanding her position as a minister's wife, and her social position in that community, that if she opened her lips she was in danger of being silenced.

| Question. | How would you have answered? | Literal renderings. |

And what could we advise under those circumstances? Reader, are you a minister belonging to a denomination which will not admit your Christian sister, however earnestly and intelligently pious, to obey the impellings of the Spirit in your church assemblies? Let me here pause and ask, Were you applied to for counsel under similar circumstances with ourselves, would you not say, as Peter and the other apostles said, " We ought to obey God rather than man "? And so said we. Do you ask what was the result? It was this : This disciple of Jesus was rejected, as was her Saviour ; and she was requested to do so no more. Not that she did not give a word in season, and was not assisted graciously in the delivery of her message. This was most obvious. The rejection of her testimony was solely on the ground that women were required to be in silence in the presence of the men. But if the letter of this prohibition were to be obeyed rather than the Spirit, with equal propriety might women be prohibited from opening their mouths to break silence under any circumstances. Does not every woman that opens her mouth in the church in the presence of a man, to sing or to cough, or, if fainting, to say, I am ill, render herself liable, on this principle, to be silenced? In either of these she breaks silence.

We at least pity the Protestant, who, by these literal renderings against the dictates of common sense, make the Scriptures contradictory, and assumes ground where the Holy Spirit and the teachings of the word would seem so continuously to disagree.

If Protestant Christians thus sever passages from their explanatory connections, and found a doctrine of such immense importance, so humiliating, and keeping back the testimony of thousands on thousands of Christ's most faithful witnesses, we see not why they may not on the same principle, and with equal propriety, take yet another relic of Popery, and adopt the literal reading of the text, "This *is* my *body* which was broken for you." We actually feel disposed to question, which doctrine, for centuries past, has done the most harm, the doctrine drawn from the isolated passage, "Let your women keep silence in the churches," or the doctrine of transubstantiation, and some other worse than senseless doctrines of Popery. We will again repeat our conviction that it is the same spirit in man that keeps the Roman Catholic women in the convent, that keeps the seal of silence in Protestant churches on the lips of woman, when assembled with her brethren for social worship.

We would not seem severe; but we know that we express the feelings of thousands of women when we say that a review of the workings of the "Man of Sin," in connection with this subject, are calculated to excite commingled emotions, which, if analyzed, might display perhaps an equal share of compassion and *righteous* indignation. We say thus because the God of the Bible has declared, that in Christ Jesus there is neither male nor female; and the more intellectual, refined, and cultivated the class of mind, the more keenly is this wrong perceived, and the more unfavorable, in a twofold sense, the reflex influence on those who are the instruments of this oppression.

We will illustrate. Here is a man of ordinary intellectual ability, but he has never taken much time to cultivate his intellect. His school studies finished, he enters upon the busy arena of life. How engrossing are its cares! From morn till eve is his attention occupied with its ever-varying whirl. Is he a professed Christian? Too seldom, during the six days of the week, does he find time for little more than a few moments to read the Holy Word in the morning and evening of the day. Doubtless the day of eternity will reveal that for years of his professed Christian life, far more of his precious time has been spent in reading the news of the day, and with interests connected with his citizenship in this world, than with interests connected with his citizenship in heaven. Can we imagine a man, whose daily routine of life is about thus, in a state of spirituality that would particularly fit him for close and effectual communion with God in leading the devotions of others, either in prayer or speaking?

Yet in thus portraying, do we not give a truthful portraiture of hundreds of business men, who take the lead in social church assemblies? But Peter, when so far off from Jesus, the light of the world, that by reason of his distance from the true light he could scarcely perceive the crookedness of his own way, or feel grieved for his derelictions, can we conceive that he would be likely to be better instructed in grace than Mary, whose supreme love disposed her to follow the Saviour closely, ever sitting at his feet?

But O, how many Marys there are still, though earthly solicitudes may press upon them, such is the absorption of their zeal that they make even their every-day cares a means of grace, and subservient to their increased ability for usefulness! Knowing that they serve the Lord Christ in serving their household, and in training their children for immortality and eternal life, being answerable to all the various social duties of life, their oft pressures of worldly care are made subservient to greater spirituality of mind, by pressing them more closely to the heart of Christ, as their almighty Friend, and the compassionate bearer of all their burdens. The Bible is their companion, and daily do they live by every word that proceedeth out of the mouth of God. Though their spiritualized affections may not have disposed them, nor their time been sufficient, to familiarize themselves particularly with many worse than useless newspaper recordings, yet with the recordings which educate the mind, and fit it for a spiritual appreciation of the responsibilities of man's short citizenship here on earth, and an eternal citizenship in heaven, they have cultivated an earnest acquaintance.

With the many women who so closely followed the incarnate Jesus in his weary journeyings, they have learned to sympathize in all the interests that appertain to his kingdom; and now that the day is past, and these Christian sisters and brethren meet in the place appointed for social prayer and conference, where is the intelligent Christian female who does not feel the inconsistency of the position in which these mistaken views have placed her? We referred to the reflex influence of this state of things on the brethren as unfavorable to themselves. We think the deduction sufficiently plain, but we are reminded of an occurrence corroborative.

A company of disciples had convened as usual in the place appointed for prayer and conference. It was a long time since that people had been visited with a revival, and the want of spiritual life in the membership was most manifest. Yet God had given an endowment of power to the church in that place, which, if it had only been brought out, might long before have resulted in reviving influences. About half a dozen of the most devout and influential Christian women in that church community had been baptized of the Spirit; and so intense were their burning desires that they would fain have communicated this flame.

This we cannot doubt would have been the order of God, and, had it been permitted, might have resulted in the flame of revival spreading through that church community. It is ever thus. The nature of grace is diffusive, and unless communicated by the recipient, the design of the divine Giver is frustrated; and thus these women felt, who had now convened with their brethren. Ignorance is not the mother of devotion, and these were not ignorant women. They could not but feel that these brethren had not received the energizing influence which the pentecostal baptism alone can impart. And yet these brethren wanted the meeting to pass off interestingly, and so one brother

exhorted the other brethren to *speak*, that they might
be refreshed.   In all this, as usual, these devoted females, whose maturity of piety was well known and
unquestioned, were not regarded any more than if they
had been infants or heathen women.   Could they, as
sensible and pious women, cherish other than a feeling of compassion for these brethren, whose want of
scriptural views of propriety was thus compelling them
to silence, when they knew that the indwelling Spirit
of truth was urging them to testify for Christ ?   There
are no such inconsistencies in the Bible, and sensible
people are not required to go beyond their senses and
believe there are.   The brethren took the advice of the
leading brother, and, as they spake, felt that they were
refreshed.   And after the meeting closed they indulged
in mutual congratulations, in relation to the excellency
and importance of speaking often one to another, as
necessary in view of receiving refreshings from the
presence of the Lord.

One of these devoted sisters, with emotion, ventured
to say, that if such refreshings were attendant on speaking, what must the sisters do, who were *never* permitted
to obey the order of God in this respect ?   Must they
content themselves to go without these refreshings ?
Is not the influence of such questionings disastrous
on the brethren, as also upon the sisters ?   Shall that
brother who has long been dwelling on the surface of
religion, and has scarcely yet come near enough to the
heart of Christ to know experimentally what it means
to be in sympathy with the Saviour in travail for souls,

indulge in boastful feelings, as though he were raised in the scale of heaven above that mother in Israel ? He who hath assured us that in Christ Jesus there is neither male nor female, and hath so ordained that the scale of divine favor shall ever preponderate on the side of that individual who has attained most of the image of the heavenly, and is most intent on *doing* the will of God, surely cannot be pleased with the boastful spirit which this error is calculated to inspire and cherish.

We are sure that those who will pursue this subject in the light of Scripture and reason, will be astonished that an inconsistency so replete with wrong, and so at variance with all the refined social qualities of our holy Christianity, should so long have been countenanced in Protestant churches. Let the reader pray that the Head of the church will arouse the churches to just perceptions of the error of having so long neglected a gift of power so evidently intrusted to the church as a speciality of the last days.

CHAPTER XII.

"There is neither male nor female in Christ Jesus. (Gal. iii. 28.) All are equal, except as grace makes them differ. All are kings, all are priests unto God. So long as the church is in the world, its external organization must be conformed to the order impressed by God on human nature here; but truly and substantially we are 'all one' in Christ Jesus. Gloriously does the gospel redeem believing woman from the disgraces of the fall." REV. GEORGE W. BETHUNE, D. D.

ND what are the indications that woman is now being endued with the spirit of prophecy, and that her mission is divine?

We will speak of one whom we have long known intimately. In early life she experienced the adopting grace of God. But though sanctified in part, she often indulged shrinkings when the duty of testifying of what the Lord had done for her was presented. Of all other duties, this was the most crucifying to the flesh. So great was the conflict, that she often felt constrained to cry out with the poet, —

> " 'Tis worse than death my God to love,
> And not my God alone."

If the flames, such as encircled the ancient martyrs, were before her, and it had been said, You are required to go through those flames to God, she might have been willing to pass through those flames; yet strange to state, when the duty of testifying of the work of the Spirit on her heart, or opening her lips by way of helping others, was suggested, she often shrank from the cross, and brought condemnation on her soul. Had

the prayer of the apostle for his Thessalonian brethren, "The very God of peace sanctify you wholly,"
been answered earlier in her experience, she might
have been saved years of painful strife.

The cross covers all the way to heaven.   Those
who conceive that they have found the way *around* the
cross at any time, or under any circumstances, will find
in the end that they have mistaken the path to heaven,
and entered upon a by-path which will end in disappointment and death.   Let those who are disposed to look
for some other way to heaven than by the way of the
cross, be careful lest they get into that way "which
seemeth right unto a man, but the end thereof are the
ways of death."

" If any man will come after me, let him deny himself, and take up his cross daily, and follow me."   "And
whosoever doth not bear his cross, and come after me,
cannot be my disciple."   So said the incarnate Jesus.
These are the *conditions* of discipleship — none ever
were received without consenting to be answerable to
them; neither was any disciple ever retained, but on
condition that he *daily* take up the cross, and follow
on after his Saviour, whether through evil or good report.
And it was in the light of the Scriptures this disciple
saw that she must either take up her cross, and walk in
the light of every duty, however crucifying to the flesh,
or recede from the path of life, and miss of heaven.

The decision was deliberately made.   She resolved
on an absolute and irrevocable surrender of her whole
being to the Lord her Redeemer, infinite in love, wis-

Convicted for holiness.　　Consideration needful.　　Command imperative.

dom, and power. And in doing this, she seemed not
to be as consciously sensible of the presence of a divine-
ly-impelling power constraining her to the act as on
some former occasions. But her judgment was assured
that, as a redeemed creature, she was the sole property
of Christ, her Redeemer — of God, her Maker; and she
was now intelligently convinced that it was a reasonable service that she should, through the redeeming,
cleansing blood of Christ, yield herself eternally to
God, her faithful Creator.

And in doing this, did she do any thing more than
the reader of these pages ought to do *now*? Should we
wait for impelling influences to do that which we have
long been consciously convinced we ought to do? Now,
do pause a few moments with me here, my dear friend.
Think! God complains of his people because they do
not *consider*. If you are not sure that you have already intelligently and deliberately come to the decision to take the steps towards God's hallowed altar
which were taken by this Christian lady, whose act of
consecration we now contemplate, does God, your Maker
and your Redeemer, leave it optional with yourself
whether you will *now* resolve on this act of entire surrender, or wait till some future period? In the presence of the God of the Bible, and in anticipation of
soon meeting you before the great white throne, when
your Redeemer will have become your Judge, and require his own with *usury*, we unhesitatingly say that
the Lord, your Redeemer, at this moment demands of
you an act of deliberate and irrevocable surrender. He

15

170 PROMISE OF THE FATHER.

Common honesty.   How to open the windows of heaven.

does not leave it optional with you, whether you will now give yourself up in the bonds of an everlasting covenant, which may be well ordered and sure. You *already* belong to him. Has he not purchased you to himself? If, from the earliest hour of your existence, you had lived in one ceaseless *act* of surrender, would you have done more than you ought to have done?

Do we call a person over and above honest because he renders to his neighbor that for which a full equivalent has been paid? Do we think of him as in a state of moral integrity so surprisingly high as to excite special observation? Do we not rather regard him as disreputable to just the degree he fails in doing this? Would we willingly unite our interests, or cultivate companionship with an individual who knowingly keeps back from his neighbor, in the least degree, that for which a full equivalent has been paid? It is therefore the eternal God who, through the blood of the everlasting covenant, hath redeemed you from all iniquity, and purchased you wholly unto himself, and hath given you friends, reputation, estate, time, and talents, with many innumerable gifts, that is saying unto you now, " Bring all the tithes into the storehouse, and prove me herewith, saith the Lord of hosts, if I will not open you the windows of heaven, and pour you out a blessing, that there shall not be room enough to receive it." And if not room to receive it, *what will be done with the overflowings* which must necessarily result from such an abundant outpouring that there is not room to contain it?

This is the question, dear reader, which we would have you most carefully ponder. Do you inquire what was the result of complying with the conditions, and thus proving God, in the case of the Christian friend we have introduced to your attentions, who came to this act of entire surrender ? The limit which we have circumscribed for ourselves forbids our portraying but the faint outlines of the career of usefulness which followed the reception of the blessing now received. It was a gift of power, so multitudinous in its outgoings, that in every direction, where multifarious duties called, its outgushings were felt. It is really wonderful to witness the remarkable transformations of grace in the case of this individual.

We have been placed in circumstances favorable to a close scrutiny of her life, and as our eye, for many years past, has followed her through all the windings of her way, in the steady yet various routine of duty, we have seen her possessed of a gift of power which has made her singularly unlike the mass of religious professors. We have seen that weak, timid disciple, who shrank once from the cross of testifying with her lips for Christ, testify repeatedly before assembled thousands. We have many times been present on occasions when she has so evidently spoken as the Holy Spirit gave utterance, that we believe scores have been arrested by the power of the Spirit, and manifestly convicted, and in a few hours converted. And these manifestations of convicting and converting power under her ministrations we have repeatedly witnessed.

We believe we should speak truly in the presence of God, were we to say that we have seen these extraordinary demonstrations of saving power scores of times, under circumstances where she has opened her mouth for God, and spake as the Spirit gave utterance. And, perhaps, in a manner still more extraordinary, have we witnessed under her labors the outpouring of the Spirit on believers. We have occasionally been present, when before hundreds of male and female disciples, she has testified, in the power of the Spirit, of her own experimental perceptions, of the blessedness of full salvation, and how she attained and retained that grace ; and we believe we have seen scores at a time, through the manifest unction attending these ministrations, tremble and weep, and rush forward to the place appointed for prayer, resolved to wrestle till the full baptism of the Spirit was given. And we are confident we speak understandingly when we say, that, in the aggregate, many hundreds have experienced the saving power of Christ, through the instrumentality of these ministrations.

We remember one occasion, when she was called to testify before a congregation of several hundreds. A series of meetings had been held a number of days preceding, but though the gospel net had been let down, little had been taken, and now the last night of that protracted service had come. The difficulty, doubtless, was the want of power in Christ's disciples. They had not obeyed the Saviour, and tarried at Jerusalem until endued with power from on high. Those early disciples, though they had obeyed the call to follow Jesus,

and were now his disciples, would have had but little
success in their endeavors to save the world, and, in
fact, could not have retained their state of discipleship,
had they not resolved to obey when Jesus commanded
that they should not depart out of Jerusalem, but wait
for the promise of the Father.

And now, on the last evening of the meeting, as
these services were about to close, this Christian lady,
who had just arrived at the place, gave in her testimony
for God. The blessing she had received on bringing
all the tithes into the Lord's storehouse, or, in other
words, laying all upon the altar of God, as a ceaseless,
ever-consuming sacrifice, was, we do not doubt, the endowment of power, such as the male and female disciples received on the day of Pentecost. And now, as
she testified, as a witness for Jesus, of the excellency of
this grace, and pointed out the steps by which it might
be attained, and by which she had received it, she
seemed to speak as with the tongue of fire.

Sudden and amazing were the effects produced.
We think the people might have been numbered by
hundreds who literally rushed forward to the place appointed for those to kneel who were resolved that they
would at once attain the grace. Such evident manifestations of intense, burning thirst after inward purity as
we now saw, has perhaps seldom been witnessed since
the wondrous day that first ushered in the glorious
Christian dispensation. The outpouring of the Spirit
continued during the whole night, and it was estimated
that not less than one hundred had been baptized with

15 *

174 PROMISE OF THE FATHER.

God's faithfulness proved. How the weak may be made strong.

the Holy Ghost and with fire during that memorable night. We might instance very many other somewhat similar manifestations of the Spirit, at various places, under the labors of this female disciple, to which we have been cognizant, and stand ready to testify, proving that God has not in these last days forgotten his ancient promise.

And on several different occasions have we witnessed these extraordinary manifestations of power, under circumstances singularly reproving to those who have withstood the Head of the church in withstanding the use of this gift of prophecy bestowed upon God's daughters. We have a number of the recordings of this servant of the church on hand, illustrative of the character and success of her labors, such as in our humble opinion would seem sufficient to convince the incredulous that the Lord of the vineyard may take the most sensitive, shrinking, and feeble members of the household of faith, and so endue them with power from on high as to make them mighty through his Spirit. Let the *weak* say, " I am strong ; " not those who have any power apart from the energizing aids of the Spirit, but those who truly, in fact, have no might, for to them who have *no* might He increaseth strength. The weaker the instrumentality, the more eminently does it exemplify the excellency of the power of grace. Surely our God is able to take the weak things of this world to confound the mighty, that no flesh should glory in his presence.

Under the old dispensation of types and shadows

there were offerings brought to the altar, which were set apart to be *whole burnt* sacrifices. And now that which before was but a type or shadow, and the things so vividly prefigured, have passed away, and we, " upon whom the ends of the world are come," have to do with eternal realities, ay, — the *substance* of the things prefigured, — are there no whole burnt sacrifices to be brought to God's altar ? — " We have an altar whereof they have no right to eat which serve the tabernacle." And has this altar no claims ? How imperative, costly, and exacting were the claims of the altar under the dispensation of types and shadows ! The individuals who failed to meet them according to their several ability were to be cut off from the community of the Israelites. Is it left optional, under the present dispensation of light and glory, whether the comers unto the Christian altar will present their offerings on the altar ? Are there no whole burnt sacrifices required now ? Yes, it is even so ; and this daughter of the Lord Almighty saw that it was not optional with herself, or any other redeemed creature, whether she should present herself on the altar of God in obedience to the command, " Be ye holy."

Constrained by the mercies of God, she presented herself a living sacrifice on the altar erected by God, whereunto the polluted may come, and be made clean — the unholy, and be made holy. It was not the worthiness of the offerer or the greatness of the gift that constituted it " holy, acceptable," but the sanctity of the altar upon which the offering was laid. And here she

resolved that the offering should remain an ever-consuming sacrifice ; that is, ever being given up to God through
Christ.   So resolved was she on this, that she asked that
she might sooner die than remove the offering. She saw
that the blessing was obtained, as also retained, by faith ;
but she also saw that she could have no scriptural
foundation for her faith to rest upon, in believing that
God accepted the sacrifice only so long as it was kept
upon the altar, and she therefore asked in faith, that
the Lord would cut short the work in righteousness, and
take her home to heaven, than ever permit her to live
and see the hour when she might stretch forth an unhallowed hand, and remove the sacrifice from the altar.

Who but may have all the grace they will live for ?
This daughter of the Lord resolved that she would live
for all that it was the will of God she might receive,
however crucifying to the flesh the processes of grace
might be.   From this point God took her, and began to
use her in a manner often surprising to herself, and perhaps equally so to her friends, and in a way that can
only be accounted for from the fact, that in demonstration of his faithfulness, he loves to take the weak things
of this world to confound the mighty, and to remind
the gainsaying and slow of heart to believe, that the
Father has not forgotten his ancient promise, but still
pours out, in these the latter part of the last days, his
Spirit upon his daughters and handmaidens, alike as
upon his sons.   In exemplification of the manner in
which the Lord is fulfilling his promise, in pouring out
his Spirit, we deem it our duty in praise of his faith-

fulness, to single out a few from many recordings we have on hand illustrative of the manner of her unsectarian teachings, and the success with which they were accompanied.

Writing to a friend, after she had been abroad at a special means of grace, she says, —

We attended a meeting held near M——, Pa., last week. The Lord was eminently present. Necessity seemed laid upon us to be abundant in labors, and our God gave ability of body and mind. To the glory of grace we would record God's abundant blessings on our souls. While engaged, instant in season and out of season, in watering others, not only did God water our own souls, but he permitted us to see fruit of our labor in the entire sanctification, and in the awakening and conversion of many. Yes, scores of redeemed sinners were brought home to Christ, and truly a measure of Christ's joy was our joy, as we saw many, who seemed to have been in most active service in the ranks of the enemy, brought to surrender to the Captain of our salvation. And as I saw numbers, one after another, of these champions in the service of sin brought to the altar of prayer, and witnessed them fall on their knees, pierced by the arrows of truth, my soul bounded up in unspeakable triumph. " Salvation, and glory, and honor, and power unto the Lord our God."

THE EFFECT OR FRUIT OF SALVATION.

Many were made perfect in love. I did not hear the number estimated. The work of awakening, justification, and sanctification went on simultaneously. My dear husband and myself labored almost incessantly; and truly did the word of the Lord have free course, and was glorified. Full salvation was also kept much before the people by the ministry. One feature of the work which we observed with peculiar satisfaction was the immediate absorption of those who received the sanctifying seal in the work of *soul-saving*. A number of those hard cases won from the ranks of the enemy, and brought to the feet of Christ, were brought by those who had first been made strong by the power of inward holiness. Yes, those who are made partakers of this grace have their fruit unto holiness.

THE ORDINATION.

It is the ordination which Christ gives his disciples, by the reception of which they are empowered to go forth and bear much fruit. I particularly noticed the experience of one Christian sister thus chosen out and ordained. Her convictions previous to receiving the Spirit's baptism were painful. She saw that it was for want of those clearer perceptions of responsibility, which the experience of entire sanctification gives, that she had been kept from making those personal and earnest efforts for the salvation of the perishing, which she now perceived to be the duty of every one wholly renewed in grace. She saw relatives and friends rapidly verging to eternity.

> 'On slippery rocks she saw them stand,
> While fiery billows rolled beneath."

We had been urging the necessity of entire holiness

in view of the Christian's high and holy responsibilities, when she seemed suddenly arrested to see what her failures had been, and she cried out in anguish of spirit, and made her humble confessions before God. In a few moments she saw not only the faithfulness, but the justice of God was pledged, for immediate forgiveness and cleansing. She resolved on exercising that violence which the kingdom of heaven suffereth, appropriated the promise, and, amid her tears, joyfully testified of the power of Christ to cleanse from all sin. At once the fruits of holiness were exhibited in her experience, and, in the spirit and might of her divine Exemplar, she began to redeem the time by being instant in season and out of season in saving souls.

WHAT, HOLINESS AGAIN!

One minister, a graduate from the Biblical Institute, and who bids fair to be an able minister of the New Testament, received the blessing in a clear and powerful manner, on the afternoon of the first day we reached the place. During the time we were at the meeting, he preached twice, and his ministrations were attended with an unction from the Holy One, which will never be forgotten. Before he had finished his second discourse, which had been an earnest effort to bring sinners to Christ, he paused, and again brought forward, as in his former discourse, the necessity of entire sanctification, and urged it earnestly on the church. In introducing the subject, he anticipated the objections of some, and exclaimed, "What, holiness again! Yes, holiness

180   PROMISE OF THE FATHER.

The pledge redeemed.   What is perfect love?   Our sister looking too high.

again. We promised the Lord if he would give us the blessing that we would have more or less of it in every sermon." He then spoke of his deep regret for former remissness in not having kept the subject more prominently before the people, in view of its all-commanding claims.

IS THAT ALL?

The presiding elder's wife also came out in the profession of perfect love that afternoon. But I think she had long loved God with all her heart ; yet, like many others, whom God has thus empowered to stand up among his witnesses, she seemed not to have recognized the fact that loving God with all the heart *is perfect love.* This reminds me of our own dear sister, who, with several other seekers of perfect love, was bending in lowly prostration at a meeting, pleading for the blessing of holiness. My dear husband, in his advices to another, in an earnest tone, said, " It is loving God with all the heart ! " " Loving God with all the heart ! Why, is that all? I love God with all my heart," she exclaimed. With many others she had thought of the blessing of holiness as an indefinite something beyond her reach ; but now, when she saw that it was simply loving God with all her heart, she found that she was already possessed of the precious pearl above all price ; and the moment she confessed what her heart now believed, the witness came with the confession, and from that hour she has been a witness of perfect love.

On an occasion when she had returned from another series of meetings, in a communication to the Rev. Mr. D——, she observes, —

You ask for reminiscences in connection with the meetings from which we have just returned. I could fill a dozen sheets with desirable recollections ; but circumstances will not admit of this. The Father of mercies, in answer to the intercessions of his Son and the pleadings of his devoted people, was most graciously present with us. In our goings out and our comings in, he was most gloriously near, imparting the constant and conscious aids of his Spirit, and causing that whereunto we turned our hands to prosper. We were permitted, during our several weeks' absence from our dear home, to witness hundreds who received the blessing of pardon, and hundreds more who were baptized of the Holy Ghost. When the invitation was given for those seeking the blessing of purity or pardon to come forward, scores would present themselves. On one occasion, about forty were blessed at one meeting — I mean on one occasion within the space of about two hours. On another occasion, in about the same space of time, about fifty, I should think, were saved. To God be all the glory. I will gather up some incidents, which may give you pleasure, and relate them in as concise a manner as possible.

THE MINISTER.

He had once enjoyed the blessing of holiness, but had now let go his hold, and was plunged in great perplexities. Our time was limited, and would not possibly admit of hearing any long recitals. But he seemed so settled in the conviction that he could not again be-

182   PROMISE OF THE FATHER.

The Holy Spirit's teachings.   Why resisted.   Effects of obedience.

lieve in his heart and attain the grace till all these perplexities were, one by one, removed, that it seemed
difficult and almost cruel to prevent him from the detail. I therefore permitted him to go on for a few
moments, till he came to a point in his narrative about
thus : " Not long since, as I was giving out the hymn,
commencing with, —

> ' There is a fountain filled with blood
> Drawn from Immanuel's veins,'

when I came to the words, —

> ' And here may I, though vile as he,'

the Holy Spirit seemed to urge the question, Why do
you not say, —

> ' And here DO I, though vile as he,
> Wash all MY sins away ' ?

But I did not say it ; if I had, I do not doubt but I
would have received the blessing." We insisted on his
pausing here, saying, " If the Holy Spirit urged you to
say it then, does he not require that you should say it
NOW ? " He would have proceeded with yet further
detailings of his difficulties and errors, but we resolutely persisted in his not proceeding one word further
till the teachings of the Holy Spirit, as far as they had
been given, were obeyed. Presently we succeeded in
getting him to repeat the words, —

> " And here DO I, though vile as he,
> Wash all MY sins away."

As he repeated the words, his faith laid hold on the
promised grace, and, overleaping all difficulties, he was

enabled to overcome by the blood of the Lamb and the word of his testimony. As he continued to *keep* hold, resolved never to doubt, though he might die in the struggle to believe, one victory of faith succeeded another, till joy unspeakable and full of glory filled his soul. It was a conscious death to sin, and a resurrection to a life of holiness. O, how he exulted in the victories of faith ! This is the victory that overcometh the world, even our faith. Great was his yearning now over those who were in like difficulties with himself; and we might mention the case of a brother minister he brought to us the next day, who was in like difficulty with himself, and who experienced a like glorious deliverance by the exercise of that faith which subdues kingdoms and turns to flight the armies of the aliens.

THE LOST SAVED.

We had been talking of the *narrow* way, the necessity of striving to enter in at the strait gate ; of the many who will seek to enter in and not be able, and setting forth the danger of deception. The Holy Spirit applied truth, and several mistaken professors were penetrated by the force of truth, and knelt at the seekers' bench, humbly confessing their sins, and pleading for mercy. Among these was a man who seemed to have been arrested by the enlightenings of the Spirit to see his deceptions, with a suddenness as marked, and well nigh as overwhelming, as that which arrested Saul when journeying to Damascus. Overwhelmed with indescribable terror, he suffered himself to be led forward to the penitent form. But while here, he seemed lost to every thing around him ; and unmindful, apparently, that he was still on the shores of time, and within the precincts of mercy, he cried out, " I am lost ! I am lost ! — lost ! — lost ! What shall I do ? O, what shall I do ? O, I am lost ! — lost ! "

I tried to get his attention by telling him that if he felt himself to be a lost sinner, he was just such as the Saviour came to seek and to save ; but my efforts were utterly vain. The curtain of eternity seemed to have been uplifted, and his naked soul, standing as it were in the awful presence of an angry God, while Christ, the light of the world and the Saviour of sinners, was wholly obscured from his vision. In vain did I entreat him to look to Jesus, and, with a louder and yet louder voice, labored to assure him that he had not yet passed the boundaries of probation, but was yet a prisoner of hope. " I am lost ! — lost ! — lost ! — damned ! — damned ! " was the fearful and only response.

My heart was agonized, and my physical ability unequal to the task of exerting my voice any more. •I was about to give up in despair of meeting his case, when I imploringly said about thus : " I wish you would only stop one moment, and listen to what I have to say." All within hearing were looking on with amazement, and others interposing. I at last succeeded in getting his attention sufficiently to listen to a few interrogatories.

" Are you a sinner ? "

" Yes," was his earnest reply.

" Is Christ the Saviour of sinners ? — then he is your Saviour."

" But I am *such* a sinner ! I have deceived myself. I have been a hypocrite. O Lord, have mercy ! — have mercy ! "

" But you are not a greater sinner than Christ is a Saviour ; are you ? "

He doubtingly shook his head, without apparently any abatement of his agony. When I said, —

" Do you believe the Bible to be the word of God ? "

" Yes."

" Well, the Bible says that Christ is able to save to the uttermost all that come unto God by him ; and if Christ is able to save to the *uttermost*, surely he is able to save *you*. Is he not ? "

Never, while life endures, can I forget the change in that countenance. Quick as the lightning's flash, amid the blackness of deepest night, was the sudden illumination of that rayless mind. The glorious Sun of Righteousness suddenly burst forth, and night of the deepest gloom was changed to midday's high noon splendors, and irradiating a countenance which, but a moment before, was defying description by the blackness of despair. And such words, such burning words as proceeded from his mouth, I will not attempt to describe. I will not attempt, because they were past description. Christ, the light of the world, had revealed himself ; and who can portray on paper the glowing, burning words called forth by the sudden dis-

16 *

186 PROMISE OF THE FATHER.

Seeker of purity.   Is the power of Christ as great on earth as in heaven.

closure of the altogether lovely, to a mind so utterly dark as the one we have described ?

SAVED ON EARTH AS IN HEAVEN.

I had been kneeling by one who was intensely hungering and thirsting after righteousness. With many others, who were longing to prove the power of Jesus to purify the heart and save from all sin, she had openly presented herself as a seeker of purity of heart.

While I was conversing with her, she was enabled to venture believingly on the Redeemer as her present Saviour from all sin. Yet, though she thus believed, still I saw solicitude depicted on her face. I marked her countenance, and inquired if she was not happy in the consciousness that Christ was her present Saviour from all sin. She assured me that she was indeed happy in the thought that Christ was now indeed her present Saviour from all sin ; but the only occasion for solicitude with her now, was the question whether she might be thus kept and saved in the future. " How do I know that he will save me next week or next year ? O, this is the only cause of present care ! "

" If you were in heaven, I suppose you would have no particular solicitude whether Christ could keep you. You think he could keep you there ; do you not ? "

" O, yes, he could keep me in heaven ! "

" Do you believe that all power is given to Christ in heaven and in earth ? "

" I do."

" Do you really believe he has just as *much* power in earth as he has in heaven ? "

" Yes."

" Can he not then keep you just as well on earth as he can keep you in heaven, if you only keep yourself wholly in his hands ? Surely, he will keep that which you have committed into his hands unto the perfect day."

Perfect confidence and unutterable joy took the place of distrust and solicitude, and her now quiet spirit, in blissful reliance, reposed on Him who is able to keep her from falling, and to present her faultless before the presence of his glory with exceeding joy. " To the only wise God, our Saviour, be glory and majesty, dominion and power, both now and forever. Amen."

THAT IS THE QUESTION.

I had not yet risen from the table, after refreshing myself with a little food, when an intelligent-looking young lady, who was an entire stranger to me, came in, and taking me convulsively by the hand, drew me aside, exclaiming, —

" I have been seeking religion for the last ten months."

" Can you not conceive of any reason why it is that God does not reveal himself to you ? Has not any thing been suggested as an object intervening between God and your soul ? "

" I know not of any thing but I would willingly sacrifice for Jesus."

" Are you sure you come to Christ renouncing the world, yourself, and all your sins ? "

" Yes, I am sure."

" Well then, if you come to him, he says, ' Him that

cometh unto me I will in no wise cast out;' and now you say you are sure you come to him, let me ask, does he not receive you?"

" That's the question," she responded quickly.

" Yes, that is indeed the *question*," I replied; "and it is a far more serious question than you imagine. O, if you could only see how it grieves and insults your precious Saviour! Now, suppose you were conversing with a number of your friends, and, unknown to you, I am within hearing. My best earthly friend, whom, of course, I honor and love greatly, is the theme of conversation. You say something by which I may plainly infer that you do not conceive him worthy to be trusted. In fact, I hear you saying, 'I would not trust him any farther than I could see him, or have some sensible demonstration apart from his word.' Would I not feel that you had greatly dishonored my friend, and do you not think I would have reason to feel myself insulted?"

" I think you would."

" You would not expect any special manifestation of my favor after you had thus dishonored my best friend?"

" I do not think I should deserve it."

" And this is just the way in which you are insulting and dishonoring my Saviour. He says, 'Him that cometh to me, I will in no wise cast out.' I ask you if you are sure you come to him. You say, 'Yes, I am sure.' And when I ask, 'Does he not receive you according to his *word*,' you say, 'That is the question,' leaving it plainly to be inferred that you have no confidence in the word of Christ. Just as though you should say, ' I will not *trust* him any farther than I can see him.' And if you were speaking thus of my best earthly friend, what could you say more disreputable ? O, how you insult the Saviour by your questionings ! Surely, you will not dare insult him thus any more."

She seemed to be covered with shame and confusion, and exclaimed, " I *will* believe. I do believe ! " And quickly she gave God the glory due to his name.

Immediately my attention was arrested from this ten months' seeker to one who came beside me, seeking the blessing of entire sanctification. While this seeker of the great salvation was believing and entering into rest, the ten months' seeker left my side, and mingling with a group of Jesus' witnesses, who had gathered a few steps beyond, she was joyfully testifying of her saving faith in the Saviour of sinners.

THE BAPTISM OF FIRE.

Seekers of pardon, and seekers of purity, were in lowly attitude bowed together. Not less than fifty in number, I think, were there, as humble suppliants pleading for promised blessings. I fixed my eye on one who, by her manifestations of fervent and absorbing nearness to the throne of grace, I imagined, was about to lay claim to the grace for which she sought. Just at this point the exercises were varied, and a song of praise was sung, preparatory to the commencement of preaching from the desk. Not more, perhaps, than three minutes had intervened when I noticed that a change of some sort had come over that suppliant. She was joining with the multitude in sacred song. Has the desire of her heart been fulfilled? or has she voluntarily given up the struggle? were questions which gave me some solicitude. I went to her, and asked whether the Lord had fulfilled the desire of her heart. She frankly acknowledged that he had not, and informed me that it was the full baptism of the Holy Spirit she felt she needed, but that she had not yet received the blessing. "Are you willing to have it on God's own terms, by coming out from the world, resolved not to touch, taste, or handle the unclean thing?" I asked. She hesitated a short time, and then responded, " Yes." She wore such worldly appendages as might seem to bespeak her as one of the children of this world rather than a child of the kingdom, and I felt that I must endeavor, in the power of the Spirit, to press the question more closely, and said, " You say you are willing to come out from the world, and be separate. The Bible says, ' Be not conformed to this world ; but be ye transformed by the renewing of your mind.' Now, I ask you in the name of the Lord, will you give up your worldly conformities? You know 'the friendship of the world is enmity with God. Whosoever, therefore, will be a friend of the world is the enemy of God.'" At this point, the struggle returned with singular intensity, so that she was unable to articulate distinctly. I could not but think of the unclean spirits as spoken of in the gospel of our Lord. For in her struggles to give up the world, it seemed as

A death to sin.   Filled with the Spirit.   Companionship with heaven's nobility.

if the god of this world was unwilling to relinquish this
his last hold of this daughter of heaven ; and with
choked utterance she expressed her inability to answer
my inquiries.   It was a crucifixion to the world — a
death to sin ; and the moment she gave up her will,
and said ' Yes,' to the inquiry I had proposed in regard
to giving up the world fully, that moment the struggle
ended, and she sunk back in my arms, overwhelmed
with the power of the Holy Spirit.   She afterwards
informed me that the moment she made the entire surrender, the Spirit suddenly fell upon her, and she felt
its hallowing, consuming influences throughout soul
and body, prostrating her for some time, so that she was
utterly unable to rise.   After this she went about
among the people, filled with the burning love of the
Spirit, inviting her friends to the Saviour.   She was
largely known, and had many friends for whom she
labored, and we trust is still laboring, as the Spirit
gives power and utterance.   O, do not our Marys need
the baptism of fire just as truly as our Peters and
Johns ?

New York, October, 1856.

Rev. Mr. W——.

My dear Brother :   How all-overcoming is faith if
we might only carry about us a living realization
of the fact that it is *faith in God,* not faith in *ourselves,* that we are commanded to exercise !   Surely it
were not difficult for the weakest believer to aspire to
companionship with those of heaven's nobility of whom
the world was not worthy, who, through faith, subdued

kingdoms, wrought righteousness, obtained promises, etc. Faith in God, though small as a grain of mustard seed, is so mighty that it will remove mountains of difficulty.

REACHINGS OF FAITH.

" Faith, mighty faith, the promise sees,
   And looks to that alone,
Laughs at impossibilities,
   And cries, ' It shall be done.' "

" Call upon me, and I will show thee great and mighty things — things which thou knowest not." So saith our wonder-working God. How important, then, that we should endeavor to assure our hearts before the Lord, and gather such inspirations as may induce us to reach out the arm of faith, so as to grasp the highest possible good for ourselves and others! Let us often say to the suppliant soul, —

" Thou art coming to a King :
   Large petitions with thee bring ;
   For his grace and power are such,
   None can ever ask too much."

On Saturday, September 13, 1856, a camp meeting commenced at M——, C. W. From the first hour of the meeting we had much to encourage our faith. The public service began about four o'clock in the afternoon. M—— is between twenty and thirty miles from Coburg, the seat of Victoria College, a very flourishing Wesleyan institution, where are being educated between two and three hundred young men, many of whom are preparing for the ministry. Several of the students were at the camp meeting.   The first sermon was by a young minister who was evidently hungering and thirsting after righteousness.   The preparations for the meeting not being quite completed, it was deemed inexpedient to have a public prayer meeting after the sermon, and some of the students desiring a conversation with us, it was proposed that we adjourn from before the stand to the prayer meeting tent, in order that all who desired might unite in the social interview. That social interview was the germ of most mighty, memorable influences.   It will make its mark, I trust, on the minds of all present for all coming time.

In answer to the invitation to converse with the company, we began by saying, In view of the fact that it is according to our faith it is to be done unto us, it seemed greatly important that our faith should reach the right point.   What had we reason to believe God would be willing to do for us as individuals ? and what would he be willing to do in answer to the prayer of faith for the success of that camp meeting?

First, how far might our faith reach for ourselves ? We live under the dispensation of the Spirit.   If the ushering in of the dispensation of the Spirit was so glorious, what ought we to expect now ?   Surely not a *decrease* of power.   Might every one of Christ's disciples receive a baptism of the Holy Ghost, which would be as penetrating, as ever abiding in its influences, as the baptism that those early disciples received on the day of Pentecost?   Is it as truly the privilege of the disciples of the present day to be filled with faith and the

17

Holy Ghost, as it was the privilege of Stephen to be thus filled? If so, privileges are *duties.* The question now before us is, May we ask in faith, believing it to be according to the will of God that we may be endued with power from on high, baptized with the Holy Ghost and with fire? Whatsoever is not of faith is sin. We must not ask unless we believe it is according to the will of God to give the grace. We must not ask to receive it now, unless we believe it is according to the will of God that we should now receive; otherwise our petition would be a vain repetition; and such we are commanded not to use. The question was then put, and understandingly settled, that we might now ask with perfect agreement, and in expectation of receiving a pentecostal baptism.

The next question was, Do we believe that it is according to the will of God that every sinner who may come upon this encampment may be so arrested by the power of the Holy Spirit as to feel his need of salvation? God will not irresistibly convert, but his word warrants us in the belief that he will irresistibly *convict*; and now may we not ask in faith, that every sinner who may tread on the encampment may feel the power of God's presence, and, as far as may consist with the economy of grace, be constrained to yield to Christ? And in this we were agreed, and the petition was presented.

The next question proposed was, Whether we might not ask that every professor who might tread upon that hallowed ground, not wholly sanctified to God, might be deeply convicted of the necessity of present holiness ; and in this also we were enabled to come to an agreement of faith.   Before we knelt to unite in presenting our petitions, we reëxamined the ground well, to see whether our faith might intelligently take all we had proposed within its grasp.   Then we solemnly bowed, and presented our petitions before the throne in the name of Jesus, believing that, to the degree the things we desired were according to the will of God, we had the petitions we asked of him.

Wonderful, indeed, were the results of that meeting.   The Lord heard, and, to an extraordinary degree, answered our petitions.   I verily believe that the day when the secrets of all hearts shall be revealed, will disclose that there was not one sinner that came on that encampment but was convinced of sin.   All did not yield to these convictions, but scores of convicted sinners were daily presenting themselves as suppliants before the Lord, and scores on scores believed and were saved.   And yet more distinctly marked was the answer in regard to the work of holiness.   So general was the work, that we could not doubt the Sun of Righteousness so penetrated unto the recesses of every professor's heart, that not one but felt keenly that without holiness no man should see the Lord.   And it is believed that none left that encampment without either having obtained the grace, or earnestly resolved that they would never rest without it.   Many also received the baptism of fire.   We have witnessed many glorious outpourings of the Spirit ; but I think in all our former labors, we have never seen a more general work of grace.

November, 1857.

Mr. E. W———.

My dear E. : We are continually meeting with varying and instructive experiences in our journeying, scarcely a tithe of which we are able to note. But I have just been reviewing with my pen a case which seems to meet so truly some points of difficulty, not only in your own, but in the experience of many others, preventing the reception of the full baptism of the Holy Ghost, that I will transcribe and send it to you.

" He loveth our nation, and hath built us a synagogue." So said a minister who was in charge of a meeting, then in progress, as he called our attention to a man of piety, whose benevolent, Christian heart was ever leading him to noble deeds becoming the Christian name. This devoted Christian gentleman, with many others who were seeking the full baptism of the Holy Spirit, was humbly kneeling, pleading with God, and this earnest minister expressed a desire that we should converse with him. We had conversed but a short time before we discerned the difficulty. The blessing of entire sanctification is received by faith, and yet the precise point of time when that faith is definitely brought into exercise, may not be as marked in the case of some as with others. But we think it a vain effort to urge seekers to the exercise of that faith by which alone the blessing is received, without previously ascertaining whether they are on the ground on which

God has promised to receive. God, though no respecter
of persons, is a respecter of *character*. The promises
are conditional. Those who comply with the conditions are already on promised ground, and sustain the
character to which the promises are made ; and to all
such the promises of God are all " Yea and Amen in
Christ Jesus."   But there are many, we are persuaded,
on this ground, who do not appropriate the promises,
and, therefore, do not obtain the witness that they are
cleansed from all filthiness of the flesh and spirit.   Too
many pause here, as though they had reached a point
from which they cannot proceed.   Here they linger as
though in helpless attitude, saying, —

"I cannot wash my heart ; "

and thus we found it with the beloved brother in
Jesus to whom our attention had been directed.

ALL CONSECRATED BUT THE WILL.

He was all consecrated with the exception of his
will. He had been waiting, that the Holy Spirit
should first speak to him in some other way than by
the " sure word of prophecy," unmindful of the fact
that in the estimation of an inspired apostle the sure
word of prophecy was of higher authority, that is, a
more sure foundation for his faith, than either eye or
ear testimony.   " This voice," said Peter, " we heard
when we were with him in the holy mount," and " were
eye witnesses of his majesty."   " We have also a more
sure word of prophecy, whereunto ye do well that ye

17 *

take heed." And in saying thus, we are far from not being earnestly cognizant of the doctrine of the Holy Spirit witnessing to the believing soul of the grace received, for this sure word of prophecy IS the voice of the Holy Ghost, for " holy men of God spake as they were moved by the Holy Ghost." And when the believing soul relies upon the written word, then does the Holy Spirit make those *words spirit* and *life* to the soul. The word of the Lord is not a dead letter. " The words that I speak unto you, they are spirit and they are life." So said our incarnate Lord, the God of the Scriptures of truth. In a word, he had been waiting for a sign or wonder; and while he had been thus lingering, the Saviour had chidingly been saying to him, " Except ye see signs and wonders ye will not believe."

But it is possible, also, to be consecrated without being fully aware of the *precise* moment when we were enabled to make the surrender; yet no one should rest one hour without the knowledge that the last object is given up, and if it has already, through grace, been done, then, though the precise point of time may not be known, it is *due* to the glory of grace that the *fact* should be *acknowledged;* for God is jealous for his glory, and requires of all his creatures the acknowledgment of every good thing that is in them. And in case the recipient believes that God, in accordance with his word, does now receive, that faith cannot be retained, neither can it be *made* effectual in the sanctification of others, unless it be communicated; inasmuch as it is written, " That the communication of your faith may be effectual by the acknowledgment of every good thing that is in you in Christ Jesus."

But the difficulty in the way of believing is, doubtless, with many, that the question, in regard to the *fact* of their entire consecration, is still unsettled.   On the part of this Christian brother, this was partially in the way ; but the difficulty was easily removed in his case the moment he resolutely subjected himself to the test of truth.

" Do you not love the Lord, your God, with all your heart, soul, mind, and strength? " we asked.

He hesitated in answering the question ; but, from what we observed of the evidently consuming ardors of his soul, and from what we had heard said of the manifest devotion and integrity of his life, we felt quite sure that the question of supreme love to God might be settled at once.

THE QUESTION SETTLED, AND THE WITNESS RECEIVED.

If the world, with all its aggrandizements, its every conceivable pleasure and honor, were concentrated and placed here, on one hand, and on the other hand were placed your once-despised Saviour, who made himself of no reputation for you, with all his disreputableness, his cross and ignominy, and the question were proposed, Which will you choose? would you not spurn the world, and a thousand times sooner say, Give me Jesus — the naked Saviour and the cross ?   " O, yes," he unhesitatingly exclaimed.   " And does not this prove that God has the supreme affections of your soul, and that you do, indeed, love him with all your heart?"

Most readily did his heart and lips respond to the fact of his supreme love to God, which he now saw might have been settled long before. What he wanted to know was, that the offering was on the altar, and that it was accepted; and, now that he believed what God had done for him, and testified of his personal realizations of the infinite efficacy of that blood that cleanseth from all sin, he rejoiced with a "joy unspeakable and full of glory." From that hour he was recognized as a joyful witness of perfect love. We were about leaving that region for another meeting. On parting with him he said, "You may hear from me again." The second hearing came in a few days, not by word of mouth, but in the form of a friendly epistle, the reading of which will, I am sure, delight every Christian heart.

THE OPEN TESTIMONY.

E——, October 5, 1857.

My dearly beloved Sister : When I said, on giving you the parting hand, that you might hear from me again, I had no idea of writing you so soon. But, as it is near the lapse of a week now, since the Lord sped your willing feet to enlighten and confirm me in the grace of sanctification, methinks you will rejoice with me, to know that the presence of the Lord has not been with me since, as the pillar of fire by night; neither has it been with me as a cloud by day, but as an unclouded sun. I have neither raptures nor transports; but, when I muse on Jesus crucified, sometimes the fire burns and the tears flow, and the thought conceived, that, if destined to the most obscure corner of heaven, that when I will give utterance to the words, " Unto him that loved me, and washed me from my sins, in his own blood, to him be glory," &c., the whole empire of the redeemed would pause and look behind them. It would afford me much pleasure, if you judge it expedient, to give testimony for me at your present meeting. In hope of being one with you and your loving and beloved husband, I remain yours,   P. S.

New York, November 12, 1857.

To the Rev. H. V. D——.

Dear Brother: A letter is before me, dated September 17, which would have received a much earlier reply if our time had been at our own command. Little did we imagine that we should have been so long detained from home. But Christ, the Captain of our salvation, has been our rereward, and, we believe, has ordered all the way before us. I trust we have deeply, and at heart, felt, for many years past, the significance of the divine declaration, " Not by might, nor by power, but by my Spirit," saith the Lord of hosts. But never before, perhaps, have we so experimentally apprehended the earnest import of this all-important truth. If good is done in the earth, it is through the might of the Lord of hosts. If holy conquests are gained, it is he who " teacheth our hands to war and our fingers to fight." But I feel that it is due to the praise of all-conquering grace to record that I have not, during the past twenty years, been prone to the temptation that I can do any thing effectually but through the might of the Holy Spirit. Human or even angelic agencies are utterly impotent, only as energized by the might of the Spirit. Though Gabriel were called to minister here on earth, by way of talking or writing, the ministrations of his lips or pen would be powerless for good otherwise than made effectual through the direct agency of the Holy Spirit.

AN EVENTFUL EVENING.

On the evening of July 26, 1837, between the hours of eight and nine o'clock, the Lord gave me such a view of my utter pollution and helplessness, apart from the cleansing, energizing influences of the purifying blood of Jesus, and the quickening aids of the Holy Spirit, that I have ever since retained a vivid realization of the fact. I feel that I have received the sentence of death in myself; that I should not trust in myself, but in him that raiseth the dead. The tempter oftener makes attempts to paralyze the energies of my faith on this wise : "You know that you have received the sentence of death in yourself, and, without the living power of a living, indwelling Christ, momentarily purifying and quickening your being, you can do nothing. And dare you, with all your unworthiness, claim momentarily this cleansing, energizing power from on high ? " Yes, I dare claim it. Alleluia !

| Offering bound to the altar. | Kept on the altar. | Witness retained. |

> " No condemnation now I dread ;
>   Jesus, and all in him, is mine !
>   Alive in him, my living Head,
>   And clothed in righteousness divine,
>   Bold I approach the eternal throne,
>   And claim the crown through Christ my own."

THE PROMISED GIFT RETAINED, AND HOW.

It was at this point, in my career of discipleship, that I received the promise of the Father.   The sacrifice of all my entire being had now been made.   The offering had not only been placed upon the altar, but it was also bound there in view of all coming time, and in contemplation of every conceivable emergency.

Daily and hourly, since that eventful period, have I claimed it.   But it is only by a *continuous act of surrender, and a ceaseless act of faith,* that I claim and retain the grace.   Not an hour, I trust, has passed since that hallowed evening, twenty years since, in which I have not felt that I would rather die than knowingly offend God.   Through grace I have been empowered to present myself to God a *living* sacrifice.   Through Christ, who strengtheneth me, I have been enabled to *keep* the sacrifice upon the altar ; and through the grace of our Lord Jesus Christ I have *retained* the witness that the blood of Jesus cleanseth from all unrighteousness.   Not because of the worthiness of the offerer, or the greatness of the gift, has the offering been accepted, but because of the infinite virtues of that ALTAR upon which the offering has been laid.   Not on the ground that I have never erred in thought, word,

or deed, but on the ground that I have, through the
enabling power of the Holy Spirit, *kept* the offering on
the altar, with a *sincere intention* to glorify God in all
things, and conscious of supreme love to my Saviour.
And while I have thus kept my unworthy offering on
the *Christian's altar*, presenting myself a *living* sacrifice to God, I have not dared to dishonor Christ, by
doubting whether the offering is "wholly acceptable
unto God." In view of the *medium* through which it is
being continually presented, that is, *through* Christ, I
dare not doubt.

Nay, rather, I will, I do believe,

> "If all the sins which men have done,
>   In thought, in will, in word or deed,
> Since worlds were made, or time begun,
>   Were laid on one poor sinner's head,
> The stream of Jesus' precious blood
> Would wash away the dreadful load."

Neither the worthiness of the offerer, nor the greatness of the gift, is the availing plea or the ground of
acceptance, but the infinitely meritorious blood of Jesus.
This is the new and living way by which alone a redeemed world may enter into the holiest. And it is
only by a continuance in this way, that is, by plunging
deeper and yet deeper into the purple flood, that we can
rise higher and yet higher in all the life of God. It
is by this purifying, energizing process, that my soul,
once dead in trespasses and sins, is being continually
raised and sustained in *newness* of life. Momentarily
am I being enabled to obey the command, " Likewise,

PROMISE OF THE FATHER. 205

New lessons of grace.   Casting anchor deeper within the veil.   Love of truth.

reckon ye also yourselves to be dead indeed unto sin, but alive to God through Jesus Christ our Lord."

MANIFESTATIONS OF SPIRITUAL LIFE.

And this spiritual life has its legitimate manifestations. If thus quickened and risen with Christ, then the life of Christ must be manifest in this mortal flesh. It is due to the glory of God to say, that, as year succeeds year, bearing me nearer to the hour when this mortal shall put on immortality, I feel yet more of the blessedness of the life-giving power within. The Spirit worketh in me yet more and more mightily to will and to do. Many new and most blessed lessons is the Spirit teaching me, as I daily cast anchor yet deeper within the veil. Instead of shrinking from the cross of Christ as formerly, it is now cause of my chief glorying. I feel that Christ has taken up his abode in my heart. He is my indwelling Saviour.

DOCTRINES OF THE CROSS UNPOPULAR.

The doctrines of the cross never have been popular with the world ; neither will they ever be until the world is renewed in righteousness. But I find, through the indwelling of Christ, that my heart is becoming yet more and more in love with *Truth.* And however disreputable its doctrines to the perceptions of the world-loving professor, my soul longs to apprehend it fully, in order that, with all the fervors of my being, I may embrace it, and set forth its excellency before a gainsaying world. But my spirit is continually reaching

18

out for more of all the fulness of God.   And while I ask, I receive, and am being enabled to apprehend yet more perfectly that for which I have been apprehended by Christ.   Now unto Him that is able to do exceeding abundantly above all that we can ask or think, according to the power that worketh in us, unto him be glory in the church by Christ Jesus throughout all ages, world without end.   Amen.

EXEMPLIFICATIONS OF POWER.

Shall I lay before you some exemplifications of this power, as we have witnessed them during the past summer and fall months ?   We can take but a slight glance as we pass on ; but I am sure you will, from the review, thank God, and take courage.

We will commence our review by saying, that quite a large portion of the scenes which we introduce to your attention are laid in Canada.   Holiness is power. And in Canada this fact has been demonstrated to a degree beyond what we have witnessed elsewhere.   The reason is obvious.   In Canada the doctrine of Christian holiness, as taught by Wesley, and set forth in our Book of Doctrines and Discipline, is not left open for controversy.   Ministers are not *permitted* to talk or preach before the people as though it were left open as a matter for doubtful disputation.   It is conceded that those who unite with the Wesleyan Church approve of her doctrines, and are, of course, bound to sustain them as scriptural.   We do not remember to have heard of but one departure from this.   It was in the case of a

minister, who, in his preaching, confounded the blessing
of justification and sanctification as one and the same
thing, as many a Methodist minister has with impunity
done in the United States.   But it was not with impunity that our Canada Methodist minister could be
recreant to his trust in sustaining the doctrines of the
church.   His case was at once reported, and at the
ensuing conference of ministers he was affectionately,
yet authoritatively, dealt with.   The consequence was,
that he renounced his error, and, at a recent camp
meeting, he, with true nobleness of mind, yet with
humility and earnestness, presented himself as a seeker
of the blessing of entire sanctification.   Before the
meeting closed, he testified, before hundreds, of the all-
cleansing efficacy of the blood of Jesus, the definite
witness of which he had that morning received.

A WESLEYAN MINISTER'S OPINION.

In speaking of the camp meetings of the last four or
five years in Canada, a superintendent of a circuit, in a
recent magazine, observes, " The history of these camp
meetings has never been written — it *can* never be written.   The light of eternity alone can unfold it.   I wish
it were in the power of my poor pen to describe some
of the scenes which we have witnessed in connection
with their progress.   We have seen a thousand persons
on their knees at a prayer meeting.   We have seen
upwards of a score of souls converted before they even
rose from their knees, and perhaps not less than fifty
saved at a single prayer meeting.   It is to be regretted,

that we have not been more careful in preserving the statistics of these meetings. The number actually saved, I am persuaded, is generally much larger than is supposed."

Seven such camp meetings have we attended in Canada during the past summer and autumn, all of which were signally owned of God in the conversion of sinners and the sanctification of believers. I am persuaded that at the most of these meetings there were not less than two hundred converted. Three others we attended in the United States were also much blessed of the Lord. So that those we have witnessed saved at camp meetings alone, number many hundreds.

THE TONGUE OF FIRE RECEIVED, AND ITS EFFECTS.

And never before have we witnessed such effusions of the Spirit on believers. Hundreds on hundreds have received the tongue of fire, and have returned to the cities and villages round about, filled with faith and the Holy Ghost to spread the pentecostal flame. Would time permit, I could tell you of instances of this sort which would fill you with admiration of the grace of God. We paused at one place, a few miles from where a camp meeting had been held. The state of the society had not been prosperous. There were, we were informed, but sixteen church members, and the minister told us that not more than half of these were available. As we passed through the village, a little before sunset, and looked at the neat and rather commodious church, and the meagre population, we thought, Can that church

The village church filled.   Awakened station master.   Pledges to work for God.

edifice be filled with this population? Evening came, and the people came pouring in from the surrounding country, so that, to our surprise, the church was filled. The circumstances, in brief, were these. Several from that little village had been at the camp meeting, and had been newly baptized. A young man, who was engaged as station master at the railroad depot, had been deeply convicted of his need of a Saviour. This young man had used all the aids afforded him by virtue of his position as station master, and also in having access to the telegraphic wires, to spread abroad the intelligence of the meeting, and thus the irreligious and people of various denominations were gathered in from the surrounding country. The power of God came down upon the people, and a number were saved. The invitation was scarcely given to come to the altar of prayer to seek salvation before it was surrounded. Among the first that were seen rushing to the altar, was the station master. He had been bowed but a few moments before he was enabled to rise and testify of the great things God had done for his soul. The work went on with still greater power, until, from the last advices we received, eighty had been newly brought into the fold.

HUNDREDS PLEDGING THEMSELVES TO WORK.

This is but a specimen of what we have heard of the spread of the holy flame from various points where we have attended meetings. At each camp meeting hundreds have pledged themselves to work daily, in endeavors to win souls to Jesus. And from various

18 *

directions are we hearing that these efforts of the laity are being greatly owned in bringing sinners to God.

At all these places much prominence has been given to the doctrine of entire sanctification. In as close connection does the doctrine of the baptism of the Holy Ghost stand with the conversion of sinners, as did the conviction and conversion of three thousand stand in necessary connection with the reception of the Holy Ghost on the part of the early disciples.

Peter might have labored five years, and not have accomplished as much as he did in five hours after he received the baptism of fire. We should speak at a low computation, should we express it as our belief that we have seen one thousand souls sanctified, and from fifteen hundred to two thousand souls justified during the past summer and autumn.

THOROUGHNESS OF THE WORK.

The characteristics of this great work have been most inspiring, and portentous of good. The thoroughness of the work has exceeded, as a whole, any thing we have before witnessed. In the unpardoned sinner, conviction of sin has been deep and pungent, and conversions unmistakably clear and powerful. In the reception of entire sanctification, there was a counting of the cost, and an absolute, unconditional, eternal surrender of all to Christ. There was an experimental apprehension of the fact that the body of the believer has been redeemed unto God, as a temple for the Holy Ghost to dwell in.

JEWELRY AND THE NOXIOUS WEED DISCARDED.

And being thus yielded up, believingly, the Spirit took conscious possession, females putting aside jewelry and artificials, and other badges of worldly conformity; the men casting aside the noxious weed, and other questionable habits, acting on the principle that their bodies, as temples for God, must not be defiled, but nourished and cherished as a habitation for God. The result has been that these earthly temples thus set apart for God were filled with the Spirit. And then the gift of utterance was given, and burning words have flowed out upon the people, penetrating the hearts of the unbelieving multitude, convincing the most sceptical that apostolic times were again being returned to the church. These, as before stated, have gone to their homes to scatter the holy fire in all the surrounding country, and revivals are breaking out in every region. May the work go on till the kingdoms of this world shall become the kingdom of our God and of his Christ.

Again she writes:

DO I WALK WORTHY OF MY FATHER?

So I asked myself, as I heard our excellent Bishop J—— discourse from Col. i. 9–12. What a prayer is this! If you have not very recently read it over, do just now get your Bible, and on your knees ponder over it, and then present it to God ceaselessly in your own behalf. Paul said he did not *cease* to pray that it might be answered for his Colossian brethren. I have presented it daily, weeks in succession, in my own behalf, since early in my heavenward career, and feel still that I cannot enter upon the duties of the day without *believing* that God will fulfil this, the *ceaseless* desire of my heart.

The bishop dwelt some time on the portion of the text, "That ye may walk *worthy* of the Lord unto all pleasing." Never has my heart been inspired with a more engrossing desire to walk carefully before the Lord. I know that the prayer, to be "filled with the knowledge of the will of God," must be first answered, or I *cannot* walk worthy of him unto all pleasing. Bishop J. mentioned an incident of a young lady who was the daughter of a minister. She was not pious; but, when asked to unite in the foolish amusement of dancing, she almost indignantly replied, "My father is a minister, and I respect him and his calling too much to do what I know would be so displeasing to him." She wished to walk *worthy of her father.* The good bishop, then addressing himself to every child of God present, affectionately asked, "Do you walk *worthy* of your Father unto all pleasing?"

AN INCIDENT IN MY EXPERIENCE.

"That ye might be filled with the knowledge of his will in all wisdom and spiritual understanding." What a privilege is here, and, in view of the fact that every prayer inspired by the Holy Spirit is equivalent to a promise, how inspiring! And here I am reminded of an incident, in my experience of many years since, in connection with this passage. And as I have often seen where an experience, such as I on this occasion had, might have been instructive to others, I will relate it, that you may gain by my failure. A short time after I gave myself wholly to the service of my Saviour, I was at a place where a series of meetings was being held. During one of the services where the ministers and people had assembled for a season of social worship, the spirit of supplication was poured out upon them in an extraordinary degree. There, in humble prostration, were bowed some seeking to be perfected in love, and others seeking pardon. O, it was a meeting of earnest pleaders, where, with strong crying and tears, they sought the promised grace. I exclaimed, Would that some one might talk about faith in Jesus, through whom alone the promised grace can be received!

If I might judge from the manifest sincerity and earnestness of these suppliants, I could not doubt but they were prepared, through the mighty inworkings of the Holy Spirit, for the reception of the proffered grace. All that now seemed to be needed was, that their attention should be turned away from themselves to an act of reliance on Christ. And O, how I longed that some one of that company might be directed by the Spirit to say, " Look away from yourselves — O, look to Jesus. Obey the divine command at once, — ' Have faith in God.' " To my spiritual perceptions it seemed as plain as noonday that but one more step was needful, and those redeemed, earnest suppliants would be ushered into a region of light, purity, and power.

It was suggested, "Why do you not let the Lord speak through your lips?" I had so recently taken the steps myself by which I had been justified, and yet more recently sanctified, that I thought surely I ought to have a more *special* commission before taking upon myself a work involving so much responsibility. Here are teachers in Israel, and other persons of prominence, and surely I should wait for a special commission for a work of such magnitude. Ah, I ought to have remembered that an emergency constitutes duty; and had I been promptly answerable to the emergency, unquestionably many would have been saved. But instead of this, I sought a place of retirement, where I might alone before God be specially instructed in relation to the duty. I had scarcely bowed my knees in the presence of the Lord, to make definite inquiry in regard to duty, in this emergency, when the Holy Spirit, somewhat chidingly, whispered to my heart, —

"Did you not, this morning, ask to be filled with the knowledge of the will of God, with all wisdom and spiritual understanding? And did you not believe, when you asked, that you received the thing you desired of God? Why, then, did you not go forward, doing that which was in your heart, knowing that the Lord was with you?" I saw my error, and hastened back to do the work; but the opportunity was gone! I had occupied the time, which ought to have been spent in doing the work, in inquiring of the Lord about that which my judgment should have made plain. And now that company was about to disperse, and the opportunity was lost. I was convicted of my error in judgment, and felt ashamed before the Lord; but I felt my heavenly Father did not condemn me, for he saw that my *intention* was to please him. I have since been endeavoring to act upon the principle of *faith*, believing, when I ask to be filled with the knowledge of God's will, that he hears me. Trusting in him for a sanctified judgment, I hasten, as emergencies call for promptness in action, believing that providential indications are manifestations of the will of God.

CAN ONE MADE MEET FOR HEAVEN REMAIN ON EARTH?

" Giving thanks unto the Father, who hath made us meet to be partakers of the inheritance of the saints in light." And can one, after having been made all ready *meet* for heaven, still remain below, carrying out the purposes of God on earth, as angels carry out the purposes of God in heaven? " This question," says Bishop J., " is satisfactorily answered in the foregoing text. Paul includes himself as among the recipients of this grace, ' made *us* meet to be partakers of the inheritance of the saints in light.' " Yet Paul remained some time on earth after this was written. And not until we are in this state are we raised to that entire newness of life contemplated in the scheme of redemption.

It was not a partial redemption, but a redemption from ALL iniquity, which was wrought out by Christ. And not until we experimentally know the power of this redemption in the entire renewal of our nature, having this meetness for the inheritance of the saints in light, are we prepared to do the will of God on earth as angels do in heaven.   Not until this is our experience have we a full fitness for our work ; for it is not until we are delivered from the hand of our enemies that we are prepared to serve him without fear, in holiness and righteousness, *all the days of our lives,* leaving it most evidently inferrible that our entire meetness to serve the Lord *on earth* just *begins* at precisely the point where the majority of professed Christians strangely persuade themselves it must end.

"We are members of the royal family, and our Father would have us wear our white robes every day." Ay, more ; we are of the royal priesthood, a holy nation.   Surely our Father will be displeased, after he has, at such an expenditure, purchased white robes for us, if, as his children, we go about with garments soiled and polluted by the world.

SAVED AFTER SHE HAD CEASED TO WEEP.

My dear S—— : I do not wonder that your heart is so sad, that you speak of yourself as undone, and that your tears are flowing so freely.   From your very childhood you have known that sin was exceedingly hateful in the sight of a pure and holy God.   You have also known that you were a sinner ; that Jesus died to redeem you from sin.   And though the Holy Spirit has been continually telling you that you ought to repent of sin, and yield yourself up to the claims of your Redeemer, and you have been constrained to think of these things, yet you have never, till within a short time, really resolved to bring these convictions of duty to a serious issue. You have never, till now, fully decided that you would break off your sins by repentance, and come to Christ, with all your heart, for salvation.

And now that you would come to your Saviour, you see a great mountain of sin intervening. You are pressing hard after Christ; but the harder you press the higher the mountain seems to rise. And I imagine the adversary tells you that this is because you are getting worse; and I know some pious people, who do not intend to do wrong, may, even without designing to favor these suggestions of the adversary, do so. They will tell you that you are getting worse because you do not submit. We will not stop to inquire whether they are right or wrong just at this point; but there is a way to account for this on what we know to be purely scriptural principles, and in a manner to encourage, rather than to discourage, your sincere endeavors in approaching to Christ. In referring to your sincerity I do not praise you, for you could no more of yourself be sincere in your endeavors to renounce sin and come to Christ, than Satan could be sincere. It is the Holy Spirit that has enabled you thus to resolve to come to your Saviour. And I do not doubt but every moment since you resolved that you would repent, and have been showing your sincerity before God by renouncing one sin after another, you have been drawing nearer to God. And while you have been drawing nigh to God,

19

he has been drawing nigh to you. God is *light*. The nearer you get to him by true repentance, the more enlightened you become. This is the reason why you see the mountain of sin higher; for as you, in getting nearer to God, get more light, you have more vivid perceptions of the exceeding sinfulness of sin. This surely does not make you more sinful. The more you see of the exceeding sinfulness of sin, the more you abhor it; and the more thoroughly you renounce it, the nearer you come to a point where God may accept you for Christ's sake. Repentance is one of the graces which brings you nigh to God —

> " True belief and *true* repentance,
> Every grace that brings you nigh."

But repentance, though a gift from God, cannot save you. Christ is the *only* Saviour. You may weep, and weep your life away, but rivers of tears will not purchase pardon.

A short time since I was called to see one who was perhaps yet more deeply distressed than yourself, in view of her condition as a sinner. The person who called for me to go and converse with her friend observed, as she was taking me to her, " She has been seeking religion six months." I found her weeping, convulsively, with her handkerchief pressed closely to her face. So desperate and engrossing was her sorrow, that, though I tried prayerfully to direct her to Christ, I could not feel satisfied that my words produced effect, or were even heard. If I had thought that there was any virtue in her sighs and tears to move the pity of God, without an exercise of faith, I should certainly have thought her in a fair way of obtaining mercy, and would not have diverted her attention from those agonizing views of herself and her sins. But I knew she would as surely perish, if she did not look to Jesus, as those Israelites, after they had been bitten in the wilderness, would have perished, if they had looked at their wounds instead of looking at the brazen serpent. My time was limited, and I knew that what I said must be said quickly ; but my heart yearned over her, and I felt that I could not leave her in such a condition. I therefore resolved on an effort to get her attention, though it might be at the expense of her weeping a few less tears, when the following ensued : —

" Will you give me your attention ? If not, my efforts to talk with you will do no good. I profess to have been a traveller in the way to heaven a number of years, and any one that has travelled a way ought to know something about it. Do you think I know any thing about the way to heaven ? Do you ? " I paused, waiting for an answer, remarking, " I cannot talk unless you give your attention to me, and answer my inquiries." I then again said, " If you think I know any thing about the way to be saved, will you listen to me, and take my advice ? "

" I will," she replied.

" Then wipe away your tears, and put your handkerchief away from your face, and let us have a little conversation. Tell me, then, do you think you are a sinner ? "

She looked surprised that I should ask a question which her heart had been so free to acknowledge, and said, " Yes."

" Well, if you are a sinner, and Christ is the Saviour of sinners, is he not *your* Saviour ? "

She hesitated, thoughtfully, and then replied, " He is *my* Saviour ! "

" Have you ever thanked the Saviour for having died to save you ? "

She lingered in replying, when I said, " If you had been condemned to death by the laws of your country, and were greatly distressed in view of the sentence awaiting you, and a friend comes to you and says, ' I will die in your stead,' and then the penalty of the law is inflicted, and he actually dies for you, how would you regard the memory of such a friend ever after ? How you would be ever thinking, I live because he died ! O, would you not love to think of that friend ? Just such a friend Jesus has been to you. He has died in your stead ! Yes, he died ! But his love did not end here. He lives again. Just now, while I am talking to you, he is making intercession for you, he is pleading your cause. What a precious Saviour ! What a glorious Redeemer ! How he has loved you ! O, I am afraid you have not been thanking him for these manifestations of love, as you should have done. If an earthly friend had shown you such love, how you would thank him ! and now will you not thank *your* Saviour for having died in your stead ? He loves to be praised ; for he says, ' Whoso offereth praise glorifieth me.' Surely you will now say, ' Glory be to Jesus, *my* Saviour ! ' "

She now seemed forgetful of her tears, for her eye had been taken off from herself and fixed on Jesus. Softly she began to breathe out, " Glory be to Jesus, *my* Saviour ! " Again and again she repeated it, with yet stronger emphasis, till her whole heart seemed to flow out in the impelling influences of praise and adoration. I think at first she began to praise the Saviour without any impelling influence to do so, feeling that it would be ungrateful not to thank him for such wonderful manifestations of love ; but as her heart began to flow out in grateful praise, the Lord poured in, till she joyously cried out from impelling influences, " O, what a precious Saviour ! what a glorious Redeemer ! "

COST OF FAITH'S SUPERSTRUCTURE.

My beloved Brother : He who hath begun a good work in you will surely carry it on, and finish it in righteousness, if you will only abide carefully in his presence, and, with earnest circumspection, attend to all the dictations of his gracious Spirit.

> " Yes, Lord, thou still dost lead
> The children of thy grace,
> The chosen, the believing seed,
> Through this vast wilderness.
>   * * *
> " Thy chart the written word,
> The Holy Ghost thy Guide,
> And Christ, thy glorious, risen Lord,
> Will in thy heart reside."

19 *

And would you indeed be willing to meet the cost of having the foundation of the superstructure of your faith deeply laid, and the building reared after the pattern shown in the holy mount ? O, would you, with every coming hour, feel yet more of the enabling, confirming, ever-abiding influences of the Spirit, causing your rapid growth and maturity in grace ? Then count the cost. Though the awards of grace are free, yet there is a sense in which the reception of grace always costs us something. That we may have all the grace we will live for, we judge a well-ascertained fact. But the answer to the prayer for an extraordinary bestowment of grace stands in connection with compliance on our part with the condition that the divine gift shall be *tested.* As in the case of the two brothers, who would have had the signal honor of sharing in the glory of Christ's coming kingdom to an extraordinary degree, so the question comes to the disciple of the present day who would covet the glorious gift of great nearness to Christ. Those brothers had not counted the cost. They knew not what they asked.

But knowledge is increased, and, by their erring, we may be instructed. We are admonished to covet earnestly the best gifts. And if the bestowment of large measures of grace implies the necessity of remarkable tests, why not stand ready for the application, and conclude to receive the grace at the well-ascertained cost. Counting the cost suggests the idea of some tax on the *intellect.* Though the claims of the blessed religion of our Lord Jesus Christ may be apprehended by persons of small mental capacity, yet it also commends itself most significantly to men of mind. Does not this divine admonition, to count the cost, call into requisition the *mental* ability ? Can cost, involving such far-reaching consequences, be counted without making some tax on the *intellect ?*

I knew one who, verily and strongly impressed with the belief that the claims of the Redeemer levied an absolute tax on the entire being, *intellectual,* spiritual, and physical, was induced thus to count the cost of living in the actual, ceaseless surrender of her whole being. Deliberately and understandingly, and unimpelled by exciting influences, she, with solemn calmness, counted the cost of entering into the bonds of an everlasting covenant, desiring that it should be well ordered and sure, so that no regrets or questionings might mar the future, now destined to entire devotedness. She looked abroad over earth, far as her mental vision could reach. Cherished ideas of worldly position and fondly-indulged objects of intellectual ambition passed in solemn review. But the assurings of the Spirit, that every mere earthly ambition must perish, and the pearl which cost all demanded all in return, prevailed. Grace triumphed. All things were counted loss. Earthly endearments, worldly preferments, and all ideas of mere intellectual ambition, were surrendered and bound everlastingly to the altar of the cross. And here sorrow and joy commingled. Nature suffers in the process of crucifixion. We cannot bind our Isaac to the altar without the cost of some unutterable heart pangs. But light emanates from the cross.

The cost being counted, and all sacrificed for the excellency of the knowledge of Christ, then Christ, as our light and our salvation, reveals himself in the soul, and becomes our life, light, and power, and we quickly find that, in giving all, we have received all in Christ. Your foundation being thus deeply laid on the Rock of Ages, the superstructure of your faith will rise rapidly in glory and strength. Having given up the citadel of your heart unconditionally and irrevocably to Christ, he comes to abide with you forever. Christ undertakes the work of your salvation, and works in you, and calls you to be a *worker together* with him, with articles of agreement clearly specified that you are to draw upon him for all your resources. In him all fulness dwells. Beginning to build thus surely, you will be able to finish. Of Christ's fulness you will ever be receiving grace for grace.

Yet we do not wish you to be unmindful of the fact that these ever-augmenting accessions of grace will be *tested*, ay, tried to the uttermost. But we do wish you to be ever mindful of this, that Christ consummates a holy *partnership* with those who enter into covenant with him by sacrifice. And the articles of agreement specify, that it is your privilege to draw upon Christ in every conceivable emergency to which your faith may be subjected. And, with the privilege of raising the superstructure, with infinite resources at command, surely you need never fear a *failure*. The foundation of your building being thus begun, you need fear no bankruptcy. Yes, you will be able to finish. Your

PROMISE OF THE FATHER. 225

Ask what ye will.   A marked point in the Christian's career.   Bible the text book.

supplies in Christ will be unfailing. Forever will your almighty Helper be saying to you, " Ask what ye will in my name, and it shall be done unto you."

After our friend received the promise of the Father, catholicity of spirit was a marked trait in her character. Speaking of the various evangelical denominations, we have heard her say, " It is the degree of conformity to the image of the Saviour that settles the nearness of my relationship. ' Whosoever doeth the will of my Father, which is in heaven, the same is my brother, and sister, and mother ; ' and such is my love to all the members of the household of faith, that I can hardly say in relation to any one denomination, Benjamin is my brother." There surely is a point in the upward career of the Christian to which Paul refers, when he says, " till we all come to the unity of the Spirit " — a point

> " Where names, and sects, and parties fall,
> And Christ alone is all in all."

Truly as our natural being seeks its affinities, and to have this social want of nature met turns to the friendly circle, thus our renewed being seeks affinities. To meet this want of the spiritual being of all of every evangelical sect who are disposed to count all things loss for the excellency of the knowledge of Christ, she has for the past twenty years had a weekly meeting established at her house, where ministers and people of various denominations meet, and the Bible alone is the text book, irrespective of denominational creeds. At this hallowed place, hundreds have, within the past twenty

years, received the endowment of power, which Christ
promises to all who in faith wait for it.

As many inquiries are being made from near and remote regions, in relation to the manner of conducting
this meeting, and in view of the fact that it has been so
signally owned of the Lord by the extraordinary
out-pourings of his Spirit, we will transfer from the
· "Guide to Holiness" an account of these highly favored meetings.

THE TUESDAY AFTERNOON MEETING.

What is the character of these meetings ? Perhaps
we may not be able to answer this question better than
by giving an extract from an editorial which we copy
from a Congregational paper. It reads thus : —

Friends, we assure you that these meetings are not
for sectarian or party purposes. A free, hearty, general invitation is extended to all, of every name, to sit
together in heavenly places in Christ Jesus. Inquirers
of different denominations are taken with equal cordial-
ity and warmth to the heart of love. Instruction is
imparted to all and every one, without distinction,
seeking higher attainments in the divine life. Prayer
to God is offered with equal fervency, and prevailing
importunity in one case as in another.

Our very soul has leaped joyfully in witnessing how
completely the Spirit of God annihilates the spirit of
sectarianism, and leaps over the boundaries of Shibbo-
leths. Here we see Methodists, Baptists, Presbyterians, Episcopalians, Quakers, United Brethren, and

Jews, in Christ, forgetting creeds, confessions, hair-splittings, and party distinctions, sitting side by side, drinking deeply of the one living fountain. And should there happen to be any one present, who, through mistake, or for want of a due sense of gospel propriety, gives a preponderance in favor of any party, creed, or sect, a cold chilliness steals over every one present. And those who follow such a one, pour in the oil and wine of gospel grace, to obliterate, if possible, the least *tincture* of the sect, and smooth off the rough edges, and calm every rising suspicion.

THE BIBLE, THE BLESSED BIBLE, IS THE TEXT BOOK.

Not Wesley, not Fletcher, not Finney, not Mahan, not Upham, but the Bible, the holy BIBLE, is the first and last, and in the midst always. The BIBLE is the standard, the groundwork, the platform, the creed. Here we stand on common ground, and nothing but the spirit of this blessed book will finally eradicate and extirpate a sectarian spirit. No meetings are attended with more direct and *special* indications of divine acceptance. God is evidently present in a very remarkable manner to bless, sanctify, and purify.

Hundreds have stepped into this Bethesda, and come out every whit whole. The atmosphere is invigorating, healthful, and heavenly. Any one has perfect liberty to rise and request prayers, or relate the dealings of God with his soul, drop a word of exhortation, exposition, or consolation, or pour out his heart in prayer or praise, always remembering to be brief, and to the *point*, and never losing sight of the main object of the meeting — " Holiness to the Lord." These meetings are not for debate, controversy, or speechifying, but for holiness. Every one that enters these consecrated halls is expected to conform strictly to the objects and purport of the meeting. Such is the nature, exercise, and spirit of these social gatherings, that we feel assured that even the sceptic, the subtile caviller, and objector will be constrained to exclaim, " The finger of God is in it."

HOW ARE THESE MEETINGS CONDUCTED?

The meeting commences at three o'clock, P. M., and is opened with reading the Scriptures, singing, and prayer. Frequently two or three succeed each other in prayer. Several ministers are generally present, and the *opening* exercises are conducted by some one of these, but much oftener than otherwise by the venerable Dr. Bangs, who, during several past years, has seldom been absent.

This meeting is far more social in its character than ordinary religious gatherings. It is rather the design of those under whose supervision it is held, that it should be regarded as a social religious company, than as a formal meeting, requiring set exactions of any sort. The children of this world have their social gatherings, where, in intelligent, social converse, heart meets heart in unrestrained fellowship. We can conceive how undesirable any set forms would be under such circumstances, and this social gathering is designed to be, in the religious world, answerable to this want of our social nature as children of the kingdom. After the opening exercises, any one is at liberty to speak, sing, or propose united prayer.

Strangers from various regions generally being present at every meeting, it is not uncommon for those in charge to say something calculated to give direction to the exercises explanatory of its objects. Many inquirers after the "way of holiness" here gather, and it is not unusual for the meeting to assume something like the form of an inquiry meeting. There are always present a goodly number who profess to have received the promise of the Father, and who are ever ready, with yearning hearts, to testify to the praise of Christ, just how they were enabled to overcome every difficulty through faith, and plunge into the open fountain that cleanseth from all unrighteousness. It must indeed be delightful to the truly pious of every sect to witness the blended sympathy of hearts made perfect in love, and those aspiring to that state.

Here you behold the streams of Heaven-originated sympathy flowing out in word, in song, and in prayer, so that the prayer of Christ becomes a heartfelt realization, "that they may all be one, even as we are one." Surely the words of the poet here become an experimental verity : —

> " The gift which he on one bestows
>   We all delight to prove ;
> The grace through every vessel flows
>   In purest streams of love."

20

Testimony follows testimony in quick succession, interspersed with occasional singing and prayer, as the circumstances may seem to demand, in sympathy with the condition of the cases brought before the meeting. In no meeting that we have ever attended have we seen the spirit of the law of Christ so sweetly fulfilled — " Bear ye one another's burdens."

The testimony of the seeker of salvation, or of the timid, lisping babe in Zion, is listened to with as much interest as that of the most deeply experienced. Whether male or female, all are one in Christ Jesus. We have often thought, in our observings, whether this meeting is not very like that gathering of the early disciples, when the one hundred and twenty were assembled with one accord in one place. Here were the chosen apostles of our Lord, and here also were the beloved Marys, Joanna, and the " many other women," who, through evil and good report, with undaunted step, followed the Man of Sorrows, receiving as their reward the first commission to proclaim the gospel of a risen Lord.

And these disciples being thus assembled, with their Lord in the midst, wait the promise of the Father, " which," saith he, " ye have heard of me." And here they continue with one accord, in prayer and supplication, looking to be endued with the gift of power from on high, which, irrespective of persons or sex, had been promised to every one of those waiting disciples. And when it fell, though there may have been dispensed gifts after some sort differing, yet it was to each, singly, *a gift of power ;* and this gift of power moved its recipient, whether male or female, to speak as the Spirit gave utterance. They had now entered upon the dispensation of the Spirit. The day of which Joel spake, in which, saith God, " I will pour out my Spirit upon my sons and daughters, upon my servants and my handmaidens."

And truly does this pentecostal scene shadow forth what we would say of this interesting weekly gathering. To the praise of God it may be said, that many have here received the full baptism of the Holy Ghost; and so penetrating, efficacious, and far-reaching have been its influences, that we verily believe that thousands will, in eternity, give God glory for the establishment of this precious means of grace. Intelligence comes on the wings of the wind from near and remote regions, of those who, through the influence of this meeting, have been led to receive Christ as a Saviour from all sin, and are now in turn bearing witness experimentally to the truth of the doctrine, and others are believing through their testimony.

In these meetings the utmost freedom prevails. The ministry does not wait for the laity, neither does the laity wait for the ministry. There are seldom less than from six to ten ministers present, and often more. These commingle as one with the laity, irrespective of theological views or dignity of position. It is not unusual for those of different denominations, who, in the religious and literary world, are the observed of all observers, sitting undistinguished in those crowded

rooms, and only brought out as they may desire the
privilege of identifying themselves openly with the interests of the meeting.　We will give a case illustrative, and also descriptive, of the prevailing spirit of the
meeting, and quite in keeping with other cases which
might be given.

The Rev. Dr. ——, known by reputation to tens of
thousands of the religious and literary world, came for
the first time to the meeting.　We were with him as
he passed through the hall before entering the rooms.
" Let me sit down in some corner — I do not care to
be brought out," said the doctor, pleasantly.　We were
well aware that he might desire the privilege of being
brought out before the meeting closed, as scores of
others had done before him, without getting the opportunity.　But we thought we would let him learn
the fact from memorable experience, and only assured
him that he need feel no uneasiness from the fear of
being brought out, and told him to choose his own seat.
The doctor chose a seat favorable to his wishes.

The meeting had progressed but a short time before
the gift of power seemed to fall upon the doctor, and
the grace of utterance, so copiously poured out upon
many present, also fell upon him, and, as if impelled
by an influence which seemed well nigh irresistible, he
made an effort to rise.　But he had crowded himself
down in a corner, and in the most ineligible place for either
seeing or being seen ; otherwise we might have observed
his desire to speak, and respect for his position and his
age would have prompted us to open the way for him.

At last, when he could forbear no longer, he reached over to one of his lay brethren who sat before him, and told him that he desired the privilege of speaking. But when he rose, another doctor of divinity, not observing him, rose also, and both were on the floor at once : which succeeded in speaking first we do not remember. And truly as those early disciples spake as the Spirit gave utterance, so we believe did this servant of Christ. After he sat down, his full soul burst out in heavenly song:

> " Our souls by love together knit,
>   Cemented, mixed in one,
> One hope, one heart, one mind, one voice,
>   'Tis heaven on earth begun ;
> Our hearts have burned while Jesus spake,
>   And glowed with heavenly fire ;
> He stooped, and talked, and fed, and blest,
>   And filled the enlarged desire.

CHORUS.

> " A Saviour ! let creation sing,
> A Saviour ! let all heaven ring ;
> He's God with us, we feel him ours,
> His fulness in our souls he pours ;
> 'Tis almost done, 'tis almost o'er ;
> We're joining those who're gone before ;
> We soon shall reach the happy shore,
> We soon shall meet to part no more.

> " The little cloud increases still,
>   The heavens are big with rain ;
> We haste to catch the teeming shower,
>   And all its moisture drain.
> A rill, a stream, a torrent flows ;
>   But pour a mighty flood ;
> O, shake the nations, fill the earth,
>   Till all proclaim thee God."

20 *

Would that we could describe the scene of melting power that succeeded — the conscious oneness of soul. O, it was a baptism of melting, uniting love. And we need not speak of the equalizing influences of such baptisms of fire. How small do all merely earthly distinctions appear, when brought under the equalizing influences of pure, perfect love! And it is this equalizing process, that, to our mind, forms one of the important characteristics of this meeting. It has not been induced as the result of human forethought, and can only be accounted for from the fact, that He who is no respecter of persons is in the midst, and so holds the minds of those who enter these consecrated rooms under a conscious realization of his presence, that each one feels in living verification that the words are ever being respoken, "Behold a greater than Solomon is here."

WHERE ARE THESE MEETINGS HELD?

They are held at a private house, 54 Rivingston, corner of Eldridge Street, New York. They were commenced over twenty years ago in the same place where they are now being held. It is estimated that the number in attendance averages about two hundred. In view of the crowded state of the rooms, the question has been asked, Why not remove them to a church? There are reasons beyond what we may now occupy space to state, why we think the recognition of the meeting as a friendly religious gathering, rather than as a formal church gathering, of any particular sect, is far more favorable to the interests of the meeting. We have desired that it should not be regarded as a sectarian meeting. Holiness is not the distinguishing doctrine of a sect merely, but the crowning doctrine of the Bible.

And many, very many among both the ministry and laity of various denominations, are being urged by the Holy Spirit, not only to investigate it as a scriptural doctrine, but greatly to desire the attainment of the experience. They have learned that there is a little social circle where experimental testimony may be heard on this subject, and where, in unreserved fellowship, they may inquire " how these things can be." If the meetings were held in a church, whether Methodist, Congregationalist, Episcopalian, Baptist, &c., it would be recognized as a meeting of the church, patronized as a matter of course. But being held at the residence of persons whose efforts to spread scriptural holiness have become more widely known than their efforts to build up a sect, inquirers of different denominations feel less restrained in pursuing their investigations. It is not unusual for ministers of three or four different denominations to be scattered about in different parts of the rooms, men whose relative position in the religious world is such, that their presence at a church gathering on the subject of holiness would expose them to observations which they might prefer not to meet until more fully established in experience and views.

Here, free from all imposing restraint, ministerial position is seemingly unthought of, and all, whether of the ministry or laity, mingle freely in testimony on the common ground of Bible truth and Bible experience.

Hundreds among various denominations of Christians who love their own people, and have no wish to manifest a preference to any other denomination than their own, are being impressed with the belief that the Bible teaches the necessity of *present holiness.* And these convictions not having been gained through the teachings of a sect, but through the teachings of the Bible, how relieving to know that they may have unrestrained access to a social gathering where they may meet Christians of various evangelical denominations, and listen to, and consult with, experimental witnesses of the desired attainment ! Many such have come to the Tuesday afternoon meetings as inquirers, and have returned as believers, to diffuse the testimony among their own people !

DO PARTIES ATTENDING COME BY SPECIAL INVITATION ?

Though a negative answer to this question may be inferred from what we have already written, yet it is due to the praise of grace to say, that, in a sense in which the deeply pious heart will appreciate, invitations are given. We acknowledge that we are willing to be classed among those little ones of the kingdom who verily believe that the humble disciple may, in childlike confidence, ask what he will, consistent with the teachings of the Word, and it shall be done unto him. We will give our idea of how the invitations are given, by transcribing some occurrences in experience, given by one who ever bears the interests of the meeting on her heart most largely before God. She says, —

I had been in the habit of devoting as much time

as I could command on Tuesday mornings to the work of preparing my own mind for the occasion, and praying for the interests of the meeting. Deeply did I feel the weight of responsibility which was continually pressing, more and more urgently, on my heart, as the meeting became increasingly extensive and commanding in its influences. I shall never forget one eventful Tuesday, as hour after hour of the day devoted to the meeting was seized by pressing emergencies, leaving no time for special preparation for the responsibilities of the afternoon. Thus hours passed on, till near the time for the commencement of the exercises. It was my midday season of devotion ; though delayed beyond my stated time, as usual I knelt, with the word of life, and opened it at my regular lesson, according to my usual custom of reading the Scriptures in course. It was the second chapter of the Gospel of St. John, where the fact that Jesus and his disciples were present at a marriage in Cana of Galilee is recorded.

Believing that *all* Scripture, whether historical or otherwise, is given by inspiration, I asked in faith that I might learn just the lesson of grace which the Holy Spirit would teach me through the presence and doings of Jesus at the marriage feast in Cana, when most inspiring, ever-memorable instructions of the Spirit were so graciously given, that, though years have passed since I received the teachings of that hour, its influences have been abiding. The instructions of the Spirit were thus : If Jesus and his disciples were at this marriage feast, it was in answer to a *special invitation* from the persons under whose supervision the feast was made. Jesus, the same yesterday, to-day, and forever, will be as truly present in answer to special invitations from those who desire his presence now, as when invited in the days of his incarnation. And why not invite Jesus to be as actually present at the meeting this afternoon, as he was present at this marriage feast ?

Ask that he will come as the Master of the assembly, and take the lead of the exercises. Ask that he will come, and also bring his disciples with him, so that just such a company shall assemble as may be drawn together through the special invitations of his Spirit, and come prepared for the reception of just such blessings as they need. Ask that he will manifest his glory to all his waiting disciples, so that every one, on entering the place, may be arrested by a divine consciousness of his presence. Ask that *Truth*, in whatever form uttered, may be felt in its deep spirituality, whether in the reading of the word, the voice of prayer, the sacred hymn, in testimony or exhortation, and, as living truth, penetrate every heart. Tell Jesus that you will, as his servant, give the entire orderings of the assembly to •him, and that " whatsoever he saith unto you, you will do it."

If we had not already occupied space quite beyond our anticipations, we would portray a faint semblance of the manner in which that afternoon meeting was divinely ordered and blest. Surely the Father sent the Son in answer to the intercessions of the Spirit. The simple prayer of faith prevailed. And such a living realization of the presence of Jesus was given, that all were constrained to feel that he spoke through the medium of all the exercises. The servant of Christ who opened the meeting, by reading the Scriptures, was so penetrated with the force of its glorious revelations that he was unable to proceed, and paused to give vent to his emotions. O, surely, in wondrous condescension, Christ manifested his glory that afternoon, giving an earnest, for all future meetings, of what we might anticipate in answer to the prayer of faith. Ever since has the presence of the Saviour been, in like manner, supplicated ; and scores or hundreds have we heard testify that they had no sooner entered those " consecrated halls," than they were arrested by a divine conviction of the presence of the Sanctifier.

In using the terms employed by our Congregational brother, in speaking of the place where these meetings are held, in his repeated commendations to his readers, our pen paused over the words " consecrated halls," and questioning whether some might not demur to the use of such phraseology in designating a private residence. And here we will take our reader back for a few moments to a scene of interest which occurred years since, when the present occupants of that residence took their abode there. Scores of the servants of Christ had assembled to participate in the solemnities of the dedication. The house being arranged on what is called the basement plan, the second floor was set apart for a chapel. By a favored minister of Christ, it was consecrated, in the name of the holy Trinity, for holy service.

Most signal were the tokens of heavenly acceptance. The cloud of the divine presence rested down upon the people. Several were enabled, through the power of the Holy Spirit, to enter by the new and living way into the holiest, and were newly added to the number of those who witness that the blood of Jesus Christ cleanseth from all unrighteousness. In conclusion, we will say that the motto of this meeting has ever been, " Not by might, nor by power, but by my Spirit, saith the Lord." We pray and trust thus it will ever be ; and we ask that every lover of heart purity will unite now with us in asking that the future, in regard to the prosperity of this means of grace, may not only be as the past, but far more abundantly signalized by the manifestations of God's saving power ; and the praise shall be given to the Father, Son, and Holy Spirit, and let all the people say, Amen.

HOW TO BECOME A MODEL CHRISTIAN.

New York, 1856.

My darling E——: Would you love to be a model Christian ? Let me encourage you by saying, it is not too late to try. And if you should fail the first, fifth, or fiftieth time, do not yield to discouragement, but —

" Try, try again."

You may and will succeed, if you depend wholly on your almighty Helper for counsel and sustainment. But you will need divine aid every moment. Do not think of your heavenly Helper as away in the distance. Help in time of need is just what he has promised. Do you need help now to aid you in forming the resolve that you will aim at perfection of moral and religious character ? Rely on Christ for strength, and then form the resolve. Say in your heart, —

> " Lord, if on thee I dare rely,
> The faith shall bring the power."

God is no respecter of persons. Your former errors of life, and your numerous failures in view of past resolves, should not, and *must* not, withhold you from a *present* reliance on Christ for the grace just now needed. Neither St. Paul, nor the most eminent saint that the world has known since the days of Paul, ever attained one step towards perfection of character but through the grace of our Lord Jesus Christ. *Grace* does not mean *merit*. Grace is a gift which has already been purchased. It was purchased for you — is just as free for you as it was for Paul.

The most unworthy and feeble have just as good a Saviour as Paul had. What an eventful hour was that to Paul when he first resolved on yielding entire obedience to Christ, and cried out, " Lord, what wilt thou have me to do ? " Humility and decision were most needful in his case, for it was to Jesus of Nazareth, whom he had persecuted, that the inquiry was addressed. But from the day that he humbly resolved on entire, absolute obedience, how rapid and wonderful were the renovations of grace !

And why may not this hour be signalized in time, and in eternity, as the most wonderful in your history? You have been changeful in your faith, and in your purposes. So greatly have you lacked stability of character, that God, your own heart, and an observant world, all stand ready to attest the fact that you have not excelled. But now, Jesus, the same yesterday, to-day, and forever, waits to transform your nature, and give you his own glorious image. He waits to clothe you with the garments of salvation. Does your heart, with loathing, turn away from self, so distrustful of fickle self that you dare not form a purpose, fearful that you again may falter? Then turn away from *self*, and look to Jesus.

I need not remind you that you have received the sentence of death in yourself, that you should not trust in yourself, but in Him that raiseth the dead. You have now come to a point where the Saviour can help you. You would fain renounce your will, and have come down into the valley of decision, and, in humbleness of spirit, are saying, " Lord, what wilt thou have me to do?" And now why may not this be a most eventful, ever-memorable hour with you? If Paul might say, "I can do all things through Christ, which strengtheneth me," why may not you say so too? Why may *you* not resolve, through Christ, on a life of entire, implicit obedience? Why not say, —

" My will in all things I resign,
To know no other will but thine" ?

Why not yield at once and forever your whole be-

PROMISE OF THE FATHER. 243

What Christ will do.   Processes of grace rapid and permanent.

ing up to Christ? He will clothe you with the garments of salvation, and will work in you to will and to do. He will work in you that which is well pleasing in his sight. The processes of grace may be as rapid and as permanent in your case as in the case of Paul. The only way that Paul attained stability of Christian character was by a continuous process, consequent on a continuous and unconditional surrender of the whole body, soul, and spirit to God through Christ. Do you now make a like surrender? If so, to you the exceeding great and precious promises are now given. By these you may be made partaker of the divine nature. Why not be made every whit whole *now*? Why not so rely on Christ, from this hour, as to have the needful salvation, wisdom, and strength, which this and every succeeding hour of life demand? O, how gloriously then will your goings be established! How truly will you become a model Christian! You will be fashioned after Christ, for he will mould you into his image.

Again she writes : —

TWO STEPS TO THE BLESSING.

The word is nigh thee, even in thy mouth and in thy heart ; that is the word of faith which we preach. PAUL.

Seest thou how faith wrought with his works, and by works was faith made perfect? JAMES.

Will you now count the cost, and deliberately set yourself apart for a life of eminent devotedness to the service of your Redeemer? In the name and in the presence of the Lord I ask this question. I have asked for a word from the Lord to you, and now come to you in the name of your Redeemer, and present this message.

"Rise! the master is come, and calleth for *thee!*" He hath need of thee in his vineyard. "The harvest is great, but the laborers are few." Will you not now, in view of all coming time, *set yourself apart* in unconditional devotedness to his service? If you will do this, God will set the seal that will proclaim you wholly his. O, you must have the seal of the Holy Spirit set upon all your powers. You must have an application of the all-cleansing blood of Jesus. You need it in order that you may have a fitness for the Master's use. It is this that will give you a readiness for every good work.

Holiness is a pearl of great price. It has already been purchased for you, and it is now ready for your acceptance, as the portion of your inheritance. O, think of the price at which it has been purchased! Surely you will not now hesitate in surrendering all for this pearl of great price. I trust now that you are ready to say, "Yea, doubtless, I count all things loss for the excellency of the knowledge of Christ Jesus, my Lord." Why may not an absolute, irrevocable, and eternal surrender be the work of the present hour?

Do you say I must first count the cost? Suppose you were to take five years to count the cost of an unreserved dedication of body, soul, spirit, time, talents, family, and estate, would you, after the most length-

PROMISE OF THE FATHER. 245

Inventory, or giving God his own.　　The two steps.　　Promised ground.

ened inventory, find any thing but what already belongs to God ? Why, then, should it take long to count the cost, when *all* that you have, or all that you ever expect to have, already belongs to God ? And if all that you have, or ever expect to have, already belongs to God, can you, for another moment, withhold any thing on any point, or in any degree, from God, without incurring condemnation ? For to him that knoweth to do good, and doeth it not, to him it is sin.

Holiness is the pearl of great price ; it cost all. And surely you will no longer linger in answering the question whether you will give all for this pearl of great price. Eminent holiness, usefulness, and happiness stand inseparably connected. Entire sanctification need not necessarily be the work of a week, or even of a whole day or hour. There are but two steps to the blessing : ENTIRE CONSECRATION is the first ; FAITH is the second. The *second step* cannot, of course, precede the *first*. How can we believe that God accepts that which we do not, through Christ, offer up to him ? How can we believe that the blood of Jesus cleanseth from all sin, before an irrevocable and eternal sacrifice of all the redeemed powers is resolved upon, and actually bound to the hallowed altar ? That moment you step on promised ground, and the promise meets you. God says, " I will receive you." And if you say, " When wilt thou receive me ? " he says, Now. " Now is the accepted time ; behold, now is the day of salvation." Do you say, " I would believe it, but I cannot sensibly feel it." Then you are seeking to walk

21 *

by *sense* rather than by *faith;* but the apostle says, "We walk by faith." Would you believe if you could *hear* a voice now saying from heaven, "I will receive you?" If you would believe it under such circumstances, then act true to your own avowed belief.

You profess to believe that the Bible is the *word of God;* and will you not now prove, before God, angels, and men, that you do in heart believe what you have long professed to believe? If you have made the consecration, and have resolutely made up your mind, in view of all coming time, to be, in the most absolute and unlimited sense, the Lord's, then take the *next step.* God commands you now to *believe.* Believe and enter into *rest.* If you hesitate to obey God, you will sin after the same similitude that the ancient Israelites sinned, when, after they were brought up to the borders of the promised land, and were commanded to go forward and possess it, they entered not in because of unbelief. Let me again ask, Do you now consecrate all? Do you now believe? If so, you are now being saved. O, hasten to give to God the glory due to his name. Hasten to confess with your *mouth* what your *heart* believes. Then will the Holy Spirit testify to your heart that it is unto salvation, free, full, complete salvation — a redemption from all iniquity.

A HOLY CALL AND A HOLY HEART.

We had a gracious season at the meeting yesterday afternoon. Two earnest disciples, who had been waiting for the full baptism of the Holy Ghost, received, I

PROMISE OF THE FATHER. **247**

Promising young man.   First step towards preparation for the ministry.

trust, the precious gift.   One of these was a most prom-ising young man, who feels himself called to preach the gospel.   He leaves this city to commence his studies for the ministry this week.   For weeks past, he says it has been sounding in his ears, " Be ye clean that bear the vessels of the Lord."   Thus we see that the Holy Spirit has been assuring his heart that the first steps to-wards a preparation for the ministry is the attainment of a holy heart.   And now sanctified, through the belief of the truth, he goes forth to commence his studies, and also his efforts, in soul-saving, under the supervis-ion of his brother, a minister, who, I trust, is doing valiant service for God.

That this conviction for purity of heart was the re-sult of the Holy Spirit's teachings who can question ? If the calling of all Christians is high and holy, how eminently so is the call of that man who is sent forth direct from the throne of God, as an ambassador in Christ's stead, to treat with dying men of divine and eternal realities !

> " * * * He alone his office held
> Immediately from God."

The case of this young man reminds me of the many, with whom I have been conversant, who have been similarly exercised in regard to the attainment of entire sanctification before entering the holy ministry.   I have co versed with scores who have thus, previous to their entrance upon the duties of their high calling, felt a keen, penetrating sense of their need of this en-dowment of power from on high.   Some have waited for the baptism of fire, others have not. We believe that there is not one truly called of God but has felt that this gift of power was an absolute prerequisite to an entrance upon their holy calling. But we fear that there are many who have not made a covenant with God by sacrifice, with an unyielding resolve to tarry at Jerusalem until the full baptism of the Spirit be given. Those who have waited have entered upon their ministerial career as men of might; but not all who have attained this grace have retained it. The baptism of fire is retained on the same principle upon which it is received. The sacrifice is ever in the process of being consumed while it remains bound on the altar. To those who thus keep the offering wholly given up to God through Christ, the prayer is ever being fulfilled —

" Jesus, confirm my heart's desire
To work, speak, think, and act for thee."

This prayer fulfilled, the whole life is an embodiment of power. Holiness insures usefulness. These, while they have continued holy and humble, by keeping the sacrifice bound on the hallowed altar, have been marked for the usefulness and appropriateness of their course. Through their ministrations Zion has risen and put on her strength, and converts have been multiplied, and thus, not unfrequently, has the eye of the multitude been attracted, and popular favor secured.

POPULAR FAVOR A TRYING TEST.

And is not popular favor a test for the Christian? It is true that on all the glory there is a defence; and this defence, if properly regarded, would only result in the reception of grace for grace. But it is, alas ! too often otherwise. I have with solicitude marked the effect of popularity on many of my friends ; and where I have seen one pass unharmed through the ordeal of reproach and disesteem for Christ, I have, I think, seen ten who have not passed unharmed. But if one maintains a steady, onward course in the way of holiness, he will find that the direct path leads through *evil* as well as good report. Good report, popular favor being gained, too many are unwilling to continue their close walk with the Saviour, but shrink from following him whithersoever he goeth, when the path leads through the vale of reproach.

When Jesus commenced his ministry, his fame went throughout all Judea. Multitudes followed him when they saw his healing power in restoring the sick, and his creating power in multiplying the bread. But there was a time when, by the wisdom of his counsels, he reproved the hypocrisy of the heart, and the various wrong-doings of the people. Then came evil report ; and such was the effect of his loss of popular favor, that many refused to follow him more. Even that chosen few, " the twelve," seemed to stand in hesitating attitude. " Will ye also go away ? " So said their Lord and Master, in expostulating tone. O, it is a lamentable fact that many prefer to lose the blessing of heart purity rather than be of no reputation for Christ's sake !

THE PRESENT DISPENSATION AND ITS RESPONSIBILITIES.

We live under the dispensation of the Spirit. Wonderful indeed are the privileges, and also the holy responsibilities, of all who name the name of Christ in these the expiring moments of the latter days. And we have only to avail ourselves of all our blood-bought privileges, and we shall be divinely empowered to meet our responsibilities. If Christ, who has purchased the entire citadel of the heart for himself, comes and brings his Father with him, — if the Holy Spirit, sent forth from the Father and the Son, comes and abides with us forever, and the body thus be made the abode of the Triune Deity, a habitation for God through the Spirit, — what an amount of responsibility may be met by one thus empowered !

Yes, we can meet our responsibilities. We can do all things through Christ, who strengtheneth us. If left one moment without the aids of his grace we should be powerless !

> " We cannot speak one useful word,
> One holy thought conceive."

But Jesus has purchased the grace for us. Thus, " As God hath said, I will dwell in them and walk in them." Glorious privileges are *ours*. And now that we are not sufficient of ourselves to think a good thought, how inspiring the consideration that all these urgings of the Spirit to win souls to Christ are divinely inspired ! And when we obey these promptings, it is by the indwelling Spirit's dictations that we walk forth

on these divine errands. It is the Holy Spirit that in-
spires our thoughts and words, when we urge the claims
of Christ on those around us. And when, through our
instrumentality, the claims of Christ are acknowledged,
it brings forth fresh incense of praise, while the lowly
instrument vibrates to the song, —

> " Thou all our works in us hast wrought;
>   Our good is all divine;
> The praise of every virtuous thought
>   And righteous act is thine."

I think much of the requirement, *" Be filled with the
Spirit."* I have resolved that I will not be satisfied
with my experience without *knowing* that I am thus
filled. Our privileges involve obligations. And if we
have received of that Spirit whereby we know the
things freely given to us of God, surely we ought not
to be satisfied with our experience without being thus
consciously *" filled with the Spirit."*

Hamilton, Canada West, October 17, 1857.

Rev. W. H. D——.

Dear Brother : What hath God wrought! Would
that I could portray on paper the wonderful works of
God, which we have witnessed in the last few days. It
is now only a little over one week since we paused, with
the intention of only tarrying for the night in this
place. We were on our way homeward from one of
the most glorious meetings we ever attended ; and had
the railroad cars favored our purpose, we should have
been with our New York friends one week yesterday.

But God's ways are not as our ways. We have witnessed, during the past twenty years, many signal displays of God's wonder-working power in saving souls, but never before have we witnessed a revival after this fashion ; so remarkable in its aspects, so singularly suggestive and inspiring. The work began only a little over one week since, and already between three and four hundred have been brought into the fold of Christ. And still the work is going on with rapidly increasing power.

It is now Monday, October 19. It was only on Friday, one week since, that this glorious work commenced; twenty-one souls were blessed with pardon, and several others, I trust, with the full baptism of the Holy Ghost, the first day that the extra effort commenced ; since which the work has steadily increased in power, the number of the newly justified varying from twenty to forty-five each day, until yesterday, when, through Christ, the Captain of our salvation, over one hundred were won over to the ranks of the redeemed. Halleluia ! the Lord God omnipotent reigneth ! And let all the redeemed say, Amen, amen !

Thanks to the Lord of the harvest for such an ingathering. And where will it end? Not, we trust, till all Canada is in a blaze. The work is taking within its range persons of all classes. Men of low degree, and men of high estate for wealth and position, old men and maidens, and even little children, are seen humbly kneeling together, pleading for grace. The mayor of the city, with other persons of like position, are not ashamed to be seen bowed at the altar of prayer beside the humble servant, pleading for the full baptism of the Spirit. My pen lingers. I might write a volume of interesting incidents, but I must forbear.

I commenced a letter, two or three days since, which I intended to have addressed to yourself, in connection with our dearly beloved pastor. In this I commenced to give, a little more in detail, a glance at our journeyings since we left New York. The recital would cheer your hearts amazingly ; but time fails. Such are the exigencies of this glorious work that every moment has its demands. But I must hasten. I have nearly filled my little sheet, yet in the multiplicity of good tidings have left unwritten that with which my pen was most heavily laden when I commenced to write. If the principle on which this revival *commenced*, and is now being carried out so wonderfully, is of God, where is there a place in God's dominions, where Christianity has the least foothold, but may be favored with a revival *at once?* This revival commenced, and is progressing, on precisely the principles laid down in the articles published in the Christian Advocate and Journal early last spring, under the caption, " *Laity for the times.*"

Though Hamilton is favored with three devoted ministers, than whom few are more marked, in our own or any other church, for eminent devotedness and ministerial ability, yet these ministers will be as free to acknowledge, to the praise of God, as ourselves, that this gust of divine power, now spreading as a pentecostal flame over this entire community, took its rise in the sudden rise of the *laity*.

In as few words as possible I will endeavor to tell you just how the work commenced ; and then tell me whether the same principles, if brought into immediate requisition in all our New York churches, would not result in the salvation of thousands of souls in less than a week. The membership in Hamilton, comprising the three Wesleyan churches, has heretofore numbered about five hundred. When we paused on our journey here, on Thursday last, one week since, with the expectation of tarrying but for the night, there was nothing in the tone of the meeting we attended which indicated the near approach of this extraordinary outpouring of the Spirit.

It was the stated prayer meeting evening, and about seventy persons were present. We were led to speak of the solemn obligation of bringing *all* the tithes into the Lord's storehouse, in order that all the tithes of time, talent, and estate might be laid on God's holy altar, and thus be brought into immediate use, by way of saving a lost world. We suggested that if the people would pledge themselves thus to bring all the Lord's tithes into his storehouse at once, and go to work on the morrow to invite their unconverted friends and neighbors to Christ, gracious results might be seen the ensuing evening. Probably over thirty of those present raised their right hand in the presence of the Lord, in solemn affirmation that they would sacrifice

that which cost them something, in earnest, specific endeavors to win souls to Christ.

A special meeting was appointed for the next evening.   Each one had obligated himself to bring at least
one with him, and to invite as many as possible.   On
coming together in the evening, the lecture room was
found wholly insufficient to contain the people, and the
large audience room was resorted to.   Ministers had
been alike diligent as the laity in giving sinners a personal invitation to come to Christ.   The invitation had
been accepted, and the glorious result of the first day's
effort was that a score of souls were added to the ranks
of the saved.   And now the newly saved were pledged,
in turn, to unite with those already in the field, in bringing their unsaved friends to Jesus.   A meeting was appointed for the next afternoon and evening, and still
the number doubled and trebled, till hundreds are now
in daily attendance on the afternoon and evening meetings, and the revival seems to be the absorbing topic of
all circles.   And who can say where it will end ?   Think
of the three or four hundred new recruits, and these all
engaged alike with those before in the field, in daily
renewal of efforts to bring one more.*

Nightly we pledged ourselves *anew* to bring yet
one more the coming day ; and thus the hosts of Zion
are enlarging daily, and new cases are being ferreted

* This, it will be remembered, was at the commencement of the
great financial difficulties, and seems to have furnished the data of the
great revival which, as a pentecostal flame, has since been spreading
over the American continent.

out, which would never have been reached but by this
system of vigorous daily effort. "Wonderful!" exclaimed one of aristocratic bearing, who had long been
unapproachable on the subject of his soul's best interest.
And now he had been approached by one who, having
newly received the baptism of fire, feared to let him
alone. The lady, who now dared to meet him in his
own home, was one among the many scores who, with
uplifted hand, was daily pledging herself to be "instant in season and out of season" in searching out
some new subject for Christ's kingdom; and now, on being thus personally addressed, and beholding the tears
of earnestness streaming from the eyes of the lady addressing him, he exclaimed with amazement, "Wonderful! What can all this mean? Never did I see any thing
like it!" He listened with interest to the expostulating tones of pious entreaty as they fell from the lips of
the lady, and though he has not yielded to the claims
of Christ, he has had a season of the Spirit's visitation,
through human agency, without which the church
might not have been clear of his blood, should he
eventually be lost.

Said another, who was a lady of some position, but
who had long been a neglecter of salvation, "Why,
here is more than half a dozen different persons who
have to-day been running to me on this subject. I do
not see what has got into the people. Why, they must
think that I am a dreadful sinner."

All classes are at work. Illustrations of exceeding
interest come up before me; but I can scarcely trust

myself to glance at them, they are so numerous and so suggestive. Seldom have I seen a more lovely convert than one in the common walks of life. After her translation from the kingdom of darkness into the kingdom of God's dear Son, she was so entranced with the glory of the inheritance upon which she had just entered, that the utterances of her new-born Spirit were singularly beautiful and sublime. I mentioned this on my return to the family where we were entertained. "O, that is the one our Eliza brought," said our hostess. Eliza is a pious servant in the family, but, though pressed with an unusual amount of service just at this time, she had, with others, lifted her hand by way of pledging herself to bring at least one.

" I did not know that our servant knew a person in the place, as we brought her from a distance, not very long since ; but she had pledged herself to bring one, and that one was converted." So said the Rev. Mr. R., the minister who superintends the work here. The work is becoming the town topic. Men of business are after men of business ; every man after his man. Surely this is a truthful demonstration of Christianity in earnest, and a return to what was said by an eminent divine of the more early Methodists — " They are all at it, and always at it."

In fact, it is only a return to primitive Christianity, when the manifestations of the Spirit were untrammelled by mere human opinions and church conventionalism, and permitted to have full sway. It is that which was foretold by the prophet Joel, and of which

22 *

258   PROMISE OF THE FATHER.

Men and women preaching.   Appeal to ministers.   Dormant power in the church.

the apostle Peter spoke, when he proclaimed, " It shall come to pass, in the last days, saith God, I will pour out my Spirit upon all flesh, and your sons and your daughters shall prophesy ; and on my servants and on my handmaidens I will pour out in those days of my Spirit, and they shall prophesy ; " furnishing a marked demonstration that the same power still continues in the church that was in the apostolic church, when Saul, breathing out threatenings and slaughter, scattered the band of disciples, comprising men and women, in every direction.   The infant church, with the exception of the apostles, were, by Saul's fearful havoc, scattered away from Jerusalem ; and being thus scattered, these *men* and *women* of the laity went every where *preaching* the word.   That is, they went abroad proclaiming the glad tidings of salvation, and urging the gospel invitation.

And why may not all these instrumentalities again be brought into use ?   Have we not men, women, and children in our various churches, whose personal realizations of the blessedness of salvation empowers them to urge others to the gospel feast ?   O, will not the ministers of the sanctuary at once bring all these instrumentalities into action ?   Dormant power is in the church, which, if brought into immediate use, would result in the salvation of thousands speedily.   Will not the captains of the hosts of Israel call upon the people to come up at once to the help of the Lord against the mighty ?   O, if we may only have a " laity for the times," how soon will this redeemed world be brought back to God !

New York, November 14, 1857.

To Rev. Mr. F——.

During the past summer and fall months we have been permitted to participate in more extraordinary outpourings of the Spirit than we have ever before witnessed. Such exemplifications of the beauty and power of holiness, and such manifest effusions of grace in the awakening and conversion of sinners, we have seldom known.

I think that in the aggregate not less than two thousand souls have been converted. I would speak with carefulness before God, and I believe this to be a low computation. Hundreds of believers have also received the baptism of the Holy Ghost ; and O, the power that has attended their ministrations ! Would that I could describe the scenes of intense interest we have witnessed ; and surely you would magnify God, and together we would exalt his name.

Our last visit was at London, C. W. While we were there a revival commenced, and many in the city of London and from the surrounding country were newly blest. The secretary of the meeting informed us that he had received about two hundred names. We remained with them twelve days, and when we left, the work was still most graciously progressing. A principle is involved in the progress of the remarkable revivals in which we have recently been engaged, we think singularly important, and which many in these regions are resolving to test. We are hearing of several encouraging things in connection with it. Companies of the laity are getting together and pledging themselves that they will go and do likewise.   A lawyer, who is an earnest class-leader, told me a few hours since, that he took the paper containing the published account of the revival at Hamilton, and read it to the members of his class, instead of engaging in the usual exercise of relating experience.   The result was, that the members united themselves into a band to carry out the principles of the letter.   The revival in Hamilton is still going on, and at the last advices we were informed that between five and six hundred had been saved.   The work of holiness is also going on with great power.   While we were there, ministers and people were coming in from the country round about to share in the holy outpourings of grace.   One man and his wife came seventy-five miles, seeking the full baptism of the Holy Spirit.   The Lord fulfilled the desire of their hearts, and they returned to their home rejoicing with joy unspeakable and full of glory.

A letter lies unsealed before me, which I have just written to the Rev. Mr. R., which introduces a subject so dear to my heart, that I can scarcely forbear transcribing it for you.   It stands in connection with the salvation of the perishing.   This is the one great work which above all others should occupy the attention of every professed servant of Christ.

> " The Christian lives to Christ alone,
> To Christ alone he dies."

It was the work of Christ to save the world.   To the

degree the disciple is Christ-like in his self-sacrificing efforts to save sinners, in a proportionate degree will he be made a partaker of Christ's joys. "That this my joy may be in them, and that their joy may be full." Christ's joy was to save the world, and bring many sons to glory. But I promised to give you my letter to the Rev. Mr. R., treating on this subject. And here it is : —

New York, November 13, 1857.

To Rev. Mr. R——.

Dear Brother : It was near the midnight hour of October 30 that we parted with our London friends. Several brethren and sisters, dearly beloved in the Lord, accompanied us to the cars. There, at that affecting, solemn hour, we strengthened each other's hands in the Lord. Here, at the dead of night, we lingered at the depot about one hour, awaiting the " lightning train," which was to bear us to our distant home. We improved this hour of waiting in proposing plans for future conquests, which we hope may be as unending as eternity for good. As a company of God's sacramental hosts, we had just left a scene of triumph ; and here, at this quiet hour, while the world was sleeping around us, we devised ways and means by which we might win the greatest possible number of souls to the Saviour. And here the whole company formed themselves into a band, which might be designated a "*Soul-saving Band.*" The company consisted of male and female followers of the Saviour. Some of these, though lovely and devoted, were timid, and comparatively uninitiated in the arts of holy warfare. Others had, during the twelve days' campaign through which we had passed, endured hardness as good soldiers. Many scores, during the twelve days we had labored together in the city of L., enlisted under the Captain of our salvation; and now, as we were about parting, we memorialized the solemn hour by forming ourselves into a band, which, we pray, may ever be signalized in the eye of God and man as a band of soul-savers. A board of direction was appointed, consisting of a presiding officer and a secretary, and the principles set forth in the accompanying preamble and resolutions were adopted. We send a copy of them to you, hoping that they may meet with your approval, and many may be induced to unite themselves in sustaining this, the most glorious enterprise that ever engaged the attention of a redeemed race. " Union is strength." And if the matter is of God, I trust many of our dear Hamilton friends will be induced to form themselves into bands for this glorious purpose. As we passed through P. H., early in June last, similar bands were formed, and we found a letter awaiting our arrival home last week, giving an inspiring account of numbers who had been converted, and others wholly sanctified, through the energetic and unwearied efforts of the members of these bands.

BANDS OF SOUL-SAVERS.

The object of those whose names are hereunto annexed shall be to use every possible means, in their individual and collective capacity, to pluck sinners as brands from the burning.

And whereas purposes, however piously formed, or strongly made, are too often failures, unless means be ordained whereby they may be made an ever-present speciality ;

And whereas the value of the soul outweighs all human considerations, and is an object to which all business or domestic avocations should be subservient and tributary ;

And whereas we believe we cannot serve the Lord Christ more effectually, either by way of bringing an increase of grace into our own souls in thus *using* the grace given, or to the individual benefit of the human family at large, than by making daily specific efforts in rescuing souls from death, for whom Christ shed his precious blood ; therefore, —

1. *Resolved,* That while we would not be unmindful of the divine injunction, " Diligent in business," we will, through the assistance of almighty grace, manifest our fervor of spirit by endeavoring to make every earthly consideration, whether it be secular business or domestic avocations, specifically subservient to the service of Christ.

2. *Resolved,* That we will endeavor to save at least ONE HALF HOUR DAILY, and more, if possible, in specific, direct efforts to win souls to Christ ; and this, God being our helper, we will endeavor to do, though it may be at the cost of a more habitual carefulness in treasuring up time, or though it may cost something in acts of self-

denial, by either rising earlier or sitting up later, or may involve the necessity of casting aside the enthusiastic doctrine that we are not to do good unless we feel free to it, or though at the cost of *pecuniary* profit ; repelling with righteous indignation the idea that *Christians* are not required to sacrifice that which costs them something.

3. *Resolved,* That we will make earnest and prayerful efforts to engage all who love our Lord Jesus Christ to unite in this, the most momentous and ennobling Christian enterprise that can command the attentions of a redeemed world ; enlisting, as far as in us lies, the interest of all professed Christians, whether young or old, and irrespective of denomination, inasmuch as all professed Christians are called to be *workers together* with God in bringing a revolted world back to the world's Redeemer.

4. *Resolved,* That we will, as far as circumstances permit, meet together weekly, at such time and place as, by mutual agreement, shall be deemed most expedient ; in order — First : To seek counsel of God, " who teacheth our hands to war and our fingers to fight," and through whom alone we can wage a successful warfare against the hosts of sin.   Second : To present cases demanding special prayer, to report conversions, or cases of hopeful interest, for mutual counsel, and especially for the encouragement of the weak and timid, in order that the graces of the Spirit, in the weakest believer, may be brought into continuous requisition, **and thereby be continually multiplied, and thus the**

timid and weak in Zion become courageous and strong as David.

5. *Resolved,* That in places where there may be more bands than one, it be recommended that they unite monthly ; and where convenient, that the minister of the church, or one or more of the ministers of the churches to which the bands belong, be invited to be present and preside. A secretary may also be appointed, whose duty it shall be to read the reports of the various bands, and be ready, if deemed expedient, to present an annual report in January of each year, when an anniversary may be held in case it be regarded by a majority of the members subservient to the cause.

In all of which we, the undersigned, do agree, and in pledge of the sustainment of which we do hereby, in the name and presence of God, affix our names.

From the eventful · hour, noted by our friend, on which she received the baptism of the Holy Spirit, she seems to have been ever intent on devising every possible means to bring souls to Jesus. This, to her mind, was the alpha and omega of the Christian's calling. It was the work that brought the Saviour from heaven to earth, and in view of promoting this, the great ultimatum of Christianity, a band was organized under her own roof to carry out these principles, in relation to which she writes thus to a friend : —

New York, January 13, 1858.

Dear Dr. B——— : You will remember we talked,

23

last Tuesday afternoon, about forming a band which might be denominated the Christian Vigilance Band, whose motto might be, " Not by might, nor by power, but by my Spirit, saith the Lord," but which, while acknowledging the utter inefficiency of all human agencies, might also aim to be properly cognizant of the fact, that true, living faith is ever active and energetic, inasmuch as faith without works is dead, being alone. We held our first meeting last evening, in view of taking this subject into consideration. We had an intensely interesting season in praying and talking over this matter. We have not yet fully organized. In fact, the subject was so suggestive of good, and so inspiring, that we found the evening quite too short, and we adjourned to meet again next Tuesday evening, when we hope that you will be present. But, though not fully organized, about twenty brethren and sisters desired to have their names affixed to the pledge to work for God.

Two ministers of different denominations were present, well known as holy adepts in the art of soul-saving. I should have said three ministers were present ; one who, though he has not yet given himself up fully to the work, anticipates doing so. He came seeking the full baptism of the Holy Ghost, not having fully understood the precise object of the meeting. But, while we were speaking of the necessity of *using* grace if we would have it multiply, and the self-sacrifice needful in view of the *natural* shrinkings of the flesh from these personal appeals to the unsaved, this brother saw that the reason why he had not before received the full baptism, was because he had not been willing to obey the gentle monitions of the Holy Spirit, which had long been urging him to these specific, personal efforts.

We had expected an interesting season ; but the meeting exceeded our anticipations.   The Saviour seemed so eminently present, and, as we talked by way of devising ways and means by which Christian men and women of the laity, as well as of the ministry, might, in a social way, win the most souls, I can hardly begin to tell you how divinely we were assured of the presence and approval of the Saviour.

This meeting, I presume, was about a sample of what future meetings may be.   Several brethren and sisters related instances in which they had been specially blessed with encouragement in seeing souls won over to Christ by their personal efforts.   Said one friend to another, as, in admiration of the grace of God, she listened to the instructive and most inspiring details of the occasion, " O, if there had been a reporter here, how thrillingly would the recitals of this meeting have told on paper ! "   " There *is* an unseen Reporter here," responded her friend.   Never, I think, under any circumstances, have I been more divinely impressed with the conviction, " The Lord hearkened and heard, and a book of remembrance was written before him."

Can we contemplate a gathering where the presence of the Saviour might be more confidently expected ? When we think of the price paid for human redemption, surely we cannot conceive it possible to be at too much pains in devising plans by which the gospel invitation may be given to every creature. And not till the professed followers of Christ feel their individual responsibility in making their secular business and domestic associations subservient to the one great object of the Christian's calling, which is the salvation of the whole redeemed family, can we hope that the gospel will be preached to *every* creature. Some thrilling recitals corroborative of this were given last evening.

Three or four different denominations were represented. And these were from various sections of the city and its environs, Brooklyn, Williamsburg, &c. This was truly encouraging, as there was little other notice of the meeting given than that which you heard at the Tuesday afternoon meeting, last week. But how reasonable that from a meeting of various denominations on the theme of holiness should emanate a social, weekly gathering, whose object may be to encourage each other in daily, specific efforts to win souls to the Saviour!

My heart glows with hallowed emotions while I write. O, I feel so sure that we may expect the guiding presence of the High and Holy One in this undertaking! We will not expect all who come to join the band at once, but will hope that the timid and weak will come, trusting that they may gather courage, and, in the end, become strong in the Lord, and in the power of his might. How often have I seen the one talent made five by reason of use! Our Congregational brother, the Rev. Mr. B., was with us, and expressed the deepest interest in the meeting. He says he thinks the Lord is going to do wonders through these simple means. If I have one passion above another, it is a passion for soul-saving.

Yours in Jesus.

O——, March 12, 1858.

Beloved Sister S——: When I tell you that we are holding four and five meetings per day, you will not wonder when I say I must be brief.

I do not know that I could have clearer demonstration to my own mind of having obeyed the divine bidding in coming here, even though the angel Gabriel had been commissioned to come and tell me so. We have much to be thankful for. He at whose mandate we have come is greatly blessing us in our work, and making our commission known, not only among our own people, but the ministers and people of other denominations seem to be well nigh equally interested with our visit. Our special commission just now appears to be to get the people one and all to come up to the help of the Lord, to the help of the Lord against the mighty.

Religion seems to be the order of the day here, or is fast becoming so, as in New York. The newspapers are taking up the theme, and reporting religious progress and revival intelligence, as in our city. Perhaps I may clip from the Gazette some intelligence of this sort for you, in which our visit is recognized. The Lord of the armies of Israel has ordered just the time of our coming. It is "court week," which brings many

23 *

strangers here. Handbills, advertising the various religious meetings, are posted all over the place, and the people are crowding the places of worship, I presume, as never before.

Yesterday we attended four meetings, one in the Baptist Church, and three in our own, all of which were attended with marked demonstrations of the divine presence and power. Last evening was especially a season of memorable interest. The battle was set fairly in array, and we had a larger number won over to the Captain of our salvation than on any former occasion. Dear husband reached here a little before five o'clock, while we were in the midst of a blessed meeting. He seemed full of the Spirit and power of his Master. Last night he had blessed liberty and power, and was most gloriously effective in his labors in winning souls to Jesus. I am now writing in much haste, preparatory to attending a special meeting, which commences in about half an hour, in the Presbyterian Church. It has been convened at the request of the minister of the church, and has been published in other churches. It is more especially in view of bringing out the *ladies* of the different sects. It seems to be rather an outspoken belief, on the part of the ministry, that the female membership of the various churches ought to be brought out to pray, and speak, and exercise their various gifts. This extra service has been appointed in view of our meeting with them, and advising them in regard to duty on this subject. It is anticipated, in view of the interest which has been manifested on the theme, that there will be many present. I feel a serious sense of responsibility on the subject, as though it might be the beginning of a work of great magnitude. The recognition of the labors of females is a characteristic of the Spirit's dispensation, which seems to have been singularly overlooked. And how remarkable it is that this request should have originated with a Presbyterian minister! And now the church bell rings, and I must leave.

Saturday Noon, March 13.

I hoped to have sent my letter yesterday, but I was peremptorily called away to meet the ladies, as anticipated. It was a meeting of intense interest. It was held in the session room, with the understanding that the gentlemen should give way to the ladies in case there should be a crowd. Some gentlemen came — I do not know how many; but they were all displaced by the ladies, with the exception of Dr. ——, the ladies crowding the place, so that it was difficult to obtain seats.

Scarcely do I remember to have felt more of the divine presence and approval. I should like to tell you how my mind was directed in addressing this meeting; but time will not permit. I saw many with tearful eyes. I talked of the blessedness of the present dispensation, and its responsibilities. Most marked indications were given that the whole matter was in the order of God; and the interested, tearful answering looks of my auditory all seemed to say that the orderings of the meeting were of God. Not a few of the aristocracy of O—— were there.

One of these earnestly entreated us to make our home with her during the remainder of our stay here. The Hon. —— married in this family. While I was talking in the church, I noticed this lady's tearful eyes, and I longed that the levelling, self-sacrificing principles of the gospel should take such fast hold on her heart that she might not be permitted to rest short of the grace of entire sanctification. In the afternoon she came to the meeting in the Methodist Church, and seemed to be still more deeply interested. This morning we have called on her, and she informs us she has had a restless night. O, indeed my convictions are so strong that God is about to raise up a holy working class of Christians in all the various denominations here, that faith almost amounts to a demonstration.

Last evening, as we were about to commence our services in the M. E. Church, a messenger came to know whether an appointment might be announced for us this morning in the Congregational Church for half past ten. So sure were we that the matter was of God, that I dared not refuse. From that meeting I have now returned. It was largely attended by persons of various denominations. And though the invitation was mainly extended to ladies, yet, as we were not restricted for room as yesterday, the meeting being held in the body of the church, the gentlemen were not crowded out; about one third, or little over, of the congregation were gentlemen. I cannot go into particulars; but I think the meeting was still more intensely interesting than the meeting of yesterday. I saw many, both among the gentlemen and ladies, in tears. As we were singing the closing hymn, one of the gentlemen of the congregation came to me, and entreated me to go to a lady on the other side of the house. I found her weeping bitterly. On inquiring the cause of her agony, she sobbed out, " O, I believe the Lord would be willing to bless me if I were only willing to do my duty."

And thus it is that the Lord of the vineyard is about to roll a burden of labor on our sisters of other denominations, and the ministers of these denominations are all intent that these female disciples of the Saviour should be brought to feel the weight of responsibility resting upon them to come out as laborers. This morning the minister of the Baptist Church came to me, and asked if a similar meeting might not be appointed in his church.

Does not all this promise a revival of Christianity after the apostolic fashion? Would it not be singular if our Presbyterian, Congregational, and Baptist friends should go beyond our Methodist friends in calling out their female laborers? Certainly they appear to bid fair for it here ; for the whole community seems to be leavening with this influence. We are having glorious seasons of the outpouring of the Spirit in our own church. Multitudes are coming out, and many are being saved. We are having three meetings per day, besides the meetings we attend elsewhere. We cannot say when we will return. Invitations are pressing upon us in every direction, but we cannot leave here just now.

Your ever-attached Sister.

Charlottetown, P. E. I., October 23, 1858.

Rev. Dr. H——— : We occasionally see a copy of your excellent paper in these British Provinces. A few weeks since we saw some reference made to our labors in these regions, and it occurred to us that it might be pleasing to the friends of Zion to receive more minute details of the outgoings of God's power in this far off land.

About three months since we passed through Boston, in answer to an official invitation from the Wesleyan Church in Frederickton, N. B., to attend a camp meeting. It was our expectation to return in two or three weeks; but at every point in our journeying we were permitted to witness such remarkable outpourings of the Holy Spirit, that we have been delayed till the present time.

The camp meeting was held near Woodstock, N. B. It was well attended in point of numbers, in view of the fact that camp meetings are considered an experiment in these parts. The secretary of the meeting reported the numbers who had been made recipients of saving grace two hundred. The flame that broke out at the camp meeting spread to the surrounding country, and we left a gracious work in progress, especially at Woodstock. A friend informs us that about six hundred have since been saved on the district in which the meeting was held. The district chairman is a man of power, filled with faith and with the Holy Ghost. On our return we paused a short time at Frederickton. Here several received sanctifying, and others justifying grace ; while here we were urgently invited to go to St. John and hold special services. We were not expecting to remain more than three or four days, but the church and the ministry began to arise and put on their strength. Many received the baptism of fire. Those holding official positions in the church were seen humbling themselves, kneeling at the altar of prayer, pleading for full salvation. Ministers and people from the surrounding country flocked in ; and we have reason to believe that as many as two hundred, if not more, were enabled to testify that " the blood of Jesus cleanseth from all sin." The church, thus endued with power, was mighty in working for God in the ingathering of sinners.

During the twenty-three days of our stay the flame of revival continued to rise and spread, every day increasing in power, the people coming out in yet greater crowds daily at both afternoon and evening meetings, till, at the time of our leaving, we think not less than four hundred had been newly gathered into the fold of Christ. The last evening of our stay here seemed to exceed all others in power and glory. Surely the Lord poured out his Spirit upon his people in floods of saving grace.

Having accepted an official invitation from the churches in Halifax, we tore ourselves away from our friends in St. John in the midst of this glorious work. Here, also, the Captain of our salvation began to work in great power, after the church membership had, in humble waiting before God, sought the full baptism of

276   PROMISE OF THE FATHER.

Work daily rising.   Truro.   Coming up to the help of the Lord.   River John.

the Holy Ghost.   The church being thus endued with power from on high, the Lord wrought most graciously. In twenty-one days one hundred and forty received the blessing of pardon ; and, judging from the many who daily presented themselves as earnest seekers of the blessing of entire sanctification, I do not doubt but at least one hundred received the witness of full salvation. The work thus gloriously commenced continued to rise during the whole period of our stay, and was at a higher point on the evening we left than at any former period.   Probably not less than forty were forward for prayers the evening preceding our departure.   But we had yielded to solicitations to engage ourselves elsewhere, and could not remain.

Our next visit was at Truro, about sixty miles from Halifax.   Here also the church was induced to listen to the call of the Spirit, and come up to the help of the Lord against the mighty.   We remained a little over a week, and witnessed, to a remarkable degree, the arm of the Lord made bare.   We heard no estimate of the number saved, but the recipients of grace were many. To God be all the glory.

From Truro we went to River John, N. S., a town of probably less than a thousand inhabitants, situated on the banks of the River John, which empties into the Straits of Northumberland.   Here the overhanging cloud of mercy began to pour out plenteous showers. We remained three days, engaged in holding day and evening meetings.   Many received the sanctifying seal, and others were newly justified.   Truly did Zion arise and put on her strength, resolving to put forth all her dormant energies in bringing lost sinners to Christ. But, by the pressure of other engagements, we were constrained to leave ere we could witness the full triumph of the promised victory.

Leaving River John, we came by the way of Pictou to Prince Edward Island. We are now at Charlottetown, the seat of government of this beautiful island, a city of about five thousand inhabitants. The population of the whole island, as we are informed, is about seventy thousand. In this place the Wesleyan body is well represented. Their church is commodious, and it is said will seat from fourteen to fifteen hundred persons; the church membership, till within a few days, was about three hundred. But what hath God wrought!

While at St. John, our friend, writing to a minister and his lady formerly resident there, says, —

Rev. Mr. and Mrs. ——: The oft-repeated name here of the beloved brother and sister in Jesus, to whom these lines are addressed, seems newly to have brought my spirit in fellowship with you. We address you as *one*, because you *are* one in Christ Jesus, and we are *one* with you.

> " One family in him we dwell."

How blessed to enter by the new and living way into the inner sanctuary, and, through the blood of the everlasting covenant, cast anchor daily yet deeper within the veil, whither Jesus, the forerunner, hath for us entered! My heart would proceed, but so prolific is the theme that my pen would fain pause. The wonderful companionship proffered to the believer, as set forth in Heb. xii. 22–24, comes up before me — "Ye are come to mount Zion," &c. Alleluia! the Lord God omnipotent reigneth!

I know you will hasten to give God the glory when I tell you that the fruit of your united labors in this place still remain. The seed you scattered here is still producing fruit; and your name is as ointment poured forth. I think we were informed that in the itinerancy this was your last field of labor. But I do not doubt that, in the field in which you by divine appointment are now laboring, an abundant harvest will in the end await you.

You will rejoice to hear that the Lord is most graciously pouring out his Spirit in this place. We came here not expecting to remain over a day or two; but such are the indications of a remarkable work of the Spirit that we hesitate in leaving.

August 2. It is now one week since we came here, and every day the interest has increased. Many have received the blessing of purity, and not a few have been newly born into the kingdom of grace. How many I cannot say, as there has not as yet any note been taken of the number. But as yet the battle has progressed on the principle set forth, 2 Chron. xx. As you will observe, here was one of the most signal victories ever gained by the hosts of Israel. Combined nations had concentrated their forces, and a won-

PROMISE OF THE FATHER. 279

Order of the battle.   How to do more in five hours than in five years.

derful conquest was achieved by *believing* and *praising*.
Singers were appointed to precede the army of Israel,
and their song was to be in praise of "the BEAUTY
OF HOLINESS." Last night, by the advice of a brother,
who is one of the leaders in Israel, we did not bring
forth the standard of holiness with quite so much
prominence before the people, and only invited those
who were seeking pardon forward. We were soon
compelled to feel that the orderings of the battle were
not in accordance with the mind of the Spirit, and
quickly retraced our steps, and invited, conjointly, both
those who were seeking either state of grace, purity, or
pardon; and, as on preceding evenings, many immediately presented themselves, some seeking pardon and
others purity.

Wed. 3. The work is going on with increasing
power. Both the afternoon and evening meetings are
largely attended. It has been estimated that not less
than seven hundred have been in daily attendance during the present week at the afternoon meetings at the
Centenary Church. At these meetings, though the neg-
lecters of salvation are not forgotten, and seekers of
pardon are earnestly invited to come to Jesus, yet the
efforts are mainly in view of inviting believers to come
up to the help of the Lord against the mighty. How
powerless is the church unless filled with the might of
the Spirit! Peter was a disciple before he received the
baptism of the Holy Ghost. But he was empowered
to do more, after he had tarried at Jerusalem and received the pentecostal baptism, in five hours, than he

could have accomplished in five years without this baptism of fire. How many disciples may still be asked, " Have ye received the Holy Ghost since ye believed ? " Glory to God and the Lamb forever for the manifestations which are daily greeting the eyes of wondering beholders, assuring the gainsaying world that we live under the dispensation of the Spirit, and that it is still being poured out upon all the disciples of the Saviour, who humbly and believingly wait for it. Alleluia ! the Lord God omnipotent reigneth. " The tongue of fire " — the prophetic flame — may not only be written about, but may be received. Many have been endued with this gift of power since we have been here. And these newly baptized ones are now going around among the unsaved inhabitants of this city, inviting them to the temple of the living God. And here the God of the temple meets them, and they are brought to a saving acquaintance with Jesus. Said I to one, who came crowding herself in among the multitude of seekers, " For what did you come ?   *What* is the petition which you would present to Jesus ? for he is *now* here to receive your petition."   " *I came to get acquainted with Jesus,*" she replied. Said I to another, who was kneeling near the one just referred to, and was weeping convulsively, " And what would you have the Saviour do for you ? for he is now saying to you, ' What wouldst thou that I should do for thee ? ' " She cried out, " O, my heart is *burdened,* so *burdened !* I feel that the Lord has blessed my own soul ; but O, my *husband* and *four* children are all unsaved ; " and then she burst into another fit of convulsive sorrow. As she lifted her head I saw that she was one who, the afternoon previous, had been kneeling, seeking the full baptism of the Spirit. And was not this manifestation of heart-breaking desire demonstrative that she had indeed been baptized into the Spirit of Him who wept over those whom he would fain have saved? O, when the Christian church is fully baptized into the Spirit of her Lord, what manifestations of yearning pity will there be over a perishing world! and how soon will this revolted yet redeemed world be brought back to the world's Redeemer!

These afternoon meetings, which are so largely attended, are made mightily subservient to the interest of the evening meeting. Here Zion puts on her strength. And in the evening meetings the hosts of Zion are seen scattered in various parts of the house, in earnest, importunate endeavors to win their friends and neighbors over from the ranks of sin. Last night about fifty were forward for prayers, and many were saved. The evening exercises are mostly directed towards the ingathering of sinners; but, as before intimated, seekers of purity are also invited forward. The large Centenary Church, where you were stationed when here, is nightly crowded — gallery filled, and people standing in the aisles and doors, unable to find seats. The ministers stand forth nobly as Captains of the Lord's hosts, and aid in leading the people forth to glorious victory. We are praying that this cloud which has arisen, small as a human hand, may spread over all British North America ; and to this we well know that your fervent hearts will respond, Amen.   Yours in Jesus.

Charlottetown, P. E. I., September 29, 1858.

Dear brother D———: Still we are delayed in these British Provinces.   We cannot doubt but the Captain of the hosts of Israel has, in ordering our steps here, led us forth by a right way.   Never have we been more fully assured of divine direction than in our detention in these Provinces.   Dr. ——— wrote you of the work in St. John.   We have since received letters from correspondents there, assuring us that the fruit remains, and that the work is most graciously widening and deepening.   A letter from the Rev. Mr. A., one of the excellent ministers resident in St. John, says, "Since your departure, although our congregations have not been so large as when you were with us, we have not forfeited the blessings which were so richly bestowed upon us during that wondrous visitation.   Our Quarterly Love Feast was held last Monday evening, at the Centenary Church ; and it was indeed one of the most hallowing and blissful seasons I ever enjoyed.   Many noble testimonies were given of the power of Christ to save to the uttermost, and many young converts spoke very sweetly of the preciousness of our Jesus.   Ten o'clock came, and every one appeared amazed, and grieved that the time for separation had come.   The language of all appeared to be, —

"My happy soul would stay
In such a frame as this,
And sit and sing herself away
To everlasting bliss."

" Glory, glory to the Lamb, for all his mercy and his grace."

One engagement has succeeded another in such rapid succession, that I cannot now remember whether we wrote you of the revival which commenced in Halifax during our visit there. While at St. John, we were induced to accept an urgent invitation from the Wesleyan churches in Halifax. Perhaps you may have seen the official recognition of this, and also of our visit to St. John, as published in the " Provincial Wesleyan " of August 26 and September 16. During our stay at Halifax, the secretaries of the meeting reported one hundred and seventy names as among the newly blessed. One hundred and forty of these were gathered from the world. From a dozen to twenty soldiers were among the newly enlisted in the service of the Captain of our salvation. They came forward in their fine scarlet uniform, and interspersed themselves among other kneeling, weeping penitents. And it was to us a most interesting sight, to see these hardy men, who, but a few months since, were engaged in bloody conflict in the Crimean war, now commencing their eternal God-service, and acknowledging allegiance to the blessed and only Potentate, the King of kings and Lord of lords. Several of these, after receiving pardon, came forward the second time, and again bowed at the communion rail. At this we at first wondered, in view of the fact that their conversion had been very clear. But on inquiry we found that the Holy Spirit had convinced them of the necessity of a further work, and they were pleading for the witness of inward purity. Nearly all of these, we trust, with several others, had not only a new song put into their mouths, but their *goings established.*

We have seen many beautiful illustrations of this in our labors at various places, of which I may write you as opportunity occurs. I cannot forbear mentioning one or two cases of entire sanctification, which occurred in but a few days after conversion, at St. John; one, of a man who received the blessing of justification one evening, in the gallery, while we were telling *how* a sinner might be saved. We were pointing out the simplicity of faith, and had asked that some one or more might be enabled to believe unto salvation. After we had finished speaking, this man came down from the gallery, and hastened forward to the altar. Soon as an opportunity was given for confession, he stepped forward, and, facing the congregation, said that he had been convicted of sin at one of the meetings two or three days previous, and had come to the meeting this evening, resolved to seek an interest in Christ. While the way to Jesus was being pointed out, he thought, Why need I *wait?* Why not trust in Christ to save me *just now?* He believed, and was saved. He had come forward now, not to profess himself as a *seeker*, but to confess that he had *found* the Saviour. He was induced, at once, to manifest his love to Jesus by constraining others to come to the gospel feast; and a brother and other of his relatives were induced to accept of the conditions of salvation.

About one week subsequent to the conversion of this earnest man, we again saw him bowed with the seekers, surrounding the communion rail.   On inquiring, we found that he was earnestly seeking the witness of entire purity, believing it to be his privilege to have the bent to backslidings taken away, and his goings established.   He did not seek in vain.   Definite and importunate petitions bring definite answers, and definite answers to prayer demand definite acknowledgments.   In less than an hour from the time he approached the altar of prayer, he rose and gave a precious testimony of the power of Christ to save to the uttermost.

One evening, as we approached the church door, we were introduced to an intelligent, gay young lady.   I urged her most affectionately to yield herself up to the service of the Saviour, and could only succeed in obtaining an answer that she would, in the strength of the Lord, try.· She did try.   That evening she presented herself among the seekers of salvation, and obtained a joyful witness that her sins were pardoned, and her name written in the book of life.   Two or three days after her conversion, she came to me, at an early hour, one morning, so distressed in mind, that I presume she had slept but little, if any, during the night.

The occasion of her distress was, that she feared she had grieved her Saviour in not having invited a gay lady to seek an interest in Christ, whom she had seen in the congregation the evening before.   Yet she had not been wholly negligent of the duty, but had endeavored to do by proxy that which the Holy Spirit assured her ought to have been done personally. Feeling as though the cross was too heavy for her to bear, she called for the Rev. Mr. A., and sent him to the lady; but he failed in speaking to the right one, and the work was left undone. Thankful to see the tenderness of conscience of this precious lamb of Christ's fold, yet longing to assuage her distress, I expressed my regret that she had not been ready to obey at once the gentle monitions of the Spirit, and by not following it, had brought upon herself a degree of condemnation. I proposed a plan, by which I suggested the cruel tempter might be more than outmatched. " Go," said I, " to the lady this morning, and tell her how distressed you feel for not having done your duty, in inviting her to the Saviour last evening." She exclaimed, " O, I would if I only knew who she was, or where I might find her ! " I had supposed that the lady who was the object of her solicitude was one of her former companions, when in friendship with the world, and could not but feel that the Lord was about to make this lovely young convert an example to believers, in the duty of being " instant in season and out of season." I advised her to manifest that she had been renewed in mind, by her outward conformity to the self-sacrificing principles of the gospel, and put aside the badges of friendship with the world. She acknowledged that my suggestions were scripturally correct; but I could see the conflict depicted in her countenance. Nature and grace were striving for the mastery. "Ye cannot serve two masters." "What agreement hath the temple of God with idols?" "What do you think," said she, "of the Christians at F—? I spent a gay winter there. I saw Christians in gay parties, and I could not see that they differed from others; indeed, I used to think that I was about as good as any of them." I assured her, in return, that such Christians were, in fact, not Christians, but mere professors, and, as such, stumbling blocks, over which, she could now perceive, she was in danger of stumbling into perdition, and entreated her to resolve that she would never thus stand in the way of others, but show that she was resolved on being a Bible Christian.

She then and there resolved that she would indeed come out from the world and be separate, and manifest her detachment from the world by laying aside her superfluities. She did so, and I was interested to see her, on the afternoon of that day, appearing more as one professing godliness. From that point she began to run on in the way of God's commandments. And why not, as she had now resolved on laying aside every weight? At one of the subsequent afternoon meetings, she came to me with a most glowing countenance. O, it seemed that my spirit's eye could see legibly written on that happy brow, "HOLINESS TO THE LORD," as she exclaimed, "I have washed my garments white in the blood of the Lamb!" The evening previous to our leaving, she rose before congregated hundreds, and testified to the power of Christ, not only to forgive sins, but to cleanse from all unrighteousness. Surely the

time has come when judgment must begin at the house
of God.   It will not do for these thousands, which are
being brought out of spiritual Egypt, to be hindered
by the example of older professors, from entering into
the Canaan of perfect love.   These masses which have
been brought out of Egypt must be led at once up into
the rest of faith.

> " A rest where all the soul's desire
> Is fixed on things above,
> Where fear and unbelief expire,
> Cast out by perfect love."

Not only must worldly-conformed professors remove
the stumbling block of their example, but those who
lead forth the hosts of Israel must furnish examples in
faith as well as in doctrine, and from their own inspiring experience be enabled to testify, " We are well
able to go up and possess the goodly land."   Authoritative or theoretical teachings are seldom effective in
leading the soul onward to the rest of perfect love.
The religion of Christ is a religion of love, and all its
indices are equalizing, and seem to say, " Ye are all
brethren."   Paul yet again and again presented his
own inspiring experiences of the grace of God to encourage others to come up to the Christian standard of
experience — " Let us, as many of us as be perfect, be
thus minded."   And in like manner does he also enforce the doctrine of conversion, by the repetition of
his own conversion.   Said a beloved young minister,
who was in attendance at one of our recent meetings,

where many, to whom he would be called to minister, had been raised up to testify that the blood of Jesus cleanseth from all sin, "What shall I do? Last night, as I saw the people crowding forward for prayers, I was so concerned about my own condition that I felt as if I could not work until I had something further done for my own soul." He had been wrestling with the Angel of the Covenant during the night. "And now," said he, "I see that I must preach holiness to the people, and I am resolved to do so; but it will be hard work to preach the doctrine theoretically unless I have experience of the grace." We presented the simple way of faith, and said, "If the prophet had told thee to do some great thing, wouldst thou not have done it? It is simply wash, and be clean. The cleansing fountain is now flowing. Christ is the Lamb, newly slain from the foundation of the world, and all you have to do is to present all your redeemed powers a living sacrifice to God, through Christ, and then rely upon the declaration, 'The blood of Jesus cleanseth.' Not that it *did* cleanse, or *will* cleanse, but *cleanseth* — cleanseth *now*. Is not an offering presented to God through Christ, 'holy, acceptable?'" He dared doubt no longer, and exclaimed, "I *will*, I *do* believe!" O, what glorious confirmation of his faith followed! Never shall I forget the affectingly interesting scene which succeeded, when, before several witnesses, he shortly afterwards nobly professed his faith in the infinitely efficacious, all-cleansing blood of Jesus.

Charlottetown, P. E. I., October 14, 1858.

Dear Brother D.: I presume you wonder that we permit ourselves to be so long detained, in view of our responsibilities.   But no apology would be needful, could either yourself or the religious community from abroad behold the great things that God is doing for this beautiful and highly-favored island.

When we accepted the invitation of the Wesleyan Church in this place, it was with the understanding that we could not permit ourselves to be detained over four or five days.   But the church began to awake and put on her strength ; and how wonderful the power she may put forth when she clothes herself with Christ, and brings her dormant energies into action !

Oct. 15.   It is now three weeks this morning since we came here ; during which time, daily and evening meetings have been held, and hundreds have been added to the Lord.   The work began with the church, and I doubt not, that from three to four hundred have received the witness of entire sanctification.   Ministers and people have come in from the surrounding country, from twenty, thirty, forty, and even eighty miles distant, and after receiving the baptism of fire, have scattered again to spread the holy flame in all the adjacent places round about.   All the ministers on the district have been present, with their beloved district chairman, all of whom are now enabled to testify, from their own experimental realizations, that the way into the holiest is open for every redeemed child of Adam, and is entered by faith in the blood of the everlasting covenant.

How important that those who are called to take the lead of the sacramental hosts of God's elect should

> " * * * themselves believe
> And put salvation on " !

The promise of the Father is received by *faith*. And as ministers are in the order of God set before the people as ensamples in *faith* as well as in doctrine, how needful that the entire ministry should be pioneers in faith, and by their experience show that the gift of power promised to all Christ's disciples is received by faith.

Never shall I forget the scene of power I witnessed at one of the afternoon meetings about two weeks since, when four or five of the ordained ministry, and others of the local ministry, and perhaps over a score of the laity, among whom were several class leaders and other prominent members, all received the baptism of fire. The circumstances were in some respects peculiar. We had observed to the people at the opening of the exercises about thus : We often have *prayer meetings*, and these surely are very important ; for what should we do if we could not approach the throne of grace by prayer ? We have also had, under some extraordinary circumstances, *"praise meetings*," and these also have been greatly blessed with remarkable manifestations of divine approval ; but neither prayer nor praise, though most needful and pleasing to God, will take the place of FAITH, inasmuch as it is written, " Without faith it is *impossible* to please God." What more proper then, than that we should have

A BELIEVING MEETING.

Many of us, perhaps, have our sacrifice already upon the altar. At least, all is there, with the exception of that *will* which requires signs and wonders. Let us get that *will* upon the altar now, and resolve at once on taking God at his word, irrespective of emotion, or any *sensible* demonstration ; for it is written, " The just *shall* live by *faith*," and to the degree we have *sensible* manifestations, faith is not necessary. It is faith that honors God. Abraham believed God, and his faith was counted to him for righteousness.

Well, we had, indeed, a believing meeting. Many now brought their sacrifices to the altar, and in faith waited for the descent of the hallowing, consuming fire. But Abraham's sacrifice became the Lord's property the moment he laid it upon the altar — just as truly the Lord's, as though he had been permitted to ascend to the throne of God in heaven, and laid the sacrifice there on Heaven's altar, before the myriads of angelic beholders. " The altar sanctifieth the gift." The moment he laid it upon the altar it became virtually God's property. All Abraham had now to do was to watch the offering. It was just as sacredly the Lord's before it was consumed as it was afterwards. When he saw the fire descend and consume the sacrifice, faith on that point was no longer necessary. It was sight. But it is faith that honors God. And now we have reason to believe that scores resolved to take God at his word.

Of course, Abraham *could not* have believed that his offering was accepted before it was laid on the altar. Neither could his offering have been consumed unless it had been placed on the altar. But the offering once laid on the altar, and kept there, God *always* does his part of the work. No danger of failure here; his name is faithful and true. Such a baptism of fire as descended on this company during the process of this believing meeting I will not attempt to describe.

From this point the work progressed with great power. I do not doubt but as many as a thousand in all have been blessed with either sanctifying or justifying grace. It is now Friday. I have not heard the number of those newly converted since last Monday. The district chairman then informed us that over five hundred names had been taken of those who had been newly gathered from the world, besides those who had been restored from their backslidings, who were before members. The work has been going on with still greater power during the present week, and the newly justified now are doubtless not less than from six to seven hundred.

What hath God wrought? Surely you will give him all the glory. My heart exclaims with the sainted Fletcher, "O for a gust of praise to go through the earth!" Let all the people praise him, and let the saints shout aloud for joy.

Yours in Jesus.

25 *

Bay of Fundy, On board Steamer Admiral, }
Nov. 22, 1858.

Dearest Sister : We have just left St. John, N. B. Jesus gives us our friends. We have just taken our last leave of scores of tearful ones, and are now on board an American steamer, on our way to Boston, where, Providence favoring, we shall probably arrive to-morrow afternoon.

Through the grace of our Lord Jesus Christ, we are what we are. Would that it were in my power to transcribe the wonderful dispensations of grace towards us since we saw you. Never have we had a deeper realization of the fact that it is "not by might, nor by power, but by my Spirit, saith the Lord," than during the entire of our present journeyings, and never have we witnessed a more extraordinary demonstration of the fact that our God loves to take of the weak things of this world to confound the mighty. I think it would be a low computation, should we say that we have witnessed, in the aggregate, two thousand newly saved at the various places we have visited, besides hundreds of believers sanctified wholly:

At every point the work has commenced with the church. Both ministers and people have, with deep humiliation and tears, sought the full baptism of the Spirit; and then, as on the day of Pentecost, the convincing power has penetrated the hearts of sinners, and multitudes have been saved. I would have written to you often ; not a week would have passed but you would have had a sheet largely filled ; but I can scarcely begin to tell you how constantly my time has been occupied. We have had three meetings a day during the past four weeks, and some of these meetings have been from three to four hours long, commencing at eight o'clock in the morning, and continuing till towards noon ; afternoon meetings commencing at three o'clock, and continuing till dark. At these meetings it is not unusual to see from twenty to fifty forward for prayers. Of course, it would be difficult to leave these earnest seekers until driven by the shades of evening and our waiting repast.

At seven o'clock we have again repaired to a still more crowded house, to be answerable to the evening service, when the Lord has generally wrought in still greater power, and we have seldom left the house till after ten o'clock. It is astonishing how the people come out from all the surrounding country, going and returning from ten to twelve miles daily, and others coming, and remaining day after day, from a distance of fifty miles and over. Wherever we have been, the ministers from the surrounding districts have come in, and few have shared more largely in the falling showers of grace than these. At the last place we visited, the chairmen of three districts were present, part of the time, with a number of other ministers. And not unlike this has it been at most places we have visited.

As you have not been with us in our campaigns, I suppose you would sometimes like to look in upon us, and see the orderings of grace. Well, it is, in short,

296　　PROMISE OF THE FATHER.

Orderings of the meeting.　　Divine call.　　Opinions of men lighter than vanity.

about like this : Dr. —— and myself generally confer together, and we select such portions of Scripture and hymns as contain such leading ideas as we wish to urge upon the attention of the people. The meetings are given in charge of husband, and after the opening hymn is sung, some minister present generally prays. A portion of the Scriptures is then read, and the peculiar gift which the Lord has given Dr. —— to read *impressively*, has, through the power of the Spirit, told most advantageously on the cause. After another hymn is sung, your humble sister aims to talk as the Spirit gives utterance. It is my intention not to exceed half an hour, but if I should say that I am often drawn out beyond my anticipations, you will not be surprised.

And now let me assure you, dear sister, that the Lord is giving most confirming evidence to thousands that he has not forgotten his ancient promise, " I will pour out my Spirit on my sons and daughters," &c. Had Gabriel been commissioned to come and assure me that the Lord would have me open my lips and speak of the power of his saving grace, and also of other things that appertain to his kingdom, I could not be more certain of a divine call. The hundreds whom we have yearly witnessed brought over to the ranks of the saved during the past twenty years since we received that memorable baptism of the Spirit, July 26, 1837, puts doubt to flight, and makes the opinions of men seem lighter than vanity, where these opinions would seem to contravene the order of God.

Were I called to pass through the vale of mortality

this hour, I should love, before entering into the more immediate presence of my faithful covenant-keeping Lord, to say, to the praise of his grace alone, that we have reason to believe thousands have been won over from the ranks of sin, whose feet, we fear, had been in the way to death, had we not gone beyond the precincts of our own home to talk to them of the way of life. I say we, because husband and myself are not only of one mind on this subject, but are also one in our labors. He always succeeds my little talk with a persuasive invitation to the lukewarm professor and the open sinner, when they often come with a rush to the altar of prayer; and it is thus that we frequently witness scores blessed daily. Alleluiah! The Lord God omnipotent reigneth. Thanks be to God, who giveth us the victory through our Lord Jesus Christ.

We would not have you infer that we have been wholly saved from the trial of our faith; but so ceaseless and triumphant have been the conquests of grace, that victory has been our constant theme. Often do we have reason to exclaim, Surely the servant is above his Lord!

Wherever we go, the Lord provides a home for us among the princes of his people. And though, in regard to leaving our own dear home, we seem literally called to test the principles of ancient discipleship, — that is, that of forsaking all and following Christ, yet at every point of need, every real want seems to have been met with singular appropriateness; so that we have most significantly exclaimed, many times,

" Lacked ye any thing? and they said, Nothing, Lord."

We have in this, as in our many other and various journeyings, had much satisfaction in our work. Truly we have a goodly heritage. I have just been reviewing the past, and should love to portray, to the praise of God and for your satisfaction, these reviewings on paper. Wherever we go, the Lord gives us the hearts of the ministry and people to a degree that humbles and amazes us. We have made it a point, wherever we have been, to work with the ministry, not *independent* of them. This is agreeable to our own preferences. Of course the people expect us to fill up the time largely ; but this the ministers also desire, and so long as the Lord works in power, all parties are satisfied, and praise redounds to God.

The last place we wrote to you from was M——. Here both minister and people were dissatisfied with each other. It is not for us to say which were in fault ; but surely there was a fault somewhere. While we were at P. E. Island we had been earnestly invited to visit M——, but had so little idea of doing so that we had actually forgotten all about the matter, until we met a number of the friends awaiting the arrival of the cars. We were on hasteful wing homeward, and Dr. —— had already sent a telegram to our beloved friends in St. John, that they might see us as we passed homeward in the steamer the next night. Added to the personal entreaties of these friends, was a written petition, signed not only by persons of the

Wesleyan Church, but of persons of standing in the place not of our denomination.

But so imperative had we regarded our call homeward, that we would still have felt it our duty to hasten onward, had not the very low state of piety in the place enlisted our sympathies. In the Wesleyan Church, the evening meetings were well nigh totally neglected, sometimes less than a half a dozen attending the lecture, and the prayer meeting an entire failure; often no class meeting at all, and, at most, not more than three or four attending. To use their own expression, " It seemed as if religion was dying out in the place, and iniquity was abounding yet more and more." It is not surprising that the dear aged minister could have had no courage to minister to such congregations. He subsequently informed us by letter, that during about a half century he had never once been called to labor on such unfruitful soil.

How could we move homeward under such circumstances? We felt that the Head of the church forbade it, and we concluded to pause three days in the place. This was about noon, and the news quickly spread abroad. We had a large congregation in the evening — perhaps about an equal division of Baptists, Presbyterians, and Wesleyans. We could not but feel the hardness of the soil, but, while laboring in spirit, felt that we had not only an almighty Helper, but a sympathizing Saviour. This was on Saturday evening. We had been informed that on Sabbath morning our friends of the Baptist Church would omit their own services in order to be present at the Wesleyan Church ; but we were pleased that this purpose was not adhered to, as we preferred to have our people by themselves, and secure their individual attention to the great work of present and personal holiness. We had a memorable time both morning and afternoon, as we saw the fallow ground breaking up, and tearful eyes in every direction.

On Monday we began to gather fruit. O, how good has the Lord of the harvest been to us ! Scarcely has the seed been sown ere it has sprung up and produced abundant fruit. Meetings were, from this time, held three times a day for two weeks, increasing constantly in interest and power, until, up to the time of our leaving, about one hundred and fifty names had been taken as newly blessed. These were not all from among our own people, nor from the immediate town, but some were from a distance, and others will attach themselves, perhaps, to other denominations ; but I presume about one hundred have given in their names to join the Wesleyan Church. Eight new classes have been formed. The converts are some of the strongest men in the community. We are informed that three or four of them are already appointed class leaders ; but you would not be surprised at this if you could only see what mature converts they are.

Here, as elsewhere, we have encouraged the newly-received disciple to look for the full baptism of the Holy Ghost. And it has not been unusual to see them **come forward again a day or two after their conversion,** seeking specifically for the fulfilment of the promise of the Father. And that the promised endowment of power from on high has been given, you would not doubt, if you could hear their lucid testimony and witness the power of their lives. We have recently received a letter from the district chairman at Charlottetown, informing us that the revival flame has burst forth at six different points on the district. The Sabbath before we left the island we were told that four or five of the young converts went to hold a meeting at a place a few miles distant from Charlottetown, when eleven convicted sinners came forward for prayers, and several were converted. O, it is the baptism of the Holy Ghost that is the great want of the church. With this how quickly would she " come up out of the wilderness, fair as the moon, clear as the sun, and terrible as an army with banners! "

It is now Monday. Two weeks ago on Saturday we left M—— for Sackville, N. B. At this I suppose you will wonder more than at any of our former removes, in view of the lateness of the season, and our oft-repeated resolve to hasten homeward. But we had been more importunately solicited to visit this place than perhaps any other since we left home, and we were now within thirty miles distance, and we feared we might resist the order of God should we refuse. At no place have we seen the hand of the Lord more signally displayed than at Sackville. The people gathered in from the surrounding country from ten to sixty miles, and a more general baptism of the church I do not think that

26

we have ever witnessed. The number newly saved we do not know, as the names were noted but part of the time. The secretary informed me that of the number of names taken he had over one hundred.

But with this triumph there was also a painful trial, which has left a sadness on our minds. The first friend to welcome us at Sackville was Charles Allison, Esq., a lovely Christian gentleman of extensive and well-earned reputation. He was in his usual health when he welcomed us to his pleasant mansion on Mount Allison, two weeks since. Now he is an inhabitant of the Eternal City. We arrived on Saturday, and he was comfortable in health till Friday of the succeeding week. While we were dining on Friday, I saw he looked feeble. We spoke of this, and he said he was in a chill. I observed it was a convenient way to take cold when at church, from the vestry door being open, by passers in and out, when we were crowded in and around the altar. Mrs. A. observed "Mr. A. did not take his cold thus; he was thrown in a perspiration this morning by assisting the sexton to sweep the church." Think of this; a man by whose means the church and the ministry was largely sustained, and whose influence and wealth was doing as much, I presume, if not more, towards supporting the institutions of piety and literature, than any man in these British Provinces. What a reproof to those who would not shut the doors of the Lord's house for nought! I was mentioning this to a minister who had been stationed in the place, and he said, "O, that was only like Mr. A., he was continually doing such things. I have known him to plant with his own hands the potatoes on the parsonage grounds."

He had been greatly blessed in his own experience during the process of the meetings. He had long been seeking the witness of entire sanctification. One night, after returning from the church, we remained up praying and talking over this subject till near midnight. We left him holding on by faith, and I said to Dr. ——, on retiring that night to our room, weary, " Well, if our coming to these Provinces may only result in such a man as Mr. A. being brought out as a clear witness of the power of Christ to save to the uttermost, I should feel myself repaid for coming all the way from New York." I then thought of what might be the weight of his testimony in that community ; but how little did I think that he was so soon to take his place among the ranks of the blood-washed in heaven! But though he had endeavored to believe his hold on the blessing was somewhat trembling until the next afternoon, when, with over a score of others, among whom were ministers and people who came forward to the altar, he sought and obtained such a baptism of the Spirit as shall ever be remembered. From this hallowed hour he seemed to rest as under the shadow of the Almighty. So peaceful was his every look and act that I could only think of him as having entered

> " The land of rest from inbred sin,
> The land of perfect holiness."

Angels had lingered over that place, and had borne

the names of scores of newly-repenting sinners to heaven. Over fifty of the students belonging to the male and female departments of the Mount Allison Seminary had, within a few days, been added to the saved, besides many from Sackville village, and the surrounding community ; and scores of his Christian brethren and sisters had received the more enlarged baptism of the Holy Ghost. And now, as we were supping with a number of his friends, for the last time, at his own generous table, as each one was in turn repeating a verse of Scripture, our dear brother A. exclaimed, " Lord, now lettest thou thy servant depart in peace, according to thy word, for mine eyes have seen thy salvation." We marked the heavenly glow that illuminated his countenance as he said this, and felt that it was invested with a singular significance, but knew not that it was the last time we were to sup with him before sitting down with him in company with all the redeemed family at the marriage supper of the Lamb. How sweetly was he prepared to enter into the rest of the redeemed in heaven ! His constitution was feeble, and he was able to endure but little ; but while his heart and flesh were failing, he felt in a preëminent degree that God was the strength of his life and his portion forever. Just as the day was about breaking that he entered upon his eternal rest, Dr. —— read to him the seventeenth chapter of John. How sublime and inexpressibly precious this last prayer of our Saviour as he was about to leave his disciples ! Both husband and myself then prayed. We could feel that his heart was with us in our approaches to the throne, but he was unable to speak. He was already buffeting the billows of Jordan. As I repeated the words, —

> " Jesus, lover of my soul,
>   Let me to thy bosom fly,
> While the nearer waters roll,
>   While the tempest still is high.
> Hide me, O my Saviour, hide,
>   Till the storm of life is past ;
> Safe into the haven guide,
>   O, receive my soul at last," —

I could feel that the fast-failing energies of his struggling spirit was with me in every line. As I pressed his hand, and kissed the forehead, now cold in death, for the last time, exclaiming, " Thanks be to God, who giveth us the victory through our Lord Jesus Christ," he raised his beaming eye, already radiant with immortality, and the utterances of that countenance spoke of light, peace, and unshaken confidence. We were constrained to leave that day at ten o'clock, and at two he entered into the joy of his Lord. He seemed only to live to glorify God, and serve his generation according to the will of God. Though not, I presume, a man of immense wealth, yet he lived not to hoard up what he had, but, as a steward, to invest in a way which might most benefit the present and future generations.

We were informed that in addition to his other outlays, by way of serving his age, his appropriations toward the erection and sustainment of the Mount Allison Sackville Seminary amounted to about forty thousand dollars. He was himself a man of fine literary

26 *

taste, munificent, yet prudent. Many have done virtuously, but perhaps few have excelled our brother as a man or a Christian. When offered the suffrages of the community, which might have secured his election as a member of Parliament, he declined the honor, and preferred a more retired way of usefulness, preferring rather, as his divine Master, to be among his friends as one that serveth. "Blessed are the dead that die in the Lord, for they rest from their labors, and their works do follow them."

Last night we took part in the exercises at the Centenary Church. We had a good season. It seemed like a renewal of the battle. Twenty were forward for prayers, the most of whom were blessed. And now, as you see, we are actually on our way to Boston, from whence we hope to mail this letter on the morrow.

We will give but one record more from the hand of our friend, and close up the testimony we would present of the faithfulness of our promise-keeping Jehovah in the case of this daughter of the Lord. That the Father has poured out his Spirit and endued her with power from on high, we trust none will doubt. If he has thus poured out his Spirit upon one, who, because of her favorable surroundings, seems to have been permitted to speak, why may he not have done it in the case of many less favorably circumstanced, who have not been permitted to open their lips for God. Well do we know those who, we judge, have felt equally irrepressible influences to labor for God, and who, seemingly, were possessed of ability equally, if not more, promising for usefulness, whose lips have been restrained. In reviewings of the labors of this daughter of the Lord by another hand,* he says, " For the last few years, we judge, she must have travelled not less than five thousand miles annually upon religious visits, always by request, to various portions of the United States and Canada. The results of these visits in the salvation of souls, and the edification of the church, cannot now be estimated with accuracy ; but we speak from personal knowledge when we say that they have been large and abiding. Our convictions are, that many thousands of persons have been brought into the enjoyment of pardon or purity through her labors."

Now, dear reader, are you a minister ? Let me ask, If this female disciple had been a member of your charge, would you not have hindered the testimony of Jesus from the lips of this servant of the church ? If so, how you would have grieved the Head of the church ?

To the Rev. Mr. D——: * * * I feel an ever-pervading, all-consuming desire to glorify God to the uttermost in all things. I have no private interests to serve, no private reputation to build up or sustain, but such as stand in connection with Christ's kingdom. Never have I written one line that has had a righteous, holy, purifying tendency, but through the enabling, constraining agency of the Holy Spirit. Most deeply do I feel the import of the passage, " Their righteousness is

* Rev. B. W. G.   Guide to Holiness, Jan. 1857.

of me, saith the Lord." If a work is being done, our attention is not occupied with the instrument. That is, if you were using a spade by way of preparing the earth for the reception of seed, I, in beholding your work, would not say, "See what that spade has accomplished, but see what my brother D. has done."

I only look upon myself as a humble instrumentality which God has condescended to use, through which to communicate simple, yet infinitely important truth, in a manner suited to the unsophisticated multitude. It is true some doctors of divinity have not disdained our simple teachings. Yet it has been my aim to avoid most carefully every thing like a display of theological technicalities. Inasmuch as the Bible is not a sectarian book, or holiness the mere doctrine of a sect, it has been my aim to present it as the absolute requirement of the Bible, and binding on all of every name, rather than as a mere doctrine of a sect. In doing this, I have kept closely to Bible terms — holiness, sanctification, and perfect love. In all my various presentations of truths, I have aimed to follow the simple Bible mode of teaching, assured that the divine Author must have suggested the most *effectual* mode of making truth palpable to the obtuse perceptions of his creatures.

By the types and historic narrations of the Old Testament Scriptures, and the illustrative emblems used by the Saviour in the New, I adopted the incidental mode of illustrating truth, apprehending it as God's way of simplifying spiritual realities, and making them tangible to the understanding of the humble. It was after this mode I began, and have continued to this day, to write and teach, carefully avoiding giving utterance to any doctrine or sentiment for which an explicit " Thus saith the Lord " may not be given. I feel that it is *due* to the praise of grace to acknowledge that God has *owned* these simple presentations of truth. To this I have hundreds of letters to testify. A large portion of these are from persons I have never seen in the flesh, of various denominations. My M—— friends ought not to love me less because my teachings assume to be Bible rather than sectarian.

But my letter is already too long, and I must pause here. In view of the fact that the uninitiated in piety and the mass of professors so seldom come in contact with the stringent, yet, in view of ultimate salvation, the absolutely important doctrines of the cross, it strikes me that the presentation of them in incidental illustrations may dispose some to acquaint themselves, when presented in this approachable form, who might shrink from the perusal of theological works, which for able argumentation might be more imposing. It has always been my aim to be useful to the masses. It was these that heard the Saviour gladly.

Pray, my dear brother, that in the recordings of eternity it may be written of me, " She hath done what she could." It is my highest ambition to be numbered at last with those of whom the Revelator says, " These are they which follow the Lamb whithersoever he goeth." O, it is, indeed, most blessed to have a name with those who follow the Lamb whithersoever he goeth here on earth.

> " My Jesus to know and feel his blood flow,
> 'Tis life everlasting, 'tis heaven below."

O, what blissful scenes open before me, as, with the ransomed company, I return to Zion with songs and everlasting joy !   I feel that I have already commenced my eternal God-service.   I would not have you infer that I have no conflicts ; but every new conflict only seems to be the harbinger of a new and yet more glorious conquest, and my heart seems ever tuned to the Christian's triumphant song, "Thanks be unto God, who giveth us the victory through our Lord Jesus Christ."   Three times have I seemingly been within hearing distance of my eternal home ; once so near that, as my spirit flickered between the two worlds, heavenly music vibrated on my spirit's ear, and, O, how sweetly did I feel that death was swallowed up in victory !   But though I write thus confidently, most deeply do I realize that I cannot stand one moment but through the power of God.   The cry of my spirit ceaselessly is, —

> " Unsustained by thee I fall ;
> Send the help for which I call ;
> Weaker than a bruised reed,
> Help I every moment need."

But while thus conscious of my momentary dependence, my heart trusts, and is not afraid.   I know I have committed my all into the hands of Him who is able to keep me from falling, and to present me faultless before the presence of his glory with exceeding joy.   "To the only wise God our Saviour be glory and majesty, dominion and power, both now and ever.   Amen."

CHAPTER XIII.

"**Even as** our beloved brother Paul also, according to the wisdom given unto him, hath written unto you; as also in all his Epistles, speaking in them of these things, in which are some things hard to be understood, which they that are unlearned and unstable wrest, as they do also the other scriptures, unto their own destruction."

PETER.

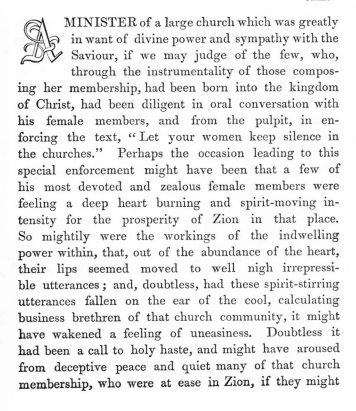 MINISTER of a large church which was greatly in want of divine power and sympathy with the Saviour, if we may judge of the few, who, through the instrumentality of those composing her membership, had been born into the kingdom of Christ, had been diligent in oral conversation with his female members, and from the pulpit, in enforcing the text, " Let your women keep silence in the churches." Perhaps the occasion leading to this special enforcement might have been that a few of his most devoted and zealous female members were feeling a deep heart burning and spirit-moving intensity for the prosperity of Zion in that place. So mightily were the workings of the indwelling power within, that, out of the abundance of the heart, their lips seemed moved to well nigh irrepressible utterances ; and, doubtless, had these spirit-stirring utterances fallen on the ear of the cool, calculating business brethren of that church community, it might have wakened a feeling of uneasiness. Doubtless it had been a call to holy haste, and might have aroused from deceptive peace and quiet many of that church membership, who were at ease in Zion, if they might

only have listened to the recital of the ardent longings of these earnest female disciples, whose hearts, in sympathy with an ancient prophet, were saying, "For Zion's sake will I not hold my peace, and for Jerusalem's sake I will not rest, until the righteousness thereof go forth as brightness, and the salvation thereof as a lamp that burneth."

But permission to give utterance to these mighty workings of the Spirit within was not granted. One of these beloved disciples, feeling, we presume, as Mary did, after the cloven tongue of fire sat on her head, felt that she *could* not restrain the utterances of the Spirit. She consequently consulted with the minister, and asked the privilege of opening her lips for Jesus. He, of course, received her affecting request with a dubious look, and told her that it was not with him to say whether she might enjoy that privilege, but that he would lay her request before the session.

Now, pause for a moment, and think, dear reader, of the process through which this disciple was required to pass before she could be permitted to obey the constrainings of the Holy Spirit, and ask yourself whether an error most grievous in the sight of God has not obtained in the Christian church. Let us conceive that after the women assembled with the other disciples, on the day of Pentecost, had received the baptism of the Holy Ghost alike with their brethren, they had been compelled to restrain those utterances until they had obtained permission from Matthew, Andrew, Peter, or other of the disciples. Can we conceive of such an inconsistency? And yet after what fashion would we desire the orderings of our church assemblies modelled, if not as nearly as may be after the fashion of this first great meeting in apostolic days?

But how was it now with this newly-baptized disciple of modern days, whose request to be permitted to speak had now gone from the minister to be laid before the official brethren of that church? And what was the decision of this company of unordained men, who took upon themselves the authority to decide whether this female disciple should obey the constrainings of the Holy Spirit? It was peremptorily decided that she should not be permitted to speak. But we do not doubt that she felt the impellings of the Spirit so that she dared not refrain. Cannot we who live in the latter part of the last days, conceive of a Mary so filled with the pentecostal flame as to speak under a divine influence, as the Spirit gives utterance? Yes, she spake in the midst of that assembly as the Spirit gave power. And that she should dare to speak when the authorities of the church of which she was a member had commanded her to keep silent, was as offensive to the rulers of that church as when those early disciples spoke in the temple after they had been commanded not to speak. And we should actually be ashamed to speak of the public and private persecution which followed, and which resulted in her removal to another place and another church community, where she was gratefully received, and her labors appreciated and blessed. The church to which she removed her membership was

27

shortly after favored with a signal outpouring of the Spirit.

And now that this persecuted Christian sister was gone, whose only fault seemed to be that she would not restrain the Holy Spirit's urgings to speak, there were still others of the most devoted female disciples who felt the urgings of the Spirit in the same direction.

Week after week did these, acknowledged by their church relation to be sisters in Christ, assemble in the prayer and conference meeting ; but though members of one household, no female member of the family was permitted to open her mouth in vocal prayer, or to speak of the interests of the household of faith, or even to tell of the dealings of her heavenly Father to her soul. We need not say that the meetings were generally cold and uninteresting. And how could it be otherwise ? We can conceive how undesirable it might be if children of one earthly parent should assemble at their father's house to subserve the interest of the family, and the female part of the household — the beloved mother, sister, or daughter — was required to be silent. How greatly would this prohibition detract from the interest and profit of this social gathering.

Think of a father who would call together his sons and daughters, to meet at the family mansion, for mutual profit and pleasure, and after thus assembling them, enjoin silence on his wife and daughters ! Should such a thing occur, we can scarcely conceive which portion of the family would feel most afflicted. Surely those attached brothers could not feel happy while their engaging mother and beloved sisters were doomed to sit in silence; neither could those beloved, affectionate, female members of the household enjoy themselves under such circumstances; and the design of the gathering would be well nigh, if not wholly, frustrated.

But the children of this world do not act thus unwisely. They are indeed "wiser in their generation than the children of light." Think of a worldly social company, where woman, with her refined sensibilities and social qualities, was not permitted to enliven and grace the circle. Worldlings are quite too wise in their own devisings to admit a suggestion of this sort. Woman may not only grace the social circle, in converse and song, but she may step out wholly beyond these precincts. A Jenny Lind, a Fanny Kemble, and a host of others, may appear on the stage, before thousands on thousands, in both hemispheres. Their names may be emblazoned in public prints, to the gaze and admiration of tens of thousands. But who reproves? Thousands do them homage, and even crowned heads bow at their shrine.

But lo! a modest Christian female comes forth. She is intellectual, and of refined sensibilities. All her antecedents and present surroundings are, and have been, beautifully chaste and becoming. With the beloved Mary she has been accustomed to sit at the Master's feet. While her more hardy brethren may have been following the Saviour afar off, or, perchance, engaged in strifes which should be the greatest, she has kept closely following the Saviour through evil and good report, and with holy carefulness has she learned to treasure up precious lessons from the lips of Jesus. So much has she been in communion with the Saviour of sinners that she has learned to sympathize with the Man of Sorrows, and ceaseless are the yearnings of her melting heart over the perishing around her. In common with her sex, the God of grace has endowed her not only with the persuasive lip and melting heart of love, but, added to this, she has, in obedience to the command of her Saviour, tarried at Jerusalem for the full baptism of the Holy Ghost; and now that God has given it to her, she feels that she knows not how to restrain the utterances of the Spirit.

Like as the beloved Marys, and the other women on the day of Pentecost, she would fain speak as the Spirit gives utterance. But who hinders her? Not the rich, gay worldling, who welcomes with thundering applause his idol of the stage or his priestess of the temple of song. No! his better nature probably might approve, and the same persuasive tones, tact, or talent which has captivated him, if turned into a sanctified channel, might long since have been instrumental in beguiling his feet from the path of folly into the way of life. O, it is not the worldling that would seal the persuasive lip of the intelligent, pious female when she would fain lift up her voice in the religious assembly, and pour out those winning strains of eloquence to which the Holy Spirit is now urging her. And who is it that would thus withstand God in withstanding the utterances of the Holy Spirit from the lips of that lovely female disciple? Who?

And now the minister of the church where the testimony of Jesus, from the lips of woman, had been so persistently repulsed, in order to quench utterly the Spirit's flame burning in the hearts of these devoted female disciples, took the oft-repeated text, " Let your women keep silence in the churches," and, without giving the explanatory connections of the text by which it is relieved of all difficulty, he condemned, *en masse,* all attempts or ideas of women speaking in assemblies as unscriptural and absurd.

And this was the state of things when the Christian lady, to whom we have referred in the preceding chapter, was called to minister in this place. The occurrences which we have narrated, in regard to females speaking in assemblies, were unknown to her; and the minister who, by his sermon, had withstood the testimony of Jesus from the lips of woman, was sitting in the altar. It was well for the blessed cause that she knew nothing of the manner in which the ever-blessed Spirit had been grieved and restrained in that place. She only knew that it was long since that place had been blessed with an outpouring of the Spirit, and, in answer to most prayerful, earnest importunities of the friends of Jesus, she was now there to help forward the interests of Zion. She spoke in the demonstration of the Spirit, and God owned his own truth, in a remarkable manner, in the awakening and conversion of multitudes, and also in the sanctification of believers. In less than a week scores of men and women were seen coming forward as seekers of salvation, desiring the

27 *

prayers of the pious, and for a time it seemed as if the whole place was literally turning to the Lord. And not a few of the precious souls gathered to Christ, amid this sudden outpouring of the Spirit, did that minister receive within his fold, who had taken so much pains to withstand the utterances of the Spirit through woman.

Now, we would not have it inferred that we imagine all women called to just such a service as the Christian lady to whom we have referred ; but we do not doubt but there are thousands whose lips would be open in the social assembly to profit, if the seal of silence were not imposed. And we also believe that some others have been, and are now being, called, perhaps in a way somewhat similar to the lady whose case we have related. We know of some whose labors have been peculiarly blessed. We remember a lovely, talented lady, who, in the days of our girlhood, proclaimed a crucified, risen Saviour to listening, weeping multitudes. Hundreds of charmed hearers crowded to hear the message of salvation from her precious, Heaven-touched lips, and many were won to Christ through her instrumentality. If she had been a child of this world, as a Fanny Kemble and other persons of this description, accustomed to minister to the tastes, intellectual pleasures, and amusements of worldlings, how her praise would have been blazoned abroad on the annals of earthly fame !

But how singular the idea that has obtained, that when the talents of a lovely female are turned into a sanctified channel, and, instead of ministering by her attractive eloquence to the intellectual pleasures and amusement of the children of this world, she seeks only to allure her audience away from the fleeting things of time and the pleasures of sense, to the Saviour of sinners and joys beyond the grave, she should be looked upon coldly by some professed followers of the Saviour, as though her call were questionable! We have sometimes thought whether that shining light, the lovely, talented, but sensitive Miss Miller, might not still have been a burning luminary here to attract thousands to Jesus by her gentle, persuasive eloquence, if she had only been as affectionately cherished as she might have been, if the gift of prophecy in woman, as a speciality of the Spirit's dispensation, had only been properly recognized.

A minister, who was well acquainted with this talented female, incidentally calling in while we were preparing these pages, bears testimony to the zeal, fidelity, and efficiency with which Miss Miller labored in New England, where crowds attended her ministry. He assures us that persons who had not been to religious meetings for years, came to hear her speak; and such was the power that attended her words, that many were awakened and converted, and became useful members of the household of faith.

We might mention several other daughters of the Lord almighty, who have received and used this gift of prophecy to profit; some who have passed away, and some who still remain: such was a Miss B——, who labored to the

320   PROMISE OF THE FATHER.

"The holy Bramwell."   His appreciation of female labor.   Presumptuous act.

profit of many in the days of the holy Bramwell. To those not acquainted with the biography of this eminent man we will say that he was known to thousands of his day as an eminent revivalist, and through whose instrumentality hundreds were brought to Christ. And it seems an admitted fact, by the thousands that were blessed through his ministrations during his lifetime, that the secret of power with him was, that he had received the full baptism of the Holy Ghost early in his ministry, and each successive year so increased in the power of the Spirit, that by general consent he seemed to have attained the appellation, " the holy Bramwell."

Having received this gift himself, he was ready to discern its mighty workings in others, whether its recipients were male or female ; and where the full baptism of the Holy Ghost has become a matter of experience, this gift of prophecy in women is generally, with thankfulness to the divine Giver, appreciatively recognized. And it was thus that this holy man, like the apostle Paul, gratefully and openly acknowledged his appreciation of female laborers. His biographer says, " If souls were saved, it occupied little of his concern to know who were the instruments employed by the Almighty. Mr. Bramwell thought that in the accomplishment of the great work of human redemption, the Almighty had a sovereign right to make his own election of instruments." His biographer further says, " To question the validity of any one's call, whose labors were clearly sanctioned by the broadseal of Heaven, appeared in his eyes a most unwarrantable act of presumption."

He regarded Joel's prophecy as containing an obvious reference to the gospel dispensation. In this view it was quoted by the apostle Peter on the day of Pentecost. But it is well known that female preachers are not peculiar to Methodism. They have been recognized as accredited teachers by the Quakers from the beginning. "It is probable that on this subject Mr. Bramwell's sentiments were much in unison with those of the respectable society of Friends."

In writing to a female laborer, he says, "From a full persuasion of your call in an extraordinary way, and believing that the design of God concerning you is to spread the flame of heavenly love in our connection, I write with all freedom," &c. On another occasion he says, "I was much affected when I came home, and found you were gone, especially as we were both promised for Dunnington circuit and Leicester, and thousands were waiting for you at Mount Sorrell. There is such an opening for you in that country as I never saw before. I bless God you ever came among us. Were it the order of God, I should not have the least objection to stand by you at every place till we take our seats in glory." Again he writes, "The Lord bring you to us soon, that you may cast your net into this deep sea of iniquity, and bring to land a few souls for glory." On another occasion he says, "I should hold a love feast at Mansfield next Monday. Is it possible that you could go in my place? I beg that you will return me an answer by the bearer. It is twelve miles from Chesterfield. I shall not rest unless I have a proper supply."

WE might speak of one personally known to ourselves, and we doubt not, as eminently called to speak for God as was Miss Miller, or Mrs. Taft, or any of the female servants of the church referred to in the preceding pages. When placed in circumstances where the gift of prophecy, with which God has endowed her, has been recognized, she has spoken as the Spirit gave utterance, to the edification of hundreds. We remember, on some special occasions, when she was thus brought out before a large audience in New York, through the instrumentality of the Rev. Mr. L——, a deeply experienced minister of Christ ; and the expectations of the people were far more than realized. There were some present, who, alike with the mass of Bible readers, seemed to have forgotten or to have passed unnoticed the fact, that it is written as characteristic of the last days, " I will pour out my Spirit on all flesh, and your sons and daughters shall prophesy."

And now that they had heard this daughter of the Lord Almighty speak with such manifest power, wisdom, and unction, so evidently betokening a divine commission, they were well nigh as much amazed as were some of the listeners, on the occasion which ushered in the last and glorious days, when woman, in common with her brethren, newly received the gift of prophecy.

But though, in thus proclaiming the unsearchable riches of Christ, she only obeyed the conscious con-strainings of the Spirit, and we heard not a dissenting voice, but that in obeying these divine convictions, she had spoken in the wisdom and demonstration of the Spirit, and multitudes desired again to hear the ut-terances of those Heaven-touched lips, still those in authority shrank from the responsibility of encouraging her to use this gift of prophecy so divinely bestowed. And she was too well taught of the Spirit to conceive that it were better for her to press her services know-ingly where such sentiments prevailed. The refine-ments of grace removes all moral obtuseness, and gives yet keener perceptions to the naturally refined sensibili-ties, rendering them still more acutely alive to every thing that is pure, and lovely, and of good report.

That the Head of the church had intrusted to this daughter of the church the gift of prophecy to speak to "edification, and exhortation, and comfort," was doubtless as unquestionable to that church community, to whom she ministered, as were the labors of those women who were Paul's helpers, for whom he kindly bespeaks the sympathizing aid of the church. But did that church lend a helpful hand to this devoted Chris-tian woman who would have labored in the gospel? No! Though it was a church community, whose apos-tolic founder, by his example, recognized the gift of

prophecy in woman, and who, by his favorable recordings, is still saying, " Help those women that labor with
me in the gospel," yet this church of her choice turned
away from the reception of this gift of prophecy intrusted to this devoted female disciple.

The attitude of this church, in regard to female speaking, authorizes us in assuming that the rejection of the
gift on this occasion was not from the improbability that
a daughter of the church might not feel the urgings of
the Spirit to duty in this direction, but that it had
become unpopular in that church to recognize such constrainings. Months passed on, and still that daughter
of the Lord Almighty felt the Spirit working in her
mightily, till she dared neglect the gift no longer, and
turned to another church community, where she might
be a worker together with God, in obeying the dictates
of his Spirit, to labor for souls in the way of God's
appointment.

Again we cannot forbear referring to the amount of
responsibility incurred in refusing to accept and use
an endowment of power, so evidently designated as a
special bestowment of the last days. If God, even
before the prophetic announcement was made, that he
would thus pour out his Spirit on his daughters, raised
up a number of acknowledged prophetesses, as we have
already shown, is it too much to suppose that he would
in these last days occasionally raise up such as he
would have openly acknowledged as helpers in the gospel? Shall it be thought a thing incredible that God,
at this remote period of the latter days, should raise

up female laborers ? Is not this just what ought to be anticipated ? We have before briefly referred to Psalm lxviii. 11; but in view of the peculiar significance of this passage, we will, for the consideration of those not familiar with the original reading of this text, give the literal rendering, as given by the Hebrew scholar, Rev. J. Benson, in his voluminous and deeply-spiritual commentary. He says, the clause here given, " The Lord gave the word, great was the company of those that published it," literally translated, is, " *Large* was the number of the women who published the glad tidings." That eminent linguist, Dr. A. Clarke, is equally explicit.

Both of these learned commentators seem surprised at the plain Hebrew rendering of this text, as though it divulged a curious fact, with which they were themselves astonished, and which might astonish their readers, but which they were forced to admit. Says Benson, " Indeed, the Hebrew word הַמְבַשְּׂרוֹת, hambasseroth, here rendered *that published it*, is in the *feminine* gender, and therefore refers chiefly to women." Dr. A. Clarke quotes the original text, הַמְבַשְּׂרוֹת צָבָא רַב, *ham-mebasaroth tsaba rab*, and follows it with the literal rendering, " *of the female preachers there was a great host.*" And then, as though he anticipated the incredulity with which this literal rendering would be received, and resolved on relieving himself of the responsibility of a non-reception of it, he affirms, " Such is the literal translation of the passage," and leaves it with the reader to make the application, with the

28

exclamation, " The reader may make of it what he pleases."

But though this excellent commentator suggests that the reader make what use of it he please, it certainly ought to be assumed that all sincere Christians, whether male or female, will in their Scripture searchings make it their highest pleasure to ascertain the mind of the Spirit. The individual who shrinks from seeking, with all holy carefulness, to know the mind of the Spirit, adopting the Bible mode of interpreting the Scriptures by comparing scripture with scripture, fearful that he may be compelled to the sustainment of some unpopular theory, is not in a state of mind to warrant the belief that he shall know of this or any other doctrine, whether it be of God.

And let no one, whatever his position may be, imagine that he is in sympathy with Christ in the upbuilding of his kingdom, who actually thus fails to acquaint himself with this or any other important truth, because of its unpopularity. Non-acquaintance with this truth, on this ground, amounts to a virtual rejection. It was on this principle that the Scribes and Pharisees, those who in fact assumed the position of teachers, and ought to have been the first to have led the people into truth, rejected the Saviour. It is true that in their gainsayings they occasionally brought up isolated portions of Scripture, as teachers in our Israel have done in this case. " Search and look," said they ; " for out of Galilee ariseth no prophet." But had they, with a sincere desire to know the truth, searched the Scriptures, comparing scripture with scripture, they would have clearly ascertained that they testified of Christ as the promised Messiah, and would not have crucified the Lord of glory.

But the truth which was now being urged upon their minds was *unpopular.* Jesus was the despised Galilean. His kingdom was not of this world. Those that confessed their belief that he was the true Messiah were cast out of the synagogue. They sought not to be convinced of the truth by scriptural searchings, as ordained by God, but preferred to remain in the dark, because they loved the praise of men more than the praise of God. It was, therefore, in their self-imposed blindness, they crucified the Son of God.

And thus, also, has Christ been crucified in his members, in connection with the greatly important truth contemplated in this volume. We believe hundreds of conscientious, sensitive Christian women have actually suffered more under the slowly crucifying process to which they have been subjected by men who bear the Christian name, than many a martyr has endured in passing through the flames. We are aware that we are using strong language, but we do not use it in bitterness, but with feelings of deep humiliation before God that the cause of truth demands the utterance of such sentiments. We conscientiously believe, and therefore must speak.

Thousands are in this day enduring this crucifying process, perhaps as never before. God has given the word, and in this wonderful season of the outpouring of the Spirit, great might be the company who would publish it. This, in a most emphatic sense, is the day of which the prophet spake, when God would pour out his Spirit on his sons and daughters. Though many men have in these last days received the baptism of fire, still greater, as in all revivals, have been the number of females. These, added to the far larger proportion before in the field, constitute a great company, who would fain, as witnesses for Christ, publish the glad tidings of their own heart experiences of his saving power, at least in the social assembly.

And when the reception of the gift of prophecy is thus recognized in all the disciples of the Saviour, whether male or female, the last act in the great drama of man's redemption will have opened. Says the distinguished Dr. Wayland, " Private believers will feel their obligation to carry the gospel to the destitute as strongly as ministers." O, if the word of the Lord, unrestrained by human hinderances, might only have free course, how great would be the company who, with burning hearts and flaming lips, would publish it !

> "The Lord shall clear his way through all ;
>   Whate'er obstructs, obstructs in vain ;
> The vale shall rise, the mountain fall,
>   Crooked be straight, and rugged plain.
> The glory of the Lord displayed
>   Shall all mankind together view ;
> And what his mouth in truth hath said,
>   His own almighty hand shall do."

CHAPTER XV.

"But who is thus to preach the gospel? What would be the answer to this question, if we listened to the voice of common humanity? When the brazen serpent was lifted up, who was to carry the good news throughout the camp? When the glad tidings of peace arrived in the city, who was to proclaim it to his fellow-citizens? When the news of peace with God, through the blood of the covenant, is proclaimed to us, who of us shall make it known to those perishing in sin? The answer in each case is, EVERY ONE."   DR. WAYLAND.

N O one would regret more deeply than ourselves the error of writing one line that might seem to diminish the influence of an officially ordained ministry; yet it has for many years been our belief, that the modern ideas of preaching, and apostolic preaching, differ greatly.

What is meant by preaching the gospel? Says the devoted Dr. Wayland, "The word *preach* in the New Testament has a different meaning from that which at present commonly attaches to it. We understand by it the delivery of an oration, or discourse on a particular theme, connected more or less closely with religion. It may be the discussion of a doctrine, an exegetical essay, a dissertation on social virtues or vices, as well as a persuasive unfolding of the teaching of the Holy Ghost. No such general idea was intended by the word, as it is used by the writers of the New Testament. The words translated *preach* in our version are two. The one signifies, simply, to herald, to announce, to proclaim, to publish. The other, with this general idea, combines the notion of good tidings, and means to publish,

28 *

or be the messenger of good news." And in this exposition of the word, we believe most, and perhaps all
other Bible expositors agree. And if this be the scriptural meaning of the word *preach*, then where is the
Christian, either of the clergy or laity, but would
have every man, woman, or child, who had an experimental knowledge of the saving power of Christ, herald
far and near the tidings of a Saviour willing and able
to save? When the ten lepers were healed, how reasonable it would have been, if they had neighbors or
friends afflicted in the same manner, to have hastened
with the glad tidings to them! And thus either men or
women who prove the power of the heavenly Healer,
the first impulse of their renewed nature is to proclaim
the good news, so that all may be induced to come to
the divine Restorer.

If this be the true scriptural idea of *preaching*, to
this we believe *every* individual called, whether male or
female, who has been brought to an experimental
knowledge of the grace of Christ, as the Saviour of
sinners. And it is thus only that the command *can* be
obeyed, and the gospel preached to every creature.
How varied are the processes of grace on the human
heart, in leading it from sin to holiness! And just so
diversified, and correspondingly varied in interest,
would be the proclamation of the healing, saving power
of Christ, in the assemblies of the saints, if the same
ideas of preaching now prevailed as in the primitive
days of Christianity.

Next to our divine Model, the Prince of preachers,

perhaps we may present the example of Paul. And judging of Paul's preaching by the specimens given by the express dictation of the Holy Spirit in the sacred records, it signally differs from the ordinary ideas of preaching of the present day. Would the Holy Spirit so have ordained that Paul should have been moved so often to refer to his own experimental testings of the grace of God, if it were not to teach those who might in all succeeding ages follow him in preaching the gospel, lessons of simplicity singularly at variance with modern ideas of preaching? And may we not also from this infer, that in proclaiming the gospel, there is no class of truths so effectual in the conviction of unbelievers as those which we have individually learned, from our *personal* experiences, of the power of the gospel? Is it not therefore that the Holy Spirit has caused it to be written for the admonition of man yet again and again, in both the Old and New Testament Scriptures, " Ye are my witnesses," saith the Lord? And of what are witnesses called to testify but of that of which they have had *personal* knowledge? " We speak that we do *know*, and testify that we have seen," says the Saviour. Have women nothing whereof to testify for their Lord? Think of the great cause pending! Behold the multitudes of unbelievers surrounding us! How these sceptical worldlings, and the yet more numerous class which compose the *many* of whom the Saviour said, they " shall seek to enter into the kingdom, and shall not be able," encompass the faithful few! They mingle in all our church assemblies and prayer circles.

And who as witnesses, who have personally tested the most precious truths of the gospel, shall be brought here to convince the unlearned or unbelievers, so that they may be constrained to acknowledge that God is of a truth with his people? Here are both male and female disciples. But above all, the Lord of the disciples is here; yes, the Head of the church is here, demanding testimony. It is his will that these unlearned or unbelieving persons should be convicted of the truth. And here in the midst is our Lord and Saviour, calling forth his witnesses. Many of the witnesses summoned to be present are females. Various are the cases to be met. Rank unbelief and a subtle scepticism have their various causes and phases. And here are a diversity of witnesses, empowered, from their diversified experiences, to meet the varieties of each case.

And now the Lord and Master of this assembly, in his own order, calls out his witnesses. Not only has he an eye to testimonies differing, but to gifts differing. For he has distributed to each severally as he will. Here are the learned and unlearned, male and female, parents and children, masters and servants; and He whose eye is minutely scanning the necessities of each, and is no respecter of persons, would have each individual case met. Unbelief is the great sin of the world; but who can tell how varied its forms.

Is it not therefore reasonable to suppose that truths not wholly suited to the tastes of the fastidious might sometimes be brought out? But does a judge rule out, in a court of law, a strong, unsophisticated testimony, because not suited to the taste of the fastidious? Is not rather its evident sincerity the ingredient of power which makes it the more effectual?

But here is a witness prepared with a class of varied, well-digested, religious truth. So closely has she followed the Saviour, and listened to his teachings, and so rich, and deep, and diversified is her experience of the grace of God, that she is prepared from this personal experience to bring out of the treasury things new and old. She is a mother in Israel, and has learned with Deborah, the ancient mother in Israel, to be valiant for God. Scores and hundreds of times has she met the demon of unbelief in his various and specious forms, and through Christ has she conquered him, and now comes forth a soul-inspiring victor. Her Saviour, who has been witness of her many conquests, in honor of his name, would now have her testify before this multitude of his all-conquering power, and in obedience to his demand she stands forth.

But who can conceive the result? "Tell it not in Gath; publish it not in the streets of Askelon!" Our hearts are indeed pained when we think of the crucifying results which have, from time to time, come to our knowledge. Were we to tell some particulars in connection with restrainings, which have occurred on the part of church communities and individuals, we fear that we might tarnish our page. But the well-known fact, that earnestly-pious and intelligent women are ever withstood, and the testimony of their lips ruled out, with but few exceptions, in the presence of the men, in nearly all church communities, seems of itself more like a return to barbarism than a perpetuation of Christianity. And the reader will, in this connection, excuse us for saying, that we have been informed, from a source which we know to be true, of a member of a church session who actually advised a brother member to resort to corporal punishment, if he could not otherwise restrain his wife, who felt that Christ would have her testify of his grace.

The lady was a deeply-experienced Christian, and we presume none doubted her blessed experience in the divine life. And we could bring up more than one case similar to this. Our heart sickens and our pen falters over such recordings, and we could not consent to the task but from the hope that these revelations, so suited to the darker ages, may have a tendency to arouse the brethren of other church communities who are withstanding in woman the testimony of Jesus, which is the spirit of prophecy, to the danger of receding from the enlightening and ennobling principles of Christianity, and going back to the dark ages.

Such recordings may seem strange; but though passing strange, similar trials are ever recurring. Within a few hours of the time we are now writing, a beloved female disciple, whom we have long known as more than ordinarily devoted and influential in her piety, has been in; she is also a member of a Christian community where the testimony of women is wholly proscribed. Her religious life, as far as we have knowledge, with all its antecedents, has set forth the power and beauty of holiness, quite beyond what is ordinarily witnessed. Occasion had recently demanded a change of residence, and she was thus about being brought under the care of another pastor.

Attending a social meeting, prior to her anticipated union with this portion of the household of faith, her heart was greatly relieved when she heard the pastor, with earnestness and importunity, press upon *all* the privilege and duty of opening their lips in testimony for Jesus. And, as with grateful surprise she heard him repeat with emphasis his wish that *all* should speak, she indulged in joyous anticipations that the Lord, in his gracious providence, was now, by her removal, opening a way for her to be answerable to those pressing convictions of duty which had been so irrepressibly urged upon her ever since the eventful time when she received the baptism of the Holy Spirit, several months previous.

We knew something of her experience personally, and if the pastor of that flock could have known of the absorption of mind, and intensity of purpose, with which this daughter of the Lord Almighty waited for this baptism of fire, we do not doubt, with his intelligent perceptions, he would have been as truly assured that she had received the grace for which she so ardently sought, as that those women on the day of Pentecost received the gift of power for which they tarried.

But though to the eye of faith he had seen the cloven tongue of fire sitting on the head of this disciple of modern days, we presume he would not have recognized the divine symbol, and his course had been

the same. Though the invitation had been thus press-
ingly given for *all* to speak, and this dear disciple,
in her simplicity, thought that the pastor recognized
females as a part of all, yet she was doomed, and in a
manner most painful to her feelings to learn, that the
identity of woman, as a witnessing disciple for Jesus,
was so entirely unrecognized, that when she went to
the pastor to inquire on the subject, he laughed at her
simplicity in thinking it were possible that she could
have imagined that women would be permitted to speak
as the Spirit gave utterance in that church. With
heart-crucifying disappointment she turns away from
this pastor over the flock of Christ. He, of course,
can have no sympathy for her in this her dilemma. But
how blessed the privilege of turning away from the
pastor who has not learned how to sympathize and lead
forward his flock through straits where church prohibi-
tions and the Holy Spirit conflict, to Jesus, the Head of
the church, and tell him all. This she did, and she
had not far to go to find him; for, since by the searching and refining fires of the Spirit he had prepared her
heart for his indwelling, she had felt the abidings of his
presence.

It is true she wept and wept, as though she would
weep her life away; but did not that barb of pain which
penetrated the tender heart of this beloved disciple first
penetrate the heart of Christ, before it sped so deeply
into her heart? If the angel of his presence is ever
with those who, through the blood of the everlasting
covenant, dwell within the veil, are not all their afflic-

tions Christ's afflictions?   And is it not thus that all the true members of Christ's body, such as at heart are in sympathy with Christ in carrying out the aggressive principles of his kingdom, are called to suffer with him?   Yes, to know a *fellowship* with Christ's sufferings, and thus made conformable to his death?   But though the Christian may, with Paul, glory in the privilege of attaining to a fellowship with Christ's sufferings, yet if offences must come, and Christ be crucified in his members, how pitiful that the instruments by which this crucifixion is accomplished should be by some specifically recognized ordainments in the church of Christ!

We know that the prohibition in this case, as in many others of like nature, came from persons who would not knowingly grieve Christ in his members.   But surely it is a significant fact, and one of which many Christian pastors are aware, that it is only the most deeply pious of their flock that feel these constrainings of the Spirit to open their lips for Jesus.   If it were those worldly conformed professors, who are at ease in Zion, that were disposed to ask the attentions of Christian pastors on this subject, there might seem to be a plea for turning aside from it.   But where is the pastor who will not bear us testimony that these convictions of duty, in regard to testifying of the work of the Spirit on the heart, come from the most intelligently pious and useful of his flock?   And to this significant fact we call the prayerful attention of all pastors.

For it is not in our heart to believe that any pastor,

29

called by the Holy Ghost to the oversight of a people, would lord it over the conscience of any member of their flock, whether male or female. But we cannot disabuse our minds of the belief that *just* what is wanting, in order to rectify this error in the church fully, is, that all ministers of Christ should seek a like baptism of the Spirit as did those early apostles. When this becomes the general experience of the ministry, then will they seek to bring out the gift of prophecy in woman. And, in fact, we have but little expectation that this neglected gift in the church will be properly recognized, as a gift of power, until the reception of the full baptism of the Holy Ghost becomes more general among the ministry. Neither do we doubt but that there are hundreds of ministers who are waiting with unutterable longings for this baptism of fire.

> " Soldiers of the eternal King,
>   Speed the watchword! give it wing!
>   Let it through the churches ring!
>   Up for Jesus stand!

> " Write it on the temple's spire!
>   Utter it with tongues of fire!
>   Sire to son and son to sire!
>   Up for Jesus stand! "

CHAPTER XVI.

"There is a resurrection power in truth, under the beams of spiritual light and heat. It is the vitality of genuine growth, as in the celebrated instance of seeds disinterred from the mummy cases of Egypt, which, after twenty centuries, have germinated in the hothouses of British naturalists."
REV. DR. ALEXANDER.

HE church estranges herself from woman's gift; or is the church a potter's field?

Just as we were about closing the preceding chapter, the activities of our pen were interrupted by the call of a valued minister of the gospel, whose early religious training was in the bosom of a sect where the testimony of Jesus, from the lips of woman, was not permitted in the church. We will introduce him to our readers. He tells us of an experience, in connection with the theme of our work, with which some husbands may sympathize. But we will let him speak for himself.

THE SEAL BROKEN.

Never shall I forget the conflicting emotions of my poor heart, when, for the first time, the voice of my wife was heard in a religious meeting. She had been trained from childhood in the Congregational Church, her father having been a deacon in the same for fifty years. I had been born and raised, and educated, for the ministry, in the Episcopal Church. All know the oppressive silence imposed on woman's lips by both these denominations in their social meetings for prayer and

Christian conference. But the voice of my wife, now for the first time, breaks upon my ear. We had only joined the Methodist Church the evening previous. I had anticipated some things in the new church not altogether in harmony with my views and tastes. But never had it entered my heart that my wife should so far forget her sense of propriety as to break that time-honored custom of silence among females in the house of God.

My mortification for a few moments was indescribably keen. I would have dissolved our union with the church instantly, and retraced our steps, had it been possible. Such license, such disobedience to custom, I felt for the moment to be intolerable. My mortification arose, not from a conviction that God was dishonored, Christ displeased, or the Holy Spirit grieved, but that the community, our former friends in the church we had just left, would be grieved, and some point the finger of scorn. It was not a care of God's pleasure, so much as a dread of violating long established customs, wounding the hearts of old friends, that troubled me.

It was suggested to my mind that I had not religion enough to allow my wife to do what she deemed to be a duty to her Saviour; that my prejudices must be her standard of activity. I at once saw the injustice, both to my wife and to my Saviour, of thus thrusting my feelings and preferences between her and the cross. I was deeply humbled, and lifting up my heart to God in prayer, forgiveness was at once bestowed. I was made happy, and blessed with power to enjoy woman's voice, in spite of former prejudices, in prayer and prophesying.

"I would have consulted you, my dear husband, had I imagined before going to church such a duty would have been impressed upon me," said my wife.

"It is well you did not, for my consent could not have been obtained. It is done now. It nearly killed me for the moment; but I have the victory, and your testimony both rebuked and encouraged me. Henceforth, please Christ, and not your husband."

I have often thought, since then, how cruel to woman it is to compel her to stifle her convictions, to grieve the Holy Spirit, to deny the Saviour the service of her noble gifts, because the pleasure of the church (not surely the world, for it favors woman's liberty) must be regarded above that of God.

The church in many places is a sort of potter's field, where the gifts of woman, as so many strangers, are buried. How long, O Lord, how long before man shall roll away the stone that we may see a resurrection?

The church a potter's field where the gifts of women are buried! And how serious will be the responsibilities of that church which does not hasten to roll away the stone, and bring out these long-buried gifts! Every church community needs aid that this endowment of power would speedily bring. And what might we not anticipate as the result of this speedy resurrection of buried power! Not, perhaps, that our churches would be suddenly filled with women who might aspire to occupy the sacred desk. But what a change would soon be witnessed in the social meetings, of all church communities! God has eminently endowed woman with gifts for the social circle. He has given her the power of persuasion and the ability to captivate. Who may *win* souls to Christ, if she may not?

And how well nigh endless her capabilities for usefulness, if there might only be a persevering effort on the part of the ministry to bring out her neglected gifts, added to a resolve, on the part of woman, to be answerable through grace to the requisition! Our friend speaks too truly of the church as the only place where woman's gifts are unrecognized; that is, the church estranges herself from woman's gifts. To doubt whether woman brings her gifts into the church would be a libel on the Christian religion.

Let us contemplate that lovely, fascinating lady, whose cultivated tastes, richly-endowed mind, and unrivalled conversational powers, made her the soul and star of every worldly circle in which she moved. Did she move in the festive hall, or the refined social circle, charmed worldlings, irrespective of sex, gathered around her, and as they greeted her gifts by unrestrained manifestations of approval, acknowledged themselves won by her endowment of power over mind.

Surely there has been no tardiness in the children of this world in acquainting themselves with her gifts. But the Holy Spirit comes to the heart of this interesting worldling, bringing to her remembrance that she is not her own, but bought with the price of her Redeemer's blood. She now apprehends, through the enlight-

PROMISE OF THE FATHER. 343

Cost counted of a death to sin. Emerging into holiness. Gifts brought into the church.

ening influence of the Holy Spirit, that all her various gifts have been purchased at an infinite price, and must all be brought into the Lord's storehouse, in order that they may be used for his glory.

Sin has its short-lived pleasures, and she has enjoyed the pleasure of securing the smiles of an appreciative world. But the Holy Spirit assures her that she must come out from the world and be separate, and she sees that she must renounce the world and sin, and through Christ give herself up to God and his church, if she would become a member of the household of faith, and secure life everlasting. How crucifying to flesh is the struggle! but she has resolved rather to endure the death of nature than to perish everlastingly. The struggle is severe. Nature, unreproved by God, will often suffer intensely, in passing through the struggle which ensues, in emerging from the death of sin to a life of holiness. God will not reprove, because he knows that nature clings to earth. But the struggle past, the emancipated soul, with all its redeemed powers, is at once taken to the heart of infinite love. This point gained, it is the divine order that all the issues of future life should flow out upon a redeemed world, in unison with the Head of the church. The church militant is Christ's visible body.

And now these gifts, so often in requisition, and so prized in the social assembly of the children of this world, have been brought into the church. We said it were a libel on the religion of Jesus to assert that natural gifts of a high order, bestowed by the God of nature, are recalled or buried, when the possessor becomes a recipient of grace and a child of the kingdom. The God of nature is also the God of all grace, and whatsoever was lovely becomes now more lovely, and that which was of good report becomes of far better report, through the refinings of grace, and far more effectual for good.

And now that these natural endowments of power, which were so captivating and commanding, and so appreciatively recognized in worldly assemblies, are laid as a sacrifice on the altar of the service of the church, what becomes of them? Does the church acquaint herself with these gifts? No! She is both a stranger to them, and estranges herself from them. In most church organizations she authorizes no church assemblies, where she brings her sons and daughters together, to call out these gifts for mutual edification and comfort. What means of grace does she acknowledge where her female members, in common with her male members, may use the gift of utterance with which God has endowed her? And if the church authorizes no means by which she may acquaint herself with the gift which God has bestowed on woman, what becomes of them? Why, of course, they are buried. And where is the sepulchre in which they are entombed? Why, the church.

And when the Head of the church comes to receive his own with *usury*, and demands that these buried gifts be brought forth, who will be required to meet the demand? Church communities are made up of individuals. Will it be some one individual member of that church session ? or will it be that minister who has failed to acquaint himself and his church session, and other members of his flock, of their responsibility before God, in thus entombing an endowment of power which might have been instrumental in the spiritual life of thousands ?   What wonder, then, that our devoted friend said, that the church is as a potter's field to bury strangers in, for the church estranges herself from woman's gifts, and buries them within her pale.

But the spirit of inspiration within us and around us, from every point, seems to say that the time is coming, and now is, when woman's gifts, so long entombed in the church, shall be resurrected.   The command, Come forth! is already penetrating the sepulchre where these gifts have been buried.   Faith sees the stone being rolled away.   And what a resurrection of power shall we witness in the church, when, in a sense answerable to the original design of God, women shall come forth, a very great army, engaging in all holy activities ; when, in the true scriptural sense, and answerable to the design of the God of the Bible, woman shall have become the "help meet" to man's spiritual nature !   The idea that woman, with all her noble gifts and qualities, was formed mainly to minister to the sensuous nature of man, is wholly unworthy a place in the heart of a Christian.

And here, in the presence of the God of the Bible, we are free to declare that a consistent Christian man — we mean one who has been baptized into the Spirit of his divine Master — will not cherish such an idea.

Nominal or meagre Christianity may tolerate it; and we think we see reasons most palpable, and such as should alarm all professing Christians, why the ancient tempter, in his enmity towards woman, should have thrust this repulsive particle of old leaven into the church, and have taken so much pains to keep it there. We sincerely believe, before God, that it is this repulsive doctrine that has so much to do towards keeping Christianity meagre — ay, so repulsively meagre that men of the world, who believe in the doctrines of Christianity, fail to see in many so-called Christian churches any thing really answerable to a social want of man's spiritual nature; — a want which the God of nature hath himself implanted in the human heart, and which would be abundantly met in the precious bosom of the church, if it were not for this ingredient of wrong which has been thrown in by the arch enemy. We speak with confidence and with carefulness in the presence of Christ, the glorious Head of the Church, who would have her stand forth before the world in symmetrical proportions of unrivalled beauty, and in inviting attitude.

In the name of the Lord Jesus, who hath purchased the church with his blood, and hath made abundant provision, not only for her purification, but for her beauty and strength, we implore those who minister at the altar of Christian churches to look at this subject. Christ would not have the church unseemly in the eyes of his enemies. How grievous in his sight that repelling influences should emanate from her whom he would call his beloved, and would fain have her stand forth without spot, wrinkle, or any such thing, so attractive in beauty and strength as to draw all men to her holy shrine!

Surely the church should present a model of all the blessed proprieties of grace. He by whose forming hand she should be modelled would have her inward construction and exterior surroundings all so truly in the *beauty* of holiness as to invite investigation and admiration. Why should she not be an embodiment of every thing pure, lovely, and of good report? And such she must, in fact, be through Christ, or her Lord can never receive her approvingly, and say to her, "Thou art all fair, my love; there is no spot in thee." Yet such she cannot be, while she entombs in her midst the gift of prophecy intrusted to her daughters.

O, the endless weight of responsibility with which the church is pressing herself earthward through the depressing influences of this error! How can she rise while the gifts of three fourths of her membership are sepulchred in her midst? Can we hope to see her clothed in strength, and coming up out of "the wilderness leaning on her Beloved, fair as the moon, clear as the sun, and terrible as an army with banners"?

> "Daughter of Zion, from the dust
> Exalt thy fallen head;
> Again in thy Redeemer trust, —
> He calls thee from the dead."

CHAPTER XVII.

" And finding certain disciples, he said unto them, Have ye received the Holy Ghost since ye believed? And they said unto him, We have not so much as heard whether there be any Holy Ghost."   PAUL.

T is possible to be acknowledged disciples in the church, and, after some sort, to *believe*, or the question, " Have ye received the Holy Ghost *since ye believed?* " had not been asked. Alas! how few out of the great body of professed believers, either male or female, have received the Holy Ghost *since* they believed! They are in the state of which the apostle speaks when he said, " And I, brethren, could not speak unto you as unto spiritual, but as unto carnal, even as unto babes in Christ," or in the state in which the disciples were before the day of Pentecost.

And never could they have made aggressive inroads on the kingdom of Satan in this state. But how quickly might a change, as marked as that which occurred to the disciples on the day of Pentecost, occur to the great mass of Christ's disciples in every region, if they would only bring the matter to a point of decision, and say, " I will have the blessing now." And why not have the blessing, the gift of the Holy Ghost, now, if it has already been purchased and promised? And He who baptizeth with the Holy Ghost and with fire is ever standing in the midst of his people, saying, " Come, for all things are *now* ready."

We were favored one morning, at quite an early hour, with a visit from a man of business, whose name stood first in the official board of the church of which he was a member. Such was his religious position that we knew many eyes were fastened upon him, and we earnestly desired that he should be made a recipient of the full baptism of the Holy Ghost, and thus be a leading spirit, under God, in arousing the membership of that church to arise and put on their strength. When we asked whether, since he believed, he had received the gift of the Holy Ghost, he hesitated, and then said, somewhat dubiously, that he did not know but he had loved the Lord with all his heart from the hour he first took upon himself the profession of Christ.

Of course we did not doubt his sincerity, and yet we could not feel that the power of his life had been answerable to such an experience. Peter might have said the same before he received the gift of the Holy Ghost on the day of Pentecost; and, in fact, he did affirm what might seem to imply as much, when he said, "Though all men forsake thee, yet will not I." It is possible for professed disciples of Jesus to follow him at such a distance as not to be aware of their true state. Christ is the light of the world; and if we follow him afar off, we can be deceived in relation to our spiritual condition. Peter was not hypocritical nor insincere when he professed so much love to the Saviour, but he surely was mistaken.

We still pressed the inquiry, and entreated our friend not to rest until he could testify explicitly that through

30

grace he " loved the Lord with all his heart, soul, mind, and strength." This is the *first* great *command*, and whether we will obey or otherwise is not left optional with ourselves. God requires *present* obedience. A wise, loving father will demand this of a child ; and can the Lord our Redeemer demand less ? We assured this friend that if he regarded the subject as important as he would soon see it to be, when viewed in the light of eternity, or as important as those early disciples perceived it to be who waited for this gift of power, that he would not rest his head on his pillow at night until it was attained. What was wanting was the will. " I will have it now, at any or every sacrifice, let it cost me what it may."

The Holy Spirit applied the truth, and our friend resolved that he would at once make every earthly project subservient to the attainment of the gift. He was a man of business ; but he decided to put aside the ordinary business of the day, and to make a point of getting the full baptism of the Holy Ghost, as marked as did those early disciples who were commanded to wait till they received the promise of the Father. And did ever one thus wait in vain ? Before the evening of that day he was rejoicing in the conscious baptism of the Holy Spirit, and he hastened with joyful lips to speak, as the Spirit gave utterance, of the great things God had done for his soul ; and we trust many believed through his testimony, and resolved in obtaining the like gift of power.

Now, who can conceive otherwise than that this

Christian brother was an infinite gainer in making his temporal business subservient to the attainment of this rich baptism of the Holy Ghost? He might have prayed for it day after day, but if he had not brought it to the point, "I will have it now," he would probably have passed on till the day of his death, and not have obtained it. Alas! how many disciples have not re-ceived the Holy Ghost since they believed, because they never really resolved that they will be holy *now!*

And this reminds us of a minister we met in our journeyings. In allusion to a letter we had written years previous, in which it was said, "Men are not holy because they never really purpose to be holy now," he asked, "Do you remember this?" We assured him in the affirmative, when he said about thus: Well, when I read that sentence, I was startled at the thought, and exclaimed, "My God, am I not a holy man because I never really purposed to be holy now!" I was in my study, and I went to the door and locked it, saying in my heart, "Never do I leave this place till I *know* that I am a holy man." Long before the day closed, this min-ister was rejoicing with a joy unspeakable and full of glory. He had received the baptism of fire, and now he was prepared to go out and speak as the Spirit gave utterance.

His wife was the first one to come to his study door, and as he told her of the gracious outpouring of the Holy Spirit, with which he was now being blessed, she also felt that she must have the same grace. He felt the urgings of the Spirit to go out among his people, and proclaim Christ a Saviour, able to save unto the uttermost. There had been no intimations of a revival; and perhaps he may not have said things vastly different from what he had said before ; but an unction, doubtless, now attended his ministrations, which made them effectual wholly beyond what they had formerly been. Many were quickened in the divine life. Those who had long resisted the Spirit began to yield, and in a short time about ninety souls were gathered into the fold of Christ. We might present scores of illustrations similar to the above, by way of exemplifying the fact that the reason why the disciples of Jesus do not now receive the gift of the Holy Ghost, is, because they do not resolve to *tarry* at Jerusalem, making every thing subservient to the present attainment of the gift.

It is a pearl of great price. It was purchased at an infinite expenditure, and, though not to be bought with silver and gold, yet not to be obtained until we sell all for it. It cost all, and can only be received by giving all. How can the offering be consumed until it is actually *laid* on the altar ? This implies the necessity of an *act* between God and the soul. The offering, when laid on the altar, becomes virtually God's property. Christ is the Christian's altar. It is not the worthiness of the offerer, or the greatness of the gift, that makes the offering " holy, acceptable," but the virtue of the altar on which the offering is laid. " The altar sanctifieth the gift."

When God was about to establish his covenant with

Abraham, by which he was to be constituted the "father of the faithful" to all generations, Abraham brought his offering. The offering was in the eye of God "holy, acceptable," the moment it was laid upon the altar. For God had thus ordained, "*Whatsoever toucheth the altar shall be holy.*" Abraham's offering, therefore, was as truly the Lord's before it was consumed as it was afterwards, when he *saw* the fire descend and consume the sacrifice. Faith on that point was no more needful. When he *saw* the holy fire consuming the sacrifice, faith was changed to sight.

Now, suppose, after he had laid this his offering on the altar, and in view of the fact that the sacred fire did not immediately descend and consume it, that he had taken the sacrifice away, would not the act have been *sacrilegious?* Yet do not many sin after this similitude? Reader, have you not sinned thus? Have you not said before the Lord repeatedly, Lord I *do* lay all upon thine altar? It was your error that you did not *wait,* as did Abraham. You should have *tarried —* *watching — waiting* for the descent of the consuming flame.

If, in the intermediate time, between laying the sacrifice on the altar and the descent of the holy fire, duty calls to present or continuous action, calculated to divide the attentions, do the duty as unto God ; for there is no duty to which you may be called in the order of God, secular or otherwise, but may be done as unto the Lord. "Whether ye eat, or drink, or whatsoever ye do," all may be done to the glory of God, and

30 *

therefore performed as an act of devotion, and consonant with the fact that body, soul, and spirit, family, reputation, and estate, are all *on the altar.* Even servants who are, in the way of duty, called to serve froward masters, may perform every act of service, as an act of devotion to Christ. "For," says the apostle, " ye serve the Lord Christ."

And while thus watching and waiting, and in view of the solemn fact that you have bound the sacrifice everlastingly to the altar, by yielding yourself up in an unconditional, irrevocable, and absolute surrender to God, acting on the principle that you are *already* the Lord's, — and how can it be otherwise, since you have bound your sacrifice to God's altar ? — while thus watching and waiting, guarding the sacrifice from the touch of pollution, the consuming fire will descend.

Perhaps it will come at some unlooked-for moment. It may be while engaging in some self-sacrificing duty that the Holy Spirit's quickening flame may fall, energizing your whole being, and the cloven tongue of fire may be given, so that you may feel intense longings to spread the sacred flame, and speak as the Spirit gives utterance. That the pentecostal fire will descend, if you will thus wait in the way of duty, resolving that you will not permit your attention to be unnecessarily scattered, is as true as God is true. This is "the promise of the Father," "which," saith Jesus, "ye have heard of me." The promise of the immutable Jehovah is pledged. The eternally "faithful and true Witness " hath said it, and heaven and earth shall pass away, ere the promise shall fail.

But let us not for one moment be unmindful of what the special promise of the Father is, here alluded to, or the imperativeness of Christ's *command*, that his disciples should, in the way of his own appointment, *wait* for it. Not one of the redeemed family, with the Bible in hand, is left to mere conjecture in regard to these, the most momentous truths of divine revelation. They are not truths of an indefinite character, in regard to which men may speculate, and then carelessly turn aside. Diversified and endless responsibilities, weighty as the worth of the soul, and solemn as eternity, will be the result of the knowledge which these truths impose. This endowment of power, which has been set forth as a speciality of the dispensation of the age in which we live, cannot knowingly be dispensed with, by either man or woman, without incurring guilt before God.

The privilege of obtaining the full baptism of the Holy Ghost is clearly set forth as the rightful heritage of every believer. *Privileges* are *duties,* because purchased by the death and sufferings of the Son of God. Dear reader, are you a professed disciple of the Saviour? If so, have you received the Holy Ghost *since* you believed? Or, are you in the state in which the disciples were, before they were endued with power from on high? If so, that endowment of power, by which you may be fitted to bear fruit, is wanting. "Herein is my Father glorified, that ye bear much fruit; so shall ye be my disciples." It is only thus that you can retain your state of discipleship. Fruitless branches must be dissevered from the vine.

Had not those early disciples obeyed the command of their Lord, and tarried at Jerusalem until they received the baptism of the Holy Ghost, they would have lost their claim to discipleship, and have been cast off as withered branches. Thus it will be with you, unless you obediently go forward, and walk while you have the light. Do not lay this volume carelessly from you, and conclude that you will to-morrow, or next week, or at some indefinite period, attend to this subject. Do it NOW. Use the light while you have it, for the night cometh. Leave the fulfilment of your purpose till to-morrow, or next week, and the keen perceptions you now have on this subject may have vanished, no more to be recalled. O, present yourself as in the more immediate presence of God *now*, and in the name of the Lord Jehovah, in whom is everlasting strength, resolve that you will never rest until you are empowered to be a witness for God of the excellency of the full baptism of the Holy Spirit.

> " Our blest Redeemer, ere he breathed
>   His last farewell,
>   A Guide, — a Comforter bequeathed,
>   With us to dwell.

> " He comes his graces to impart,
>   A willing guest,
>   While he can find one humble heart
>   Wherein to rest."

CHAPTER XVIII.

WE have had opportunities to witness wonderful renovations in opinion, both in the clergy and laity, on this subject, immediately consequent on the reception of the full baptism of the Holy Spirit. We remember a distinguished minister of literary fame, whose talented wife, while listening to the utterances of a female disciple who had received the gift of the Holy Ghost, was convinced that herself and the mass of Christian professors were living far below the gospel standard of Christian privilege.

She had incidentally stepped over the precincts of her own church fold, where female testimony was ruled out or not permitted. Otherwise she never would have heard that simple yet wonderful testimony, whose inspirations, as a link of light, were destined to enchain all her future destinies to the throne of God, and to lead scores of redeemed spirits thitherward through her instrumentality. After she had heard this testimony, she did as all who name the name of Christ should do; that is, she concentrated her attention with the most earnest and absorbing diligence, to the study of the

Scriptures, in order that she might ascertain, beyond all controversy, whether the testimony to which she had listened was clearly set forth, in the Scriptures of truth, as the privilege of all believers. The result of these scriptural searchings was, that she saw that God required present holiness; and the reception of the full baptism of the Holy Ghost was not only the privilege, but the fact that it is the privilege constitutes it the present duty of all believers.

Just as soon as she became convinced that this is the heritage that the Redeemer of the world has purchased for all the redeemed family, she felt that it was not left optional with herself whether she would obey the command, and wait for the promise of the Father. In the way of God's appointment, she set herself apart to seek with all her heart for the promised grace. And who ever sought with singleness of purpose and unyielding faith the purchased blessings of grace without attaining them? Who ever brought all the tithes into the Lord's storehouse without proving that God, true to his promise, opens windows in heaven, and pours out blessings beyond what there is room to receive; and then the lips, as on the day of Pentecost, are constrained to utter abundantly the memory of God's great goodness. And it was thus in the case of this our friend. She received the overflowing blessing, and felt a constraining influence to testify of it.

And God would have honored his name by making her a channel of communication to others. The grace she had received was not her *own*. It was God's grace.

God had opened the windows of heaven, and this blessing, which poured out through those open windows directly from the throne of the Father, through the Son of his love, God would have poured out through her upon others. But she belonged to a church where the testimony of women is not received. Still she felt that she must obey God rather than man, and she dared not refrain her lips. The Lord our righteousness had now become her all in all, and she felt the imperativeness of the command, " Give unto the Lord the glory due unto his name," and that she must say with David, " I have not hid thy righteousness within my heart ; I have declared thy faithfulness and thy salvation; I have not concealed thy loving kindness and thy truth from the great congregation ; " " I have not refrained my lips, O Lord, thou knowest."

But not a sympathetic chord leading to the heart of the church could be touched, by which her way might be open to speak as the Spirit gave utterance. The church was not in sympathy with her Lord on this subject. The testimony of Jesus from the lips of woman was not to be received, even though it might be an acknowledged belief that she was filled with the Holy Ghost. O, what a serious responsibility does it involve for a church not to be in sympathy with its Head, who is her wisdom, righteousness, sanctification, and redemption !

Christ had taken up his abode in the heart of this precious disciple, and now he would have used her lips to testify of the blessedness of the full baptism of the Holy Spirit. Had she been permitted freely to have given in her testimony, many might have believed through her instrumentality. So irrepressible were the constrainings of her heart that she could not endure. She turned to a loving, sympathizing one, in whom, above all others under God, she had confidence; but, though a most affectionate sharer in her former solicitudes, she had now come to a point where she could not find a responsive chord, even here.

He did not doubt her sincerity, but he probably hoped that she was mistaken, and assumed a dissuasive attitude, and, mentioning the officiating minister's name, he exclaimed, " What will Mr. A —— say ! " And what does St. Paul say in regard to women's speaking in the churches ? Perhaps on no other subject could she have sought for sympathy in that ever-accessible, loving heart, and not have found it. But it would seem as if there were no subject within the range of our religious observations on which the tempter has more successfully and cruelly, as an angel of light, withstood the order of God, than in regard to the gift of prophecy as bestowed upon women.

But there was no conceivable point to which she might turn for sympathy but to the heart of her ever-sympathizing Saviour. Yet, O, how consoling and strengthening, under such desolations from without, to turn to the ever-abiding Comforter within, and say, —

> " I dwell forever on his heart,
> Forever he on mine."

On no subject, seemingly, has the church manifested

such an aversion to sympathize with her female membership as on this. It is humiliating to refer to the manner in which female gifts of the highest order, and most manifestly intrusted by Christ, have been slighted and ultimately rejected. Women whose wisdom is acknowledged, and whose position is venerated, when thrown in the society of men of refinement, either of the ministry or laity in polite circles, are, when brought into the church circle, treated by the same men with a coldness which shows that her opinions are lightly esteemed, and her position but little regarded.

Will not men of piety look at the inconsistency of their position in relation to this matter? We delight to talk before the world of the lovely proprieties of grace — the beauties of holiness; but would the men who sympathize with this error in the church in many places, love to have brought out before men of the world just what her bearing has been towards some of the most deeply pious and talented women of the church? " Be courteous " is a divine admonition; but do men of the church take as much pains to manifest courtesy towards women in the social church assembly as men of the world do in social assemblies?

That the general principles of Christianity are calculated to exalt woman is a fact too obvious to need comment. Where Christianity is not acknowledged, men are barbarous in their treatment of the female sex. Might is right, and man, wholly depraved, manifests his supreme selfishness by making woman his slave. But where Christianity is acknowledged, though it be but a general acknowledgment of its principles, there woman is honored and her opinions regarded, and a breach of courtesy towards the sex is summarily condemned as unchivalric and disreputable. Says the author of Distinguished Women, "To degrade and demoralize the female sex is one of the first and most persevering offorts of false religions, of bad governments, and of wicked men." Again this author says, "I venture to assert that in the moral progress of mankind, woman has been God's most efficient agent, the co-worker with his providence in those remarkable events which have changed the fate of nations, brought light out of darkness, and given impulse and direction to the souls of men, when these sought to advance the cause of righteousness."

Would we have the world infer that the general principles of Christianity, when brought to those specific and personal realizations which result in the formation of church organizations, diverge from these *general* principles, and favor such a course towards woman as would be calculated to provoke the courteous worldling to hostility?

But it gives us satisfaction to record, in the case of our friend, to whom we have just referred, that but a few months had passed before the distinguished husband of this devoted lady also set himself apart for the attainment of the same grace, and received the promise of the Father. We said we had witnessed wonderful transformations of opinion in regard to the gift of utterance, as bestowed upon woman, consequent on the reception of the gift of the Holy Ghost on the part of those who have withstood the use of this gift in women ; and thus, doubtless, it has ever been.

It was a marked interest with us to observe the change of opinion consequent on the change of experience of this devoted husband, whose faith had led him to such glorious experiences that he seemed well nigh ready to out-distance the faith of his pioneer wife. How far was he now from manifesting a disposition to withstand the testimony of a Christian woman in the church !　He had now cast off every weight, and entered upon the highway cast up for the ransomed of the Lord to walk in.　And as he daily made progress in this way, light, beaming more directly from Him who sitteth on the throne, shone more clearly on his upward path, and the more clear and comprehensive views did he obtain of Bible truths, and of the various hinderances which prevent the Christian church from putting on her beauty and strength, and coming up out of the wilderness, terrible as an army with banners.

And we have heard him express it as his deliberate opinion, that of all the machinations of the arch adversary to prevent the aggressions of Christianity, this neglected gift of prophecy, as intrusted by the Head of the church to woman, is the greatest.　And let the Christian reader mark the man, the demonstrations of whose life show that he has received a similar baptism to that which the disciples received on the day of Pentecost, and he will see a man who has a most appreciative sense of the gift of prophecy, as bestowed upon woman, regarding her as the " help meet " for man in the gospel; and, with the apostle Paul and the most apostolic men who have lived in all ages of the church, he will endeavor not to bury her talents by crowding them out of use, but he will regard the refined sensibilities of her nature, and courteously avail himself of her aid, by bringing her talents into use, and will ever be ready to say with Paul, " Help those women who labored with me in the gospel," and thus will incite others to a similar courteous, consistent course of action.

And this, unquestionably, will be the true state of things in the Christian church just so soon as the reception of the full baptism of the Holy Spirit becomes the general experience of the Christian ministry and membership. A man who has himself experimentally apprehended the significance of the promise, " I will pour out of my Spirit upon my sons and daughters," and daily lives under the influence of these outpourings of the Spirit, will have been too correctly taught of the Spirit not to discern that the promise made to him, as a son or servant of the Lord, was, with equal explicitness, made to his sister in Christ, as a daughter or handmaiden of the Lord. He will, if favored with the abidings of the Spirit, have learned, that in Christ Jesus there is neither male nor female. The same constraining spirit of prophecy which moves him to earnest, holy utterances, he is aware, has also been given to that female disciple, who, alike with himself, has claimed the promise of the Father; and he would no sooner be guilty of the sacrilegious act of withstanding the Holy Spirit's utterances through her, than would any of those ancient disciples, who were baptized with the Spirit on the day of Pentecost.

It is our purpose to close up this volume with portrayings from real life of some of those who profess to have received the gift of which the prophet Joel spoke, and of which Peter gave confirmation on the day of Pentecost. We say portrayings from real life. We will present no overwrought picture of ideal goodness of which the lives of other Christians may not be a transcript. The cause of truth needs no such effort, neither is it advantaged by them. The sketches we will present shall be those of whose daily walk and conversation we have personal knowledge. That they have received the endowment from on high of which they affirm, the power of their lives for extensive good evidently exhibits.

For many years have we known personally of the excellency of the walk of these devoted ones. And we only state what we believe scores and hundreds of responsible witnesses would gladly unite with us in affirming, were we to record that these witnesses, which we now bring forward, have long and largely been received as "living epistles, known and read of all men." The minutiæ of their every-day life furnishes a living comment on what they profess. And what do they profess? Why, only that God is faithful to his ancient promise; that is, that the promise of the Father is, in these last days, being fulfilled to his sons and daughters, his servants and handmaidens. And it is our purpose to bring the testimony of well-accredited witnesses, both male and female.

It is reasonable, as the promise has been specifically made to both God's sons and daughters, that, before we take our leave of the reader, a few of each should be specifically called out to testify to the faithfulness of God. "Ye are my witnesses, saith the Lord." If God fulfils his ancient promise in these last days, he demands testimony to that effect. Who would dare to assume that he does not fulfil his promise? To doubt whether he has witnesses in these last days, who are empowered, from their experimental realizations, to testify to this fact, is impious. Yes, *impious,* inasmuch as by the sure word of prophecy God has declared that he would do it; and they that would assume that there are no witnesses in these days of the fulfilment of the promise of the Father, assume the ground that God has not fulfilled his promise; and surely such a suggestion is impious.

And, if there *are* witnesses who stand ready to testify of the faithfulness of God in fulfilling his promise in bestowing this endowment from on high, where are these witnesses? The Christian world demands their testimony. And to withhold it would be to withstand God, and grieve the Spirit of eternal truth. Witnesses are called to speak of that they know, and testify of that they have seen. Other testimony is not regarded as valid in a court of law, and only such is received in the court of heaven. We might bring forward scores and even hundreds of witnesses, attesting the faithfulness of God in the bestowment of this gift, personally known to ourselves ; but our limits will only permit us to present a few. We will commence with the testimony of a friend, the light of whose example has emitted a steady flame for many years past. And as we present these examples, setting forth how the baptism of the Holy Ghost was obtained, and how it has been retained through a series of years, let the reader remember that God is no respecter of persons, and resolve to sacrifice all for this pearl of great price.

> " Were I a persuasive female voice,
>   That could travel the wide world through,
> I would fly on the beams of the morning light,
> And speak to men with a gentle might,
>   And tell them to be true ;
> I would fly, I would fly, o'er land and sea,
> Where'er a human heart might be,
> Telling a tale or singing a song
> In praise of the right, in blame of the wrong.

> " Were I a consoling female voice,
>   I'd fly on the wings of air ;
> The homes of sorrow and guilt I'd seek,
> And calm and truthful words I'd speak,
>   To save them from despair ;
> I would fly, I would fly, o'er the guarded town,
> And drop, like the beautiful sunlight, down
> Into the hearts of suffering men,
> And teach them to look up again."

CHAPTER XIX.

"The things unknown to feeble sense,
    Unseen by reason's glimmering ray,
With strong, commanding evidence,
    Their heavenly origin display.
Faith lends its realizing light, —
    The clouds disperse, the shadows fly,
Th' Invisible appears in sight,
    And God is seen by mortal eye."

HOW THE PROMISE OF THE FATHER WAS RECEIVED.

A FEMALE friend testifies of her reception of this grace thus : "The subject of heart holiness has been to me one of all-absorbing interest ; and not only heart holiness, but a holy walk, a holy life, a holy conversation, a life of entire *symmetrical* holiness — an aiming to be in the world as he was, our blessed Pattern, our holy Redeemer. I had been a professor of religion sixteen years, but I never heard of the doctrine of entire holiness as a thing to be realized in this life until February, 1839. When I tell you that I had never been associated with a people of this belief, you will be able to account better for my ignorance. In the good providence of God, I went, last February, into a protracted meeting. I heard a sister there speak as I never before heard man or woman speak. A holy composure sat on her countenance, and she seemed to be breathing the atmosphere of heaven. She spoke with the simplicity and love of the beloved disciple who leaned on Jesus' bosom.

I sought a private interview with her. I opened to her my heart. I told her I lived in a state of daily condemnation, and I had never indulged a hope of living above this state. Then, for the first time in my life, I heard of Jesus, a present Saviour from all sin. We knelt side by side, and prayed — she to a present God, clearly seen in and through Jesus ; I to God afar off. The news of this salvation, a salvation from sin, was good news, glad tidings. This, thought I, is worthy of the Son of God ; this is, indeed, *peace on earth.* I seemed to see, if this were true, it was the healing balm for all my woes. I will not undertake to describe my past experience. I will turn away from this long, dark chapter of my history, only with saying, I remember three different periods of this experience, when, it now seems to me, I might easily have entered into this state of entire consecration to God, and perfect love in the soul, had I met with such a friend to guide me.

But I cannot excuse my sins, my unbelief of God's word. There God, *even my God professedly,* had always called me to holiness ; and I may say in truth that I never read and meditated upon his word without seeing and feeling the difference between the gospel standard and that by which I was living. I had only one interview with this sister, as she left town, having been here only on a visit. Alone, unaided, except by the Spirit of God, I pursued the doctrine of heart holiness.

NOBLE-MINDEDNESS.

When a doctrine is pressed on the attention, where there is a contrariety of opinions, and human teachings seem dark and contradictory, thrice blessed the privilege of turning aside from all human counsellors to the unadulterated teachings of the Wonderful Counsellor, the Everlasting Father, the Prince of Peace. "To the law and the testimony;" if not according to these, it is because there is no light in them. It is thus alone that we can arrive at unerring conclusions.

Those we have esteemed the most pious may err. Though those who sit in Moses' seat may teach us, and we should, with due deference, regard the opinions of God's appointed ministers, yet even these, from educational trainings or denominational prejudices, may not always know the mind of the Spirit. The most important truths, those that stand in vital connection with human salvation, are generally the most unpopular. When questions of vital interest to the soul are proposed, it were better not to ask the question, "Have any of the Scribes and Pharisees believed?" but to do as did those Bereans, who were pronounced by the voice of inspiration more *noble-minded* than the Thessalonians, in that they received the word with all readiness of mind, and *searched* the Scriptures *daily*, whether these things were so. And those who would know of the full baptism of the Holy Ghost must surely pursue a similar course, or never will they know experimentally of the doctrine. This we see in a scriptural sense betokens noble-mindedness. And this was the course pursued by our friend. The glorious results which followed her prayerful Scripture searchings we will lay before our readers, with earnest importunity that they will go and do likewise.

Our witness continues her testimony : —

I came to the word of God with a determination to lay aside my former creed; to forget the experience of of those dear servants of Christ I had long known and loved, and understand for myself what the salvation of the gospel was. Being so situated as to be able to control my time, I laid aside all work, excepting the more necessary and peculiarly pressing family duties, and devoted my time, for eight weeks, to the study of the Bible. I commenced with Paul's writings, and often read one epistle through four or five times before I went to another, dwelling on his expressions, and endeavoring to find out all his meaning. From the Epistles I went to the Gospels, and from the Gospels to Isaiah's glowing descriptions of the church. I soon became speculatively convinced, not only of the extent of God's requirements, but of the obligation and the *ability* of the Christian to fulfil these requirements in and through Jesus, who, I saw, was manifested to take away our sins.

I now set myself, by prayer and supplication, to seek the Lord. I fasted, wept, and prayed. Passages of this import, " If any man love the world, the love of the Father is not in him." " If ye have not the Spirit of Christ, ye are none of his," were searching texts. The

Spirit of God accompanied the word, and it was like a two-edged sword, piercing my heart. But I had come to the Bible to receive and believe it all, and my eye fastened on the promise of our Saviour, " Blessed are they that hunger and thirst after righteousness ; for they shall be filled." Blessed, sweet promise ! my heart swells with emotion while I repeat it. While pleading this promise, kneeling before God with the words on my lips, I felt a sweet assurance that my prayer was heard ; a sensible peace entered into my soul. I arose and returned to my Bible with new emotions. Now I saw and believed.

I should have said that as soon as I believed that holiness was to be *attained* in this life, I immediately commenced perfecting myself — that is, I labored to control every sinful emotion ; and herein I advanced externally, but found my *heart* was ill at rest. But after this peace or love entered into my soul, nothing moved me. I thought if every friend on earth should die, my happiness could not be affected. I had but one desire, namely, that God's will might be done. I seemed to have no will of my own. I could conceive fully of the feelings of martyrs, and it seemed to me an easy thing to yield up life for Christ's sake. Indeed, I felt, *to die is gain.* I read my own heart's emotions in the strong language of Paul and David. Christ was my all in all. I could say, " Whom have I in heaven but thee ? and there is none on earth that I desire beside thee."

The presence of Christ was as much a reality as if

he had been in the flesh, sitting by my side ; and as I read the gracious words which proceeded out of his mouth, I received them as fully as if I had heard his own voice. Thus my feelings ran for several weeks ; my soul seemed completely under the power of love. I knew of no contrary emotion existing there. I had been conscious, in weeks prior to this state of love, of the Spirit's power on my heart, particularly in setting home the truths of God's word ; but I now received a special manifestation, as much of a reality to my soul as the sunlight to my eye.

BAPTISM OF THE HOLY GHOST.

It came gently, yet powerfully and overpowering ; it was like a mighty, rushing wind in the soul, extending itself through all my bodily frame. I said, " Lord, I am thine, eternally thine ; come life, or come death, I am wholly consecrated to thee." I seemed now to know what is meant by the Holy Ghost. This manifestation brought me nigher to God than ever before. I could now say, Father, Abba, Father. I seemed joined to Christ ; the oneness I cannot define, but our Saviour prays, " that they all may be one, as thou, Father, art in me, and I in thee, that they also may be one in us," and I think I know what he meant, and received the very thing he then prayed for. I could now say, " I live, yet not I, Christ liveth in me." I felt strong in the Lord, and in the power of his might.

Now came various temptations, and in various ways ; but out of them all the Lord delivered me, and he doth yet deliver, and I believe he ever will if I only confide in him. I do know that my Saviour hath power over Satan, and through him I expect to conquer every foe. Sometimes I have been in heaviness, through manifold temptations, doubtful of the path of duty, and *variously tried;* yet have I never lost my faith and love. As with the desperation of a drowning man, clinging to some rope, extended to draw him to shore, thus have I held on to the promises of God, determined never to cease my hold. Often have I come, pleading, "I will never leave thee, nor forsake thee," and on his promise anchored my soul, though in darkness, beset with temptations. For the last year, I can say, the life which I now live in the flesh I live by faith on the Son of God. Blessed be God, his word is as immutable as himself.

I have known much of this world's happiness. Riches, friends, and intellectual pleasures have ever been spread out before me; but all, all I have ever enjoyed now seems as nothing compared with my happiness the past year. I have now found *rest to my soul;* everlasting life and blessedness have dawned there, and the prospect is widening, and I sometimes get an open vista into heaven. The sunlight of God's countenance, the *great* God, whose beautiful works I every where behold, and have so often admired, — even the terrible God, who rideth in the chariot of his anger, to destroy the rebellious nations from off the earth — this God is my God. The sunbeams of his love rest upon me; upon *me*, a poor, frail child of dust, once all polluted with sin, but now a joint heir with Christ, a partaker of his holiness, with immortal glory full in view. Glory, glory be to God, glory and praise forever and ever. Amen.

Do I then shrink to give up all for Christ? Do I withhold my heart, my *whole heart?* O, no! How much I love the first and great command I cannot tell; how much I love that Saviour who atones for past offences, and now frees from condemnation, by enabling me to fulfil this command, I cannot say in words. I trust my life will tell the story of my love, and in death I expect to praise his name, and throughout eternity to love and adore. O, could I speak to the Christian world, I would proclaim, " His name is Jesus, to save us from our sins. Be it unto thee according to thy faith."

KEPT FROM FALLING.

" I trust my life will tell the story of my love." Well, years have passed since our friend, whom we have brought as a witness before you, thus made mention of her humble trust. Has she been kept? Yes, though encompassed about by a great cloud of witnesses, she has been, and is still being, kept by the power of God, through *faith.* Yes, through faith, not in herself, but faith in the *ability of God* to keep her. Dear reader, were you now required to answer the question, before congregated thousands, whether you believe before God that he is at this moment able to keep *you* from falling, and to preserve you blameless, and present *you* faultless before the presence of his glory with exceeding joy, what would you answer ? Would you limit the Holy One of Israel, and hesitate in giving an answer ? Surely, you would not sin against your Almighty Lord, and against your own soul, and say, No ! If you would not dare say no, then why not glorify the God of your salvation, and say, Yes ? Do you say yes ? Then you will appreciate the testimony of our friend, who, year after year, has been enabled to trust in Him who is able to keep her from falling.

RECORDINGS BY THE WAY.

In this continuation of my experience, in the summing up of the feelings of several years, I am at a loss where to begin, and what to say — how to give the right expression the average weight of feeling. But through every change I think I can say, in truth, I have maintained *one* purpose — one fixed and unalterable desire to glorify God, by the constant exhibition of the spirit and temper of my Lord and Master. I account it my highest happiness to have known the Lord Jesus as a *pattern* for *imitation* in interior purity and in outward conformity to the will of God. I have been made happy (as happy, it seems to me, as a mortal in the body can be) in the love of God.

WALKING IN THE WAY.

The way upon which our friend had now entered, being a way cast up for the ransomed of the Lord to *walk* in, it will be interesting to our readers to know something of the manner of her progress. A singular idea has obtained with some persons, that, when the redeemed of the Lord have, through the blood of the everlasting covenant, entered upon this way, they have arrived at a point in their heavenward career from which they may not progress. Does not our wonderful Counsellor, in the chart he has given us, direct our attentions to this as the *only* way leading directly from earth to heaven, in which the ransomed of the Lord shall *walk?* It is by this way that they are to return to Zion.

And that there may be no mistake in a matter so momentous, and in view of the fact that there are many by-paths, he does not leave the matter in indefiniteness, as some good meaning people would have us infer. No, he gives the way a *name,* and as we will observe, it is a *highway;* a way above the grovelling walk of ordinary professors. " An highway shall be there, and it shall be *called* The Way of Holiness." Blessed way of purity, over which the unclean shall not pass, but so plain and free from obstructions to the earnest, simple follower of the Lamb, that even "wayfaring men, though fools, shall not err therein." But let us not say that it were a matter of small moment what we shall call *this* way, when God, in his infinite wisdom, has given it a definite *name.* " It shall be *called* THE WAY OF HOLINESS."

We will give some recordings by the way, setting forth how truly our friend found it to be a way in which she might return to Zion with songs and everlasting joy upon her head. Yes, she found it a blissful way, and thus, as year after year passed, she proved yet more gloriously that the joy of the Lord was her *strength.* " Ye shall receive power after that the Holy Ghost hath come upon you," said the incarnate Saviour, as he was about ascending to his Father and our Father; and now, we will see by the recordings of our friend that she was enabled to retain this gift of power, and pursue a steady, onward and upward course, gathering at every point strength and joy to work more efficiently for God.

May. Have an abiding sense of God's presence, and at times my heart seems not only filled, but to overflow with the love of God. No clouds nor darkness overshadow my path; my faith receives no check; it seems fixed immovably on God. Have a strong desire to declare publicly, yea, to all the world, could my voice be heard, what a Saviour I have found—one that makes whole; but am hindered. I mourn as a child who so loves, he fears to grieve his parent; as one whose heart is full, and yet is forbidden to speak. Was greatly comforted in this strife of feeling between love and fear, as I opened to, and read again and again, (1 Peter iv. 1,) " Forasmuch, then, as Christ has suffered for us in the flesh, arm *yourselves likewise with the same mind.*" O, what sustaining power did I find in this chapter! Verily I went in the strength of that meat many days. O Lord, thou knowest I desire only to do thy will. Let me but know thy will, and it is done, if all the world despise me. I sacrifice nothing when I give up all the world for thee.

May 25. After much deliberation, and many weeks

of prayerful study of God's word with reference to this duty, was led this evening, at a public prayer meeting, to declare the *greatness* of the salvation I had experienced. Now, Lord, have I sacrificed all to thee ; a willing sacrifice, thou knowest. Be thou still my God, and joyfully will I bear reproach and shame.

June 20. My peace this month has been abundant, like the river ever flowing ; and my joy, at times, has risen high, even as the swollen river, overflowing its banks. New sources of joy arise in my contemplations of God, and God alone is the object on which my mind rests. It seems a waste of thought to dwell upon myself, on my past sins. God's forgiveness is so complete, my sins so blotted out, as if no more remembered, that I cannot name them. My poor, famished soul, so long oppressed in darkness and in sin, having found new wings on which to rise and soar, scarcely dares look back, but hastens on to know more and more of God.

August 31. Received, a few nights since, a special token of God's remembrance of me, which greatly cheered and comforted my heart. I returned from church conference depressed, not finding in the breasts of others any response to my own feelings, and, under the influence of much that was discouraging, committed myself to sleep. I awoke at dead of night, surrounded by God's presence. Surely he had come, or sent some angel visitant to bear up my spirit, which was drooping. My reflection was, what can I not do, what can I not bear, sustained by God ? One other such angel visit, at dead of night, I would here record, two months since :

it was light, glory, and blessedness in my soul, which banished all sleep, and kept my eyes waking, and strengthened me for the performance of a cross bearing duty, which immediately awaited me, and I knew it not.

O, sacred temple, has it since been polluted? Father, thou knowest. I hope, I believe not. The foul breath of disease and death has often blown upon it, but the breath of the Eternal has consumed it; and, O, shall I not say it? left the temple still his own. Lord, if it is so, I am wholly a debtor to thy grace. Thou knowest my weakness — through what straits of temptation I have sometimes passed; how near my feet have come to slipping, if I have not slipped; and thou hast seen the anguish that has almost overpowered my spirit from the dread of sin. Yes, the thought of *thy presence* has supported, has comforted, has cheered, when my soul was bordering on hell, on sin; and I still live, my soul is still alive to praise thee — to declare thy great goodness, thy faithfulness, to one of the children of dust, of emptiness, of very weakness itself.

O, come, ye hearts of love, let us worship, and adore, and praise the Lord our Maker, our Redeemer, our Sanctifier — the holy, holy, holy Three and One, in whom our salvation is complete. In the beauty of holiness, in the secret depths of the soul, let us worship, and love, and adore, now and forevermore. Amen.

And now we must leave our friend steadily pursuing her heavenward way. Nearly a score of years have passed since, as a disciple of Jesus, she tarried at Jerusalem in obedience to the command of the Saviour. You have her testimony before you, dear reader, that she did not wait in vain. Does not the testimony she has given prove that God has not forgotten his ancient promise, but that he does, in verity, as truly pour out his spirit in these last days upon his daughters as on the day of Pentecost?

You will also observe, from the testimony of this female disciple, a development of the principles which we have endeavored to urge on your attention. With what unutterable longings did she seek opportunities to testify before her fellow-disciples as they assembled for social worship, in the conference room and elsewhere. But cruel custom forbade her; and when occasionally she did obey these constrainings of the Spirit, we see how *crucifying* to the flesh was the coldness with which this testimony was received. O, it is a serious matter that the professors of the religion of the cross should, at this late day, crucify Christ in his members! Let us refer you to points in the testimony of this witness, where she speaks of her heart as " not only *filled*, but overflowing, with the love of God." No clouds nor darkness, but with a faith in exercise, which receives no check, but immovably fixed on God. Could David have testified of more, when he proclaimed, " My heart is fixed, O God; my heart is fixed " ? Or could Mary have said more when the cloven tongue of fire rested on her head, and she spake as the Spirit gave utterance? Mary was filled to overflowing, and this

382   PROMISE OF THE FATHER.

The privileges of modern and ancient disciples contrasted.   Witness recalled.

precious female disciple of these latter days testifies that she is filled to overflowing.

But where is the difference of the two? Mary was permitted to speak as the Spirit gave utterance, and, doubtless, by her testimony, added her full quota, in company with the other disciples, to the great amount of good that was done when such a multitude believed, when, not only Peter, but all the other disciples, spake as the Spirit gave utterance. But this Mary of later days was not permitted to speak as the Spirit gave utterance. Had she been permitted to do so in an unrestrained manner, who can tell what a message might have been delivered through the lips of this daughter of the Lord Almighty, now being so almost irrepressibly urged by the Spirit to speak?

Let us review her testimony on this point, and let those male disciples, whether of the clergy or laity, who prohibit women from testifying as the Spirit gives utterance, see how they will be able to answer in the day of reckoning to the Head of the church for prohibiting the use of this gift of prophecy in woman. In view of the momentousness of this matter, then, we will not apologize for again bringing forth our witness, and for a few moments reviewing her testimony, in order that you may see the difference between the religion of the brethren of apostolic days and the present. That Mary and the other female disciples were permitted to speak, as the Spirit gave utterance, before the apostles and other male disciples, is too evident to need comment. But how was it with this disciple? Listen to her testimony : " Have a strong desire to declare publicly, yea, to all the world, could my voice be heard, what a Saviour I have found — one that makes whole ; but am *hindered.* I mourn as a child who so loves, he fears to grieve his parent ; as one whose heart is full, and yet is forbidden to speak." She then speaks of being greatly comforted between this strife of love and fear by the Holy Comforter bringing to her remembrance the sufferings of her Saviour in the flesh, and the necessity of arming herself with the same mind ; and then she resolves " to do the will of God, though all the world despise." What a pity that fellow-disciples in church communion with herself should have been made the occasion of thus crucifying the Saviour afresh in one of his precious members ! Again, under another date, " after many weeks of prayerful study of God's word," she records her deliberate conviction of duty on the point of testifying of the greatness of the salvation she had experienced, and she dares refrain no longer, but, as a consequence, she is made to feel the reproach of the cross ; but she exclaims, " Be thou still my God, and gladly will I bear reproach and shame." But how passing strange to be reproached for bearing a testimony of the saving power of Christ before a company of the disciples of Jesus ! O, how unlike Christianity in the days of its primitive freshness !

CHAPTER XX.

"We for Christ our Master stand,
Lights in a benighted land;
We our dying Lord confess;
We are Jesus' witnesses."

"Let the people be assembled; who among them can declare this, and show us former things? let them bring forth their witnesses, that they may be justified; or let them hear and say, 'It is truth: Ye are my witnesses, saith the Lord.'"

WITNESS SECOND.

THE witness we now present is one, the record of whose life has been minutely passing before the eye of our mind during the lapse of over a quarter of a century. We will only make such records for your eye as we shall wish to read, and be answerable for, when we meet the account on the pages of eternity. But could we bring up the testimony of this life before you, as you will see it in the other world, we do not doubt but you would see scores, if not hundreds, saved through her instrumentality. Happy for her, and thrice blessed for the interests of the Redeemer's kingdom, that she has been placed under genial influences in regard to laboring for God. In the Christian assembly she is permitted to speak as the Spirit gives utterance. We do not doubt but hundreds of the most eminently pious would join us in giving thanks to the Triune Deity that they ever heard her voice in the public assembly, both in prayer and speaking.

Though we have many times heard her precious

voice uplifted in the social assemblies of the pious, where both male and female disciples have convened for worship, never do we remember to have heard her once speak or pray, under such circumstances, but we have been impressed with the conviction that she was divinely aided. And we are confident that hundreds will to all eternity give glory to the God of all grace that she was permitted to open her mouth and speak as the Spirit gave utterance.

How disastrous would it have been for her, and for the glorious cause she represents, had she fallen under the trainings of a ministry or people who assume to themselves the authority to silence the spirit of prophecy in woman. We have observed her under almost every variety of circumstances, advantageous and disadvantageous, prosperous and adverse, abundant and singularly effective in labors. Through the gift of prophecy with which she has been so richly endowed, and her varied labors in season and out of season, the wilderness and solitary place have been made to bud and blossom as the rose, both in a religious and moral sense.

She was on one occasion called, in the order of Providence, to remove to a place where spiritual and moral desolation reigned.

> " The sound of the church-going bell
> Those valleys and rocks never heard."

There was neither church nor Sabbath school, and the Sabbath seemed only known to be desecrated. But God in the order of his providence, had placed her there, and she believed Christians were called to be a light in a *dark* place. She took within her range a circuit of three or four miles, and visited every family, gathering in all the children of the region, with scarcely an exception, to Sabbath school, and their parents to attend worship, which she established regularly at her own house.

And now that she had been enabled, through the aid of the Head of the church, to establish the means of grace, and the people came out largely, what would those who would prohibit the use of the gift of prophecy in woman advise, under such circumstances, in case a regularly ordained ministry could not be sustained? Would they say, Let the people perish for lack of knowledge? or would they close in with the order of God, and say, Let those Heaven-touched lips of that servant of the church at C——, minister to the people of the things that appertain to the kingdom, as the Spirit gives utterance? And thus did she minister to this little church in the wilderness, with such other help as she could obtain, as occasion required, for years in succession, till truly the solitary place was made glad, and the desert rejoiced and blossomed as the rose. Yet this, though characteristic of the sort of labors in which she has engaged, presents but a small part of her ministry for good.

In the church and in the prison, in the garret and the cellar, among the sick and the well, the rich and the poor, and as a visitor for various benevolent societies, sustained by public and private charities, and by various denominations, is she accomplishing her ministry as an angel of mercy. We heard of eighteen during one winter among the sick poor, who were, when she began to visit them, without God or Christ in the world, and who, through her ministrations under God, were brought to the Saviour, and departed this life expressing blissful hopes of immortality beyond the grave. Often have we thought, as we have seen her accomplishing her Christ-like mission early and late, proclaiming the gospel of salvation to the poor, and ministering the healing balm of grace to the broken-hearted, and presenting deliverance through Christ to the captive soul, that she had received a divine anointing for her work, which neither men nor angels might question.

Of the hundreds who know her, we are disposed to believe that there are none but what will be ready to join us in saying that she has received an endowment of power beyond what many professed Christians enjoy, but which all may laudably covet, and all possess. "Covet earnestly the best gifts" is the command. Surely this was an excellent gift obtained by this beloved disciple, that has made her life such an embodiment of power. Do you ask how this gift was obtained? We can only answer that this witness also, as those before introduced, tarried at Jerusalem until endued with power from on high. That is, she made every earthly project subservient to the attainment of the grace. Soul and body, family, friends, reputation, estate, ease, *all* was laid upon the altar of sacrifice, never to be resumed.   We will not further anticipate her testimony, but will listen to hear her interesting recital of the manner in which she received this endowment from on high.

BORN INTO THE KINGDOM OF GRACE.

In compliance with the requisition of Him who hath said, " Ye are my witnesses," I will endeavor, briefly, to give in my testimony.   One Monday morning, between thirty and forty years since, when but a feeble child, seeing a minister apparently very happy, I desired the same enjoyment, and was instantly prompted to secure it by seeking to become a child of God.   And on the Wednesday following, after an earnest struggle for pardon, I heard Jesus whisper, —

> " ' Thy sins are forgiven ;
> Accepted thou art !'
> I listened, and heaven
> Sprang up in my heart."

My transported soul, perfectly unconscious of earthly objects, was permitted, as if disembodied, to mingle with the heavenly choir in praise and adoration.   The witness imparted that moment has never been questioned.   For weeks my joys were uninterrupted; not even a temptation was permitted to cloud my sky. About two years after, I was presented with Wesley's Views of Christian Perfection.   My mind was peculiarly happy at the time, but I began to pray earnestly for all that it was my privilege to enjoy.   For the first time I now heard the voice with power — " I am the

Almighty : walk before me and be thou perfect.'' My desires were intense — my temptations powerful. But O, how often, in flying to Jesus for refuge, have I felt all the sweetness and security of a babe in its mother's arms! I was a babe, and felt as a babe. My soul was also frequently encouraged by the consideration — it is the *"Almighty"* who commands. Then, endeavoring to take hold of Omnipotence, I would be enabled for a season to rejoice in hope.

REMAINS OF THE CARNAL MIND.

" And I, brethren, could not speak unto you as spiritual, but as unto carnal, even as unto babes in Christ." — *Paul to the Corinthians.*

That any degree of the carnal mind may remain, after forgiveness and adoption, is a doctrine which many are not willing to receive. Yet, though open in their avowal of their belief, alas! it is too often the case that we find such among those whose lives do not furnish demonstration that the remains of the carnal mind are removed. We would earnestly entreat those who maintain this doctrine, and teach others so, that they lose no time in seeking the enlightening influences of the Holy Spirit. If any degree of the old leaven of sin is in the heart, nothing is gained by permitting it to remain undiscovered. " If we say that we have no sin, we deceive ourselves, and the truth is not in us. If we confess our sins, He is faithful and just to forgive us our sins, and to cleanse us from all unrighteousness."

Here we see in clear, scriptural light, the distinctness

33 *

of the two states, as set forth by the testimony of this witness. We are not disposed to doubt the sincerity of some who hold that the body of sin is totally destroyed at the hour of conversion. But the comfort arising from a mistake, even though it be a sincere mistake, will be cause of great discomfort when viewed in the light of eternity. But let us not be unmindful that on condition that we *confess* our sins, the faithfulness and justice of God stand pledged to forgive us our sins and to cleanse us from all unrighteousness. This, through grace, our witness was enabled to do. And after she had complied with the condition, and became an experimental witness of the faithfulness of God in cleansing her from all sin, — what was her duty under such circumstances? Was it not to *testify* of it to his praise? Could she have retained the grace, had she not given to God the glory due to his name? She says, —

" It was not until 1824 the veil was lifted, that I might glance at the corruptions of my nature. Then I was almost overwhelmed at the sight, and while abhorring myself, was perfectly astonished that even the infinite love of Jesus could look on one so impure. My views of sin, its awful demerit, and the anguish felt in consequence, were now much, *much* more clear and keen than before justification. It now seemed as if the enemy must be forced to surrender by continued resistance, and the conflict was sore. In the early part of 1825, I obtained the Christian's Manual, and through this means was led to expect deliverance through faith in the atonement.

While in this state of extreme anxiety, I dreamed one night of being alone in a large, beautiful field of snow, on a lovely moonlight evening. Nature looked so pure and heavenly, that I thought surely God is here. I will kneel, and ask him to purify my heart just now. I did so, and was immediately filled with light and inexpressible glory, and exclaimed, This is not holiness, but *heaven.* I awoke, filled with holy rapture, and said, if I had only been awake, I should have no doubt but that God had purified my heart. I immediately arose, and fell on my knees to ask the blessing; but prayer was lost in praise; yet I could not confidently claim the witness of holiness; but my soul was all athirst for the full impress of the image of the heavenly. My views of faith became more clear, and I often attempted to believe *now.* Thus I went forward for about three months, generally rejoicing, and sometimes believing that the blood of Jesus now cleanseth.

WRESTLING WITH THE ANGEL OF THE COVENANT.

"And he said, Let me go, for the day breaketh. And he said, I will not let thee go except thou bless me. And he said, What is thy name? And he said, Jacob. And he said, Thy name shall no more be called Jacob, but Israel, for as a prince hast thou power with God and man, and hast prevailed."

One Saturday evening I resolved not to rise from my knees the whole night, or even the next day, without the witness of *holiness.* Earnestly did I plead. Several times the words were presented, "The blood of Jesus cleanseth." Tremblingly faith would take hold,

and say, I do believe ; but impatient for further manifestations, I would again resume pleading. About one
o'clock in the morning, I opened the precious Bible on
" Ye have need of patience, that after ye have done the
will of God ye might receive the promises. For yet a
little while, and he that shall come will come, and will
not tarry. Now the just shall live by faith." I felt
the reproof, also the encouragement, and calmly said,
Lord, I will believe ; I am wholly thine ; help me to
abide in thee. I then retired, resolving to live by faith.

At the dawn of day I awoke, desiring the Lord,
almost as a condition of perseverance, to confirm my
faith, by directing my eye to some special passage, and
for that purpose reached to take a Bible. The suggestion came, " It will open on some passage you have
marked." Indulging the impression, I withdrew my
hand, and took another which I had not used, when the
Holy Spirit, in infinite condescension, directed my eye
to " Now the just shall live by faith ; but if any man
draw back, my soul shall have no pleasure in him." A
thrilling sensation came over me ; I felt to draw back
would be death, and cried, Lord, keep me.

Throughout the day, a most profound solemnity rested
on my mind. Holiness seemed written on every object.
On Monday, the enemy said, " It is possible you may
yet be deceived ; you have not received this blessing as
you expected." But my heavenly Father soon assured
me, if an earthly parent would not give a stone for
bread, or a scorpion for fish, neither would he. My
soul was now sweetly and continually sustained by the

precious promises. It was only to ask and receive. On Tuesday morning, a very powerful temptation being presented, I hastened to my closet, and pleading my youth and inexperience, felt encouraged to ask another and still more powerful assurance of purity. The answer was instantly given, by a most powerful application of " Now ye are clean through the word which I have spoken unto you." It was enough, and my enraptured soul could only adore such infinite condescension. For nearly a week, I was permitted, in a manner unknown before, to walk and talk with God, continually receiving repeated and powerful assurances of purity.

And here for a few moments we will pause over the testimony of this witness, and say, that subsequently for a time she lost the direct witness of purity which she had with so much prayerful intensity sought, and which was so inexpressibly precious to her. O, what a blessing is conscious purity ! Blessed indeed to know that the fountain from which motive emanates is pure. And how can we assuredly *know* that our labor *is* in the Lord, unless we may know that the spring from whence action emanates is pure. But she lost that conscious nearness and repose in Christ which she once possessed, and a degree of power of faith which made her labors less effectual for good, and felt her spiritual energies variously incapacitated by the loss of this gift of power. Do you ask how she lost it ? It was solely by yielding to a well-circumstanced temptation, *not to testify explicitly* of the grace she had received. " Ye are my witnesses, saith the Lord." Neither this nor any other gift can be retained otherwise than by obeying the order of God. "With the heart man believeth unto righteousness, and with the mouth confession is made unto salvation." But she felt that she could not live without this gift of power; and who that has once known the excellency of this grace but will feel that it is a pearl of infinite price, and will, with utterable longings, seek till they regain it? and thus it was with this precious disciple. Again we will listen to her testimony in relation to her regaining the witness of inward purity.

POSITIVE ASSURANCE OF INWARD PURITY SOUGHT.

In the former part of May, 1835, an impression was felt so much like unhallowed emotion, that it caused extreme pain. I then again resolved, if it was possible to have the positive assurance of *inward purity*, I would have it. I immediately went to my room, and in the most solemn manner entered into covenant with God, to withdraw my mind from every object that might divert it from this point, and to leave no means unused to which he might direct, most earnestly imploring divine guidance. I now withdrew as much as possible from society, and with much fasting and reading the Scriptures, with continual prayer, waited before the Lord. Temptations over which the Lord had enabled me to triumph for months, were now presented with renewed force; each motive, purpose, and practice was required to undergo a renewed investigation, and the result was too clear for even Satan to question. My only desire was to walk in the narrowest part of the narrow way. I now waited, expecting an immediate baptism of the Holy Ghost. I had not once thought of claiming the blessing without it ; but it did not come. It seemed as if my heart would break with desire to be filled with God.

One day, while thus breathing out my desires, too great for utterance, it was suggested, " Emptied, then filled : " this turned my attention, and instead of *fill*, I now cried empty, thoroughly purify my heart. That moment, as if directed by God, I opened the Life of H. A. Rogers, and read, " Reckon thyself dead unto sin, and thou art alive unto God from this hour. O, begin, begin to reckon now ; fear not ; believe, believe, continue to believe ; so shalt thou continue free." I fell on my knees, and cried, Lord, I will believe, I now believe. " Help thou my unbelief." I *now* believe the blood of Jesus cleanseth from *all* sin. Thou hast purchased pardon and holiness for me, even me. I will from this moment reckon myself " dead indeed unto sin."

Perfectly composed, I looked at the time, and continued to say, " Yes, Lord, from this hour, half past two, P. M., the twenty-first of May, I dare reckon myself dead indeed unto sin." I waited speechless and motionless, expecting an instantaneous baptism, but felt no emotion except a sacred stillness. The word of life was lying before me ; I cast my eye on it, and read, " I am the way, the truth, and the life ; no man cometh unto the Father but by me. If ye had known me ye should have known the Father also ; and from henceforth ye know him, and have seen him." *A new and inexpressible consciousness of having come to the Father through the Son was now given ;* and I cried, O, fill me with the Holy Ghost ; but all was calm and stillness ; I had none of the expected emotion.

FIGHTING IN CANAAN.

"Surely fighting in Canaan is far beyond journeying through the wilderness, and I should think comparatively few Christians come to that reality of conflict." — *Adelaide Newton.*

I arose from my knees, fully determined to rest in God, when the enemy immediately suggested, "You have no more evidence now than before ; you might have believed long since ; who ever heard of believing and continuing to believe without evidence ? " Immediately the Spirit replied, " Blessed are they that have not seen, and yet have believed." For nearly a week, I do not think there was a joyous emotion, but an unceasing effort to believe. Presumption, enthusiasm, antinomianism, were the constant cry of the enemy. But the sword of the Spirit prevailed, though the contest was very, *very* severe. To draw back, I knew, was death to the soul, and I resolved to endure the conflict while mortal life should last, if no other evidence was given. Just after forming this resolution the promise came with more power than ever, " Blessed is she that believeth, for there shall be a performance of those things which were told her from the Lord." Thus nerved afresh, I was enabled to obey the oft-repeated exhortation, —

> " Drooping soul, shake off thy fears ;
>   Fearful soul, be strong, be bold ;
>   Tarry till thy Lord appears ;
>   Never, never quit thy hold ;
>   Murmur not at his delay ;
>   Dare not set thy God a time ;
>   Calmly for his coming stay ;
>   Leave it, leave it all to him."

The whole of that hymn was made a blessed means of sustaining my soul under this severe trial of faith. The next Wednesday afternoon, in a prayer meeting, I was sorely tried by having no liberty in prayer. This, for the enemy, was a powerful argument ; but I could only reply, with the holy Fletcher, —

> " Be it I myself deceive,
>   Yet I *must*, I *will* believe."

On my return from this meeting, business required me to call on a beloved minister. Speaking of holiness, he said, " Sister, you know something of this by experience, do you not ? " I was startled, and replied, " I am not prepared to answer that question ; " but after a moment's hesitation said, " I have made a bold venture ; I have dared, though perhaps presumptuously, to believe, and reckon myself dead indeed unto sin." He gave me much encouragement ; said, " Never fear presumption in believing God ; presumption lies in daring to doubt." All fears now vanished, and on leaving the door I began to glory in being *wholly* the Lord's, and immediately my soul was filled, —

> " Unutterably full
>   Of glory and of God."

34

For a week my mortal powers could scarcely contain the weight of love. I had such a deep consciousness of *purity* as is utterly inexpressible ; nor do I think there has been an hour since but I have been enabled to rest in the atonement, and much of the time with the most indubitable assurance that the blood of Christ *now* cleanseth. And O, with what holy rapture, with what triumph, have I since been permitted to dwell in God !

> " 'Tis more than angel tongues can tell,
>   Or angel minds conceive."

Though, as before stated, the witness of the Spirit has not been withdrawn for an hour, yet there have been instances when sudden temptation has assumed so much the appearance of sinful emotion as to cause severe sensations ; but I have been invariably enabled almost instantly to appropriate that blood which *now* cleanseth from *all* sin, known and unknown. These acts of faith have generally been immediately succeeded by a most joyous assurance of acceptance ; and but a very short season has at any time intervened before the Comforter has come. There are also on record seasons when, almost positively convinced of yielding to temptation, I could

> " Weep my life away, for having grieved his love."

But O infinite condescension ! Glorious plan ! My Advocate has prevailed ; the fountain has been opened, and I have been permitted immediately to wash and be made clean.

My consciousness of the necessity of the momentary

intercession of our Lord Jesus Christ is much more clear than ever ; and never was the petition, " Forgive us our trespasses," presented with more fervor than it has been since I have been kept from voluntary transgression.   There have also been seasons when, for days in succession, the arch enemy has seemed to rally all his forces to wrest from me the shield of faith ; especially on one occasion recently, the powers of darkness were permitted so to prevail that I seemed almost constrained to cry out, " Hast thou forsaken me ? "   But deliverance came, Omnipotence prevailed, and his feeble one was enabled to rejoice in Him " who always causeth us to triumph."

Since I have been enabled to abide in Christ, I believe the language of my heart has been, —

> " No cross, no suffering, I decline,
> Only let my whole heart be thine."

The honor of being an agent for God seems very, *very* great ; and yet I fear I often lose opportunities of acting for want of wisdom.   Perhaps there is no grace of which I *feel* so much the need.   I *feel* that I am *nothing*, I have *nothing*, I *know nothing*, and am therefore constrained to cry continually, " Teach me thy way ; lead me in a plain path."   And O, how precious I find the promise, " I will instruct thee, and teach thee in the way which thou shalt go ; I will guide thee by mine eye " !   The WORD OF GOD is increasingly precious. It is principally through this medium I am permitted to hold converse with Deity.

CHAPTER XXI.

Let the press, whose wheels of might
Roll for reason, and for right,
Flash it on the nation's sight!
Up for Jesus stand.

"I have not refrained my lips, O Lord, thou knowest. I have not hid thy righteousness within my heart; I have declared thy faithfulness and thy salvation: I have
not concealed thy loving-kindness and thy truth from the great congregation."—*David*.

THE BAPTISM OF FIRE.

Testimony of a Congregational Pastor.

Years ago, sitting in Sabbath school, while my
teacher spoke of God, it seemed a worthy thing to love
and serve him. The flow of sweetness then went
through my heart at such a thought. Was it, therefore, renewed? No! only the moral sense was awakened. That was the approval, not the reception, of God.
For afterwards the sins of boyhood and youth swept
through my heart with a black surge. Nevertheless,
conscience was yet alive, unseared, itself burning like a
hot iron into my life. This often made me moody,
morbid, and misanthropic, even to thoughts of suicide.

Amid all this, still there was a wild joy, a reckless
flippancy, which seemed to mark the outer life as free
from stings within. But that was only the flower
blooming on the crater's verge, the bird's song in the
tempest cloud. Sickness came, more than once, sore
and terrible, swinging me close to the dark pit. Fear-
struck, I cried to God for life, and promised him my

service. Though all forgotten when health came, there dwelt black phantoms of remorse in my soul. College days dawned. In the heat of study, under the spur of ambition, and with an awakened love of the beautiful in letters and art, a glare of glory brightened the cloud. No thoughts of duty to God and a religious life intruded. Fame, greatness, learning, and honors, these were the goads of endeavor, dulled only by vanities and vices of youth. But in the midst of deadness to divine things, even in the hearts of God's so-named children, one gay, frivolous fellow-student was converted. Converted? As I had been taught, or rather left untaught, this sounded strangely.

At times before, I had proposed to be religious, and so went to church oftener, read the Bible and the Episcopal prayer book solemnly, and thought I was doing right well. This, however, was only the cloud and the dew of a wayward soul. But now I heard and saw that there was in another, and must be in me, a change, deep and radical, before I could be God's child. Who would show it to me? Who might tell me? Alas! none spoke a word. I asked one, who had named Christ, to point me to salvation. He thought me in sport. Never before had I spoken a serious word to him, and he treated me as one who mocked. But when I urged my question vehemently, he was confounded, and, in his own blindness, told me to believe. Believe! Believe what? "What the Bible says — on Christ." There was no prayer offered, no advice otherwise given to my benighted soul.

I read God's word. It said to me, " *Now* is the day of salvation." So the preacher said ; so my soul said. Now or never. It was done. Darkly and imperfectly I gave my heart to God. Vaguely and gropingly I accepted Christ, and followed him. But it was yet afar off, and through the mist. Still I had peace — no joy. How should I serve him? By preaching the gospel. So I studied theology, as it is called, — the science of God, — but after the traditions of men, not the commandments of Christ. A dry, barren, outward life of religion mine was. Enough of services, and ordinances, and ceremonies, broken cisterns, holding no water ; nothing of the inward spring, flowing with eternal life. Though the peace of justification breathed low, the tide of joy in holiness did not stir.

Something was wanting. Ah, a great void within, chasm-like and abysmal, yawned deep and dark below, threatening to swallow up in death all my hope. Reason only came to my aid, and out of its fragments I patched up a many-colored coat of complicated belief. Simplicity and single-mindedness in Christ I knew not. The garment of faith I wore needed to be dipped and soaked in his blood, my soul to be baptized into his life, making it of one divine hue. Prayer was audible speech and outward form, not inward utterance and power. Truth was a creed, not a life. So I began to preach.

Young, enthusiastic, and impulsive, my zeal was without knowledge, and to the unwise appeared spiritual. Souls became thoughtful and inquiring. What

could I say to them? Nothing which they could understand; if any thing were spoken, it might not be
heard through what seemed a wall of granite, many
feet thick and miles high, between the soul and me.
What should I do? I read the lives, and works, and
words of sainted men. Alas! they only smote and
burned my soul. I could not think, and feel, and act,
like them. "No," said the deceiver, "nature un-
fits you for this." That was not all. At prayer he
knelt with me, and whispered, "Ah! you are no Christian at all, but a fool, a hypocrite. Why waste your
powers and resources here? Go back to the great
city, where fame, wealth, and influence await you, and
be something." I was agonized. Pledged to God, yet
drawn to desert. On the threshold, yet hesitating.
Could I dare, should I not be ashamed, to look back
and leave the plough in the furrow? Yet can I preach?
shall I lead souls to God without his truth and life in
me? I cannot; I shall not. So I spoke to a good and
wise man in the church. He, too, smote me, but in
love. "Young man, who sent you here? If God,
what for? If to preach, do it. No matter, if as yet
you are no Christian; as a vessel of dishonor God may
use you to his glory; do his will; even if you are
damned, you will be less wretched than if you had
basely fled from duty. I obeyed. Soon the grim list
of my sins was written out and laid before God. Within was a selfish will, a sensual mind, an ambitious heart.
Chief among my transgressions was an intense, burning love of literature. This and all else was yielded.

Essays, poems, tales were bundled up, sealed over, and stowed away. What gifts seemed worthy were given to God; what seemed useless were thrown to the winds. Consecration, full and perfect, so far as knowledge went, was thus rendered. God entered then the open door, and took the vacated throne within. O, in full glory, with a pure breath of love, and a chorus of joys, in ermined holiness, was his coronation made. Peace deeper than any river, raptures transcending mountain exhilarations, then followed. It was meat and drink to do his will. It was ease and infant play to bear his cross. It was inspiration and creation to speak his words. Souls listened, and were saved. How long did this transfiguration-glory last? Only one week. In that time, the consciousness of perfect love, in full exercise, was clear and strong. But fatigue overcame emotion, exhaustion deadened thought, till, ignorant of the true and abiding way of faith, my soul pitched into the breakers and began to split.

Ah, there was the rock of death, which so many strike. Had I only known that emotion, and exercise, and vision were only the beams of the sun, and not the orb itself, the fruits, and not the roots, of God's life in the soul, I had not sunk. What was to be done? Bring out the idols bundled up; burn them to ashes; go over the smoky catalogue of sins again; renew confession, and increase endeavor. Nay, this was all useless. The foundation was already laid. Faith only was needed to lay up the walls aright. But I had not learned, was never taught by man, this "highway of holiness." So the old life again gradually came back, with its ups and downs, its fears and trials, its griefs and toils. Yet not so dimly and stiffly did I walk then as before. The light had been kindled, and was not all gone out ; the life, the true eternal life, had begun to breathe ; the well-spring of Christ was opened in my soul, and, at times more than ever before, religion was a vitality, a reality, an immortality, though much dimmed and down-dragged by a worldly life.

Now God began the keener work. His pruning-knife went deeper than ever, — cutting away from me my beloved ; sending me out into the wild, where prairie solitudes and forest glooms were made darker by men's iniquities. Toil, sacrifice, disappointment, sickness, weighed and haunted. New scenes, new relations, brought new interests and endeavors, with their hopes and aspirations. Revivals occurred ; but as each one came, a deep gloom, a keen in-search, a fearful sifting, preceded, till joy and peace returned. Then, as pressure and excitement afterwards passed away, softly the world stepped in, and circled its meshes round my unsuspecting soul.

So I lived and labored, wept and prayed, through twelve long years of ministerial life — years not deficient in tokens of God's love, that could not but awaken grateful joy, though marked by selfish plans, dark repinings, personal ambitions, and conscious unfaithfulness. No storm on the Black Sea, shipwrecking the mariner, and surging him on its shores naked and companionless, could be more dark in its memories

than is that past to me. God hides much of its ter-
rors, yet reveals enough of them to humble and melt
me even now. Yet, amid all those waves of evil,
yearnings for life, wrestlings for liberty, were like
root-growths in the rock and oak-throes in the storm.
The day of glory was coming ; the blind soul was being led by an unknown way. Placed where I wished
not to be, called to a work I desired not, yet obeying,
as by necessity, the divine finger, God kept near
to me.

I had often tried to escape the duty of preaching ;
never did I love the work except as an intellectual one,
unless in revivals, when the present glow of interest
charmed. Nevertheless, God kept me in it, and when
I turned drove me back to it, as with a cherub's sword
of fire. Two years ago, the great political contest of
the nation commenced. Plainly I saw it expedient to
preach on civil duties. Many said that such as preached
thus would be cursed of God, with loss of spirituality.
I began then to pray more ; for I had nothing to spare
from my soul, and wanted to do right. In the very
teeth of some opposition, though with many favoring,
I gave sermon after sermon for a month.

As I preached I prayed ; never so much before.
Men listened unwontedly. Why ? Satan said, " Pol-
itics." God said, " Truth." I saw that not their understanding only, but their moral sense, was moved, as
I had not moved men the like. This was because my
heart was in the utterance. Then I asked God why the
simpler, more radical truths of the gospel could not be

thus impressively and successfully urged by me. This was the answering voice : —

"Because you are not *wholly* consecrated to me. You think you *are,* because you *were* once ; but you have taken back the gift as often as made ; your heart is not in the work ; you strive to please men, not ME ; you preach yourself, not Christ."

All true, — sadly, fearfully true ; this was my soul's deep conviction. Then I said, —

"Lord, I will be thine, — thine wholly and forever."

So I gave up all things, all literary schemes, all lecturing tours, all purposes of foreign travel ; every thing of life went into God's hands, till I felt that nothing remained, not an atom or hair of my own, which was not yielded. Then I *felt,* I BELIEVED, I KNEW, that between me and Him no stone of separation was left standing. But then, how shall I stand ? what will make me endure unto the end ? Ah, how often before was this self-renunciation made, and then lost ! What did I need ? Not the witness of my personal acceptance ; that I had gained before, and had never fully lost, though I had held it with a tremulous, loosening grasp, as a mariner overboard in the ice waves of the Pole clings to a floating berg. I wanted the proof of my call to the ministry ; that only could fix me. I had been taught that reason, Providence, and such outward signs enough proved a man's call, and that any thing inward was vanity, yea, fanaticism. But now I said, —

"Lord, if there truly be such a thing as an inward

call, a clear, positive witness of my fitness for the ministry, and thy purpose for me in it, give it to me ; for without such assurance I shall never abide."

Two weeks of prayer brought it. O, it came, blessed be God, clear, strong, full, unmistakable. The Spirit witnessed thus : —

" Yes, you were born for this, created, foreordained for it, and in this work you are henceforth to live and die, so that no authorship, professorship, or teachership, nothing whatever, shall allure."

"Ah, then," I said, " I shall stand now, sure, firm, fixed, never wavering. The problem is solved, doubt is all gone, and my work is settled."

How the future's path then glowed ! How life then charmed ! How toil became pastime ! Two years have passed since then, and daily, hourly, even amid trials, hatreds, curses, and afflictions, this pillar of fire by night goes before me, brightening at each step. But this was only the opening eyelid of the morn : full-orbed glory was yet to come. One ray but wakened the breath for more and many. Christ, too much to me as to others, had been one far off, over the sea, a proprietor or principal for whom I was steward and agent, and to whom I sent back my account, imperfect, indeed, but true, for which I received the recompensing commission. That was not sufficient. Ah, I wanted him to come to me, or myself to go to him, and be united in a life-partnership, in an eternal fellowship.

I went. He came. We met in mid-ocean, and on

the dark wave; like Peter, trembling, I cried and grasped his hand, the right, while he embraced me with his left, and took me into his heart, putting his into mine. Then I could say, and say it now, God being my witness, Christ is my life; he is hid in me, formed in my soul, the hope of glory. That was another stride which the angels of my soul, in its aspiring thoughts and affections, made on the Jacob's ladder of faith towards the New Jerusalem, which I saw now coming down to me out of heaven. I panted then for further heights. Not only to recognize, but to realize, God in all things, inward and outward; in the framework of man and of the universe; in the insect, bird, and flower, as in the thought, desire, and affection,— this I desired. Every where, at all times, in all circumstances, I wished to know and *feel* that God came and spoke to me, breathed upon and touched me — a sensible presence, a living inspiration. Ah, how long I prayed for this! how much I agonized! Did I not need it? Could I speak and work for him truly, fully, unless my soul appprehended his smiling presence, his truthful voice? All through the winter's remnant and the summer's fulness, the prayer for this divine realization was offered. One more speciality was added to it, and sought amid other things. I had bid souls to God because he was great and worthy, because his service was their duty and mine, because if it was not given, they and I should be lost. If loss came, then it was just and right. But, O, there was not in my soul tender compassion, ardent, burning love for the poor, sinking sinner. I wanted this, for it was needed ; so my prayer was, —

" Lord, give me an *unction* for souls, the baptism of the Holy Ghost, that I may compassionate the lost and win them to Christ."

Alas ! it seemed as if these two prayers, daily, hourly going up to God in clouds of importunity, would never be answered ; but the delay was only to accumulate the blessing. One day, in the first autumn month, the Methodist brother having charge here came to me. He told how that at camp meeting, just closed, God was present ; how that the Spirit had come with his brethren as with a cloud into the sanctuary ; how that his faith foresaw, nay, that present sight even declared, a great work of God. He told me that if I and my people wished to be blessed, " it would be well to follow where God led, dropping all distinctions, and working together in Christian fellowship."

I listened doubtfully, shrugged my shoulders, shut up my heart, and called it secretly a spasm. Candidly I told him that I did not like his sect, its shouts and groans, its methods and teachings, and that neither I nor my people could labor well with him and his.

Like Abraham, but without the old saint's largeness of heart, I bid him, as Lot, go his way and I would go mine. This was not like Christ ; but, as Paul did, I sinned ignorantly in unbelief, and God had mercy on me. My brother begged me to come and see. I went. I saw young men, but a little while ago thoughtless and hardened, now bowing there at God's feet, and I said,

"This is a divine work; only the Spirit could thus humble." So at once I laid all my bigotry, my prejudices, my conventionalisms, and my sectarianism in one black bundle at Christ's feet, and pledged myself to my brother, in my Master's name, to help him as the Lord should will. My own people were not alive; it seemed as if a little before, the blessing had been offered them and was not received: besides, we had no place for public week-day meetings. Never dreaming but that they would more than approve of the step, and follow me as their spiritual shepherd, I went on calling to my sheep. Alas! they did not at first hear my own or their Master's voice; and I went on alone and un-approved.

Sabbath night came, when my Methodist brother asked me to preach for him. I consented, there not being service with us. God gave me the right text— "Rejoice, O young man," &c. While I spoke, the veil was lifted, time fled away, and eternity, with its judgment, appeared. O, God! I saw poor souls, precious more than myriad worlds, sweeping up thither without hope. My heart broke; it melted, it ran. So much did the power of truth and love flow together within, that I was like an over-freighted bark, nigh to sinking. Therefore I cried out for God to stay his hand; for it seemed more than I could bear and live. It *was* stayed, but to my grief; for, though that night many souls were pricked and wounded, and though I went home peaceful at first, the light within was veiled, the chains around were renewed. Again, two evenings after, I preached. Ah, what damp, dripping walls, what cold, rusty links, encircled me! No freedom, no fulness. Agonized in my study that night, I cried, "Lord, why is this? What sin, what difficulty walls THEE from my soul?" God replied, —

"That Sabbath night I was ready to answer your prayers — to give you all your heart's desires But two things you interposed. First, your pride — your personal, denominational, intellectual pride — stood in the way. You were not willing to seem, or be accounted as a fool, yea, a fanatic even, before that people. Then again you feared for your poor, weak body, wishing to save it up for yourself and your own people, to do a work for them; not knowing that if I had such a work to do by you, I could even raise you up from the dead; if not, that it were better for you to die." Then I said, "Lord, it is even so. With shame and grief I confess the evil. If, therefore, it be not now too late, and thou wilt return bringing back that rejected gift, I will yield up my pride, my reputation, my life, my all, believing that thou wilt protect, provide, and sustain me." In that hour I let go my hold on self; my will was put into the hands of God.

The evening before Sabbath came. Meantime I had peace again. Then we met, disciples, young and old, to tell of love. It was a pleasant, cheerful meeting; no excitement whatever there, but a sweet pervading breath of joy. At its close, souls were called to the altar. Then a neighboring Congregational brother spoke, telling his own experience. His word was powerful. As he exhorted, I stood beside the pastor, and my eye ranged over the souls yet unborn, many of whom I had warned and prayed over in love. These, and others of my own flock, dead in sin, came to my thought. Alas! how dreadfully gleamed their guilt! how luridly flashed their sins on my soul! The terror of their doom in unbelief blackened on my view. What if they should be lost? What a death must be theirs forever! At that moment a strange sensation filled me. My heart began, as it were, to collapse, and shrivel far within, like a parchment scroll in the flame. What spiritual agony was that!

I turned to the pastor and said, "My brother, I am dying." "You are not sick, or faint?" he asked. "O, no," I answered; "my soul is sorrowful, even unto death: I shall fall." "No matter," he replied "let go of yourself." I fell; instantly his arms embraced me. Then it seemed, (I say it *seemed*, not because it was not reality, for it was, deep and intense; but because figures only, and those but faint, can express what imagination did *not do*,) it seemed as if a heart, ten thousand times greater than my own, was projected into it, till it filled, swelled, cracked, burst, and scattered into pieces like an exploded bomb. Then came arms, as if infinite and omnipotent, passing up through my soul, and reaching towards those and other souls, with wide sweep gathering them up, and bringing them into me, to press them through my soul, till, like a travailing woman, I writhed, and groaned, and cried. Then, as out on a broad sea of desolation and darkness, I was hurled,

35 *

cast overboard, and sinking down, down, down, till a deep, majestic current came sweeping on, and surging me up high over the eternal shores, where the judgment throne was fixed.

Ah, there it rose, the Sinai of eternity, where blackness and darkness rolled in massive clouds, frighting the soul of sin. There Holiness, Justice, and Truth reigned over the guilty. "Before Jehovah's awful throne" souls wept, receiving their doom. My soul was tortured with grief for them, as through that gloom a voice of divine wrath spoke in spiritual tones — " Tell them — tell those unbelieving souls, that here, if they come in sin, I will say to them, 'Because I called and ye refused, I stretched out my hand and ye regarded not,' therefore your fear and desolation shall come as a whirlwind." I told them so. Some believed, some feared, while others mocked. All this while personal consciousness of time, place, and circumstances remained. Neither air nor water I wanted ; for I was not faint nor sick in body — only in soul. At last the calm came, when prayer began. Then faith lived ; then peace flowed. Souls yet unborn in fact were seen passing through birth. Troubles, fears, anxieties, doubts, cares, were all sunk in an ocean of love, and I was borne along, in an ark of faith, on the upper wave.

They lifted me up ; for I was weak of frame, though strong of soul. I spoke to them of unbelief ; of the sin against the Holy Ghost, which I then saw ; of the judgment to come ; of the celestial home ; of the eternal hell. Ah, it was the place of God's presence there — the ante-chamber of the great future. Souls trembled and wondered. They took me home, a wonder to many, not less a wonder to myself. It was all a new and strange thing to me, for I had never seen an instance of the so-called "power" which this was, although I had never doubted its reality. After sweet and tender prayer I lay down to rest. Nights before I had tossed and groaned till past midnight, with a burning brain and a burdened heart, for my unawakened people. I thought it would be so again. To-morrow the Sabbath was to dawn, and but an imperfect preparation made. At once I was stilled. God bade me, like a child, leave it all to him — my body, my mind, my preaching, and my people; I did so. Almost instantly, like a tired babe embraced in love, I dropped into a slumber such as never before since childhood I have ever known for its sweetness and fulness. Long before dawn it ceased.

Waking as by a touch, the divine Spirit communed to my soul; bade me in clear, unmistakable language, what to do. Among many things that Sabbath night, I was to preach, at God's bidding, on the words, "Greater love hath no man than this : that a man lay down his life for his friends." It must be in the Methodist Church. Though I had not been invited, my brother, on being told of it, recognized the divine direction. God promised to show me Christ's love as I had never before known it. That morning, on rising, strength came into my frame. O, how like a giant's members mine seemed. It was Elijah's power, — or rather, like it.   Never before had I felt so strong in body ; never, likewise, so clear in mind, so bold of soul.

Thus did I go to the sanctuary.   My text was this : " There shall be weeping and gnashing of teeth when ye shall see Abraham, and Isaac, and Jacob, and all the prophets in the kingdom of God, and you yourselves thrust out."   God aided me in speech.   He seemed to give me the spirit of one of the old prophets.   I cried aloud and spared not, telling my people of their sins, seeing them at the judgment seat, and alarmed in soul at their danger.   They looked aghast, and listened amazed.   Some were frightened, others angered, while many deemed me crazed.   Alas ! they were as yet not raised enough above the earth to discern the Lord's presence.   God knows, — and I am sure now, — that I was truly rational, though filled with a divine unction.

Night came, and with it a crowd to the Methodist church — not to hear my poor speech, but drawn thither by the Unseen.   I told them of Christ's love — for it came to me then as a present reality — an intense conception — almost like a pictured vision.   The Father's bosom opened, the life-star descending, the infant mangered, the wanderings and persecutions, the long, long trial of men's scorn, the bitter cup in Gethsemane, the cruel judgment, the piercing cross, the dark sepulchre, the coming forth and the passing away, — all these appeared in clear, full view ; all as tokens of love.   Ah, such love, so marvellous, so infinite !   But alas ! the guilt so terrible of its rejection — the baseness so damning of its despisal !   This made that love a terror to the soul of sin. Yes, this was the new light in which God showed to me Christ's love. It did not melt, but smote; it did not comfort, but condemn. Nevertheless, it saved; though Satan hissed, and said only evil was done.

Now, then, came the power of that tempter. Next day complaints, censures, revilings, sunk like spears and arrows into the already wounded heart. Even women, otherwise kind, reproached. They called the preacher wild and mad. Only a few spoke words of kindness. One chiefly, and most tenderly of all, was the brother who stood to receive the smitten. I said to him, in anguish, "My brother, they pierce, they crucify me — even my own people." "No matter," he replied; "so it was with the Lord." At my request, we went into his empty church, and sat down in the pulpit. I told him the sad story of all my past; of rebellions, and wanderings, and ambitions; of God's crosses and burdens upon me; of my unworthiness and nothingness, till the whole was unfolded.

We agreed to a mutual consecration, and together knelt in prayer. He poured out his soul for me and my people, as for himself and his own. Then I opened my heart to God. At the very outset he took my soul into his hands, and bore me up to the presence of ineffable glory. Through this, the Spirit of his Son, with a clearness and definiteness of tone that spoke with power, in my heart and through my lips, asked me for each and every one of my life's cherished treasures: "Will you give up to me your beloved wife, for me to take her from you if I will, by separation or death? Will you put your children, not their bodies only, but their minds, into my hands, willing to have them know nothing, and be nothing, if that shall glorify me? Will you employ all your time, and devote all your talents, even the smallest and seemingly most useless, to my service? Will you resign your reputation, personal and professional, to me, so that, if I require, you may be disgraced, contemned, even by your friends and brethren, as by the world? Will you part with your people, ready to suffer reproach from them, and be discarded by the most attached? Will you yield to me your few possessions, your books, and your home, that you may become destitute and shelterless? All, *all*, ALL. Will you now and forevermore, without condition, without reservation, without any expectation of earthly good, without any return but my own life, consecrate thus yourself and your all to me?" Ah, Lord, how those questions came with searching, sifting power! They burnt into my bones; they ate my flesh; they flayed my heart. I pleaded with God, and reasoned with him at every step, to let me keep but one gift. No! all or none! I yielded all, and he took all. O, in that hour I felt like an outcast seaman left on a desert island in mid-ocean. Inwardly I suffered the loss of all things more keenly than if outwardly they had been in reality taken away; for then I had still retained the affection and anticipation of them. But now all ties of life were broken, all interests of time lost, all joys of earth quenched.

When this was done, the voice said, "Go now and

preach my gospel, baptizing men with truth and love, in power." In that hour my future spread before me ; my path of duty lay plain, and my mission henceforth was definite to my view. In that hour I saw before me in the world only tribulations, sneers, censures, oppositions ; but in Christ, I beheld, inwardly, truth, love, and divine glory as mine. That was the "sealing of the Spirit." Under that process — a fiery ordeal indeed — I cried like a babe torn from its mother's heart. I sobbed like an orphan at the grave of both parents. All hopes, all ambitions, all interests, all affections, every thing of life, then stripped off, passed completely into God's hands. That was the "inward crucifixion" — "the circumcision of the heart." The will of self then fell into the will of God, as a rain-drop or snow-flake falls into the sea and becomes a part of its current. Thus began the union of the human soul with the divine nature. What were the results of all this ? Let others speak of those external to myself. Nothing do I see to glory in or commend. Only of that which is within can I tell, and that imperfectly. At first I felt as if a besieged city, overcome and prostrate, lay in my life, amid ruins ; as if a dissected frame were mine, yet intensely alive and sensitive to every touch of evil, every word of error. Men frowned, and I wept ; lips cursed, and I warned. * * * Intellectually, thought was quickened and intensified, conceptions of truth were clear and strong, speech was fuller and truer ; only the old habitudes of mind hampered the utterance.

The former poetic and ornate sentences, which gave

pleasure to the earthly taste, with just enough truth in them to save from damnation, were gone to ashes, burned up as hay, wood, and stubble. In their place, plain speech, simple thought, yea, even sometimes common-place expression, entered, displeasing to minds who think that popularity and success with ministers depend upon beauty, and not upon truth. Preaching became and now is attractive, glorious. The Sabbaths come not often and nigh enough. Study, and prayer, and converse on religious themes are an intense delight unceasingly. The interests of earth excite but little; it is child's play to talk of or attend to them. Time is a shortened duration, in which all the energies must be enlisted to the utmost. O, it is a glory thus to live.

I never knew before what that term "*glory*" meant. It has been like the flashing of a rocket wheel, expiring in the moment that it shines. Now it is the pathway of suns, the sweep of comets through my soul's firmament. Night and day God *realizes* himself to my soul.

Spiritually, this life is indeed beyond description; truly, its peace passes understanding; its joy is unspeakable. Amid trials, tests of faith and sincerity, which God has brought to me over and over again; by seeming death agonies of my beloved; by insults to my face, and slanders at my back; by desertions and distresses multiplied and severe, I am still kept sustained by all-sufficient grace, with the harmonies of God's truth, the great choruses of his promises in my soul, with the pulsations of love in deepening tides beating evermore into my central life. God be praised.

The tempter comes, hisses with hate, allures with smiles, assails with questionings, in vain. Knowing that victory is sure, though the battle is keen, I am never overwhelmed. Blessed be God, who causeth me to triumph. Though weakness, defects, and infirmities abound, — though ignorance, and failure, and difficulty retard, — the step is progressive, the movement upward. How can I unfold all the sweet, transcendent blessings of this new life in Christ? Whatever he commands I obey, though it be to stand in the fire with the Three. Ah, I know that the form of the Fourth will be there, and that the smell of fire even shall not be found upon me. If God be with me, who can be against me? If Christ be my *All*, how can I need more? No! the world may take from me all its own ; I claim and need it not. The church, yet half-born, in the twilight of the valley, may grope and doze, may cast the spawn and slime of its earth-life along my path. My soul shall be cleansed therefrom by the ever-cleansing blood of Him who walked that path before. My feet shall tread the air as though they were wings, and the mountain tops only shall be my stepping-stones of glory — my ascension ladder to the mid-heaven of God's great city. There and thence I shall cry, "O, church of God! O, souls on whose lintel the blood of Christ is sprinkled, be ye wholly cleansed. Lion, arise! Israel, come out of Egypt, pass from the wilderness, possess the land of rest in the blaze of God's shekinah, and shout, 'Enter thou, O Lord, with us, and dwell in thy temple evermore. Amen.'"

NOTICES OF MRS, PALMER'S WORKS,

The chief characteristic of Mrs. Palmer's productions may be briefly summed up thus: 1. A lofty and pure ideal of Christianity and the Christian life. 2. She is deeply in earnest to exemplify this ideal, not by fitful endeavors, but by a steady, persistent strife. In her there is no tinge of quietism. 3. Her writings are well adapted to set every body in motion with whom they come in contact. We know of no human book that will so stir a person's soul to its lowest depths as her "Faith and its Effects." We once circulated a few dozen of that book among a church spiritually dead, and the result was a gracious revival. *Her books make working Christians.* 4. They exhibit a rare insight into the Scriptures, a clear view of the temptations of the enemy, and the method provided for our escape ; while, at the same time, they open up so clearly the great doctrine of Holiness, that no one in earnest to find it need stumble. 5. As a crowning excellence, they indicate a *present salvation.* Many have a way of talking and writing about religion very convincing, indeed, but then the hearer or reader, after swallowing the nostrum, falls asleep, without thinking or making any effort for the next twenty years. Not so with our author : every line is an exhortation to present duty. First shedding light on the subject patiently, till all the phases of it become clear, the next is action — present, steady, persistent *action.* Many receive the doctrine of holiness in a vague and general manner, which leaves them at liberty to act now, by and by, or never ; but in these works they are driven to the wall, and made to feel that *now* is the accepted time. The perusal of these works will always be attended with happy results. They are excellent to put in the hands of young converts. — *Zion's Herald.*

THE WAY OF HOLINESS, WITH NOTES BY THE WAY. Thirty-sixth American Edition.

We regard the reading of this book as an era in the progress of our Christian experience. So it is also regarded by numbers who have read it in this place. We wish those who oppose the doctrine of holiness would read this book, and then ask themselves whether that doctrine really tends to let down, as has been reported, the standard of the gospel, and whether such an experience can originate from other than the Spirit of truth. We recommend it as one of the best books that can be placed in the hands of inquirers after full salvation in Christ. It bears the stamp of no one particular sect, but teaches the way of holiness in truth and love. — *Evangelist.*

" The Way of Holiness " is pure in sentiment, correct in theology, and beautiful in composition. Of all that has been written on the blessed theme of entire sanctification, it is doubtful whether any thing is better calculated to rouse pious desire, and guide the soul in its seeking. — *Ladies' Repository.*

We are led to admire the common sense and judicious manner in which Mrs. Palmer writes on the subject of Christian perfection. This volume combines religious experience and Bible argument. It contains enough of the former to illustrate, and enough of the latter to prevent, its being insipid. — *Christian Repository.*

We would commend this work to all who are perplexed as to the nature of true faith, as well as to the confident Christian. The work has been highly commended by many, and great has been the demand for it. — *Weekly Message.*

" The Way of Holiness, with Notes by the Way." 1st English, from 34th American Edition. Contains a remarkably clear exposition of the doctrine of entire sanctification, and of the scriptural way of attaining to the experience of this inestimable blessing. The Notes, which constitute the second part of the book, relate the experience of the writer, a singularly devoted American Methodist. The book has been well received in America, and is well worthy of acceptance in England, where we trust it will arouse and instruct many to walk in the way of holiness. — *Wesleyan Methodist Magazine, England.*

One of the best books of its class which has been issued from the press for a long time. We envy not the feelings of the individual who can read it without resolving on entire devotion to God. If such books were more in vogue, more holiness of life would be exemplified by professed Christians. — *Methodist Association Magazine, England.*

We do most heartily desire and pray that such zeal and piety as Mrs. Palmer's may every where be kindled, and that such narratives of experience may be greatly multiplied. — *London Watchman, England.*

A deeply interesting book, on a most important subject. It is true to the experience of almost every Christian. It cannot be perused, with thought and prayer, without much spiritual benefit resulting therefrom. We cordially commend it to our readers. — *Methodist Pilot, England.*

It is a book rich in experience, and breathing a spirit full of humility and love. — *Primitive Methodist Magazine, England.*

We do not expect our friends to buy and peruse every book mentioned in these notices ; but here is one which we are not willing to suppose will escape the examination of any Christian whose eye may light upon this recommendation of it. There is an unusual degree of simplicity in the narrative, such as we think could not be arrived at except by the chastening power of the Sanctifier. The author has but one aim ; namely, to present pictures — daguerreotype impressions — of her states of mind, from the time she started in the way to seek Holiness until after she attained it. The difficulties she encountered, their effect upon her mind, and the manner of her escape, are also so represented that the pious reader readily apprehends them, and often finds that as in water face answereth to face, so does heart to heart in religious experience. We earnestly commend this little volume to all who hunger and thirst after righteousness. — *Bishop Hamline : Ladies' Repository.*

FAITH AND ITS EFFECTS; OR, FRAGMENTS FROM MY PORTFOLIO. Twenty-fourth American Edition. By Mrs. Phœbe Palmer.

We know of few who have labored more, or more successfully, in promoting the cause of Holiness than the author of these "Fragments." It is a delightful fact that the works written by her have met with a most unprecedented sale. The author shows clearly that it is the will of God that believers should be wholly sanctified. In doing this, she exposes and corrects the errors into which some had fallen, points out the short and good old way of attaining this state of grace, and supports all she advances by direct and incidental appeals to the *Word of God.* — *Christian Advocate and Journal.*

In this work such light is thrown upon the precise point of transit from condemnation to favor, bondage to liberty, partial to full salvation, as is not perhaps so clearly done in any other human composition. The prevailing error of waiting for greater preparedness of mind, and for impulses and manifestations from on high, *before* we may consider ourselves called upon to trust God for justification and sanctification, is exposed, and the *simplicity* of faith, and manner of its exercise, so logically presented as to be nearly if not quite unmistakable to the least discerning mind. — *Zion's Herald.*

It treats of every stage of religious experience and practice, from the dawn of conviction for sin to the stage of hallowed intimacy with God enjoyed by the mature veteran believer. The reader will find here the best thoughts on a thousand points of Christian truth of a mind highly endued by nature, constantly impelled by a consuming zeal for the salvation of souls, and enlightened and guided by long-continued habits of communion with God and his word. The whole is illustrated and enlivened by a happy intermixture of fact and incident, never, perhaps, to be met with in a work on experimental divinity, save the book in question. — *Northern Christian Advocate.*

It is calculated to instruct and interest every believer, and it seems particularly adapted to Sabbath school teachers. It will greatly assist them in explaining *the way of faith* to their scholars, and, if prayerfully read, will not fail to increase in their own hearts the work of faith with power. — *Sabbath School Advocate.*

This work has met with a remarkable sale, bespeaking a growing piety in the church. A revival of religion on the right basis is that which carries believers on to perfection. In the Methodist and other churches such a revival was perhaps never more general than at present; and in the United States and in Canada this has in no small degree been promoted by Mrs. Palmer's writings. It is only a truism to assert that Mrs. Palmer is eminently *scriptural.* — *Christian Guardian, Canada.*

An 18mo volume of 352 pages, illustrating very fully the nature of " Faith and its Effects." It is written in a simple, concise, and persuasive style. The child or the adult, the Christian or the unbeliever, may be profited by its perusal. — *Family Guardian.*

"Faith and its Effects, by Mrs. Phœbe Palmer." 1st English, from 22d American Edition. This little work is rich in all the best experiences of the Christian life. If the rationale of faith is still to seek, its reality and power are put beyond all doubt or controversy, and the believer stands immeasurably in advance of the philosopher. — *London Quarterly, England.*

The work consists of a series of letters, which, for simplicity, religious beauty, and adaptation for usefulness, were never surpassed. They are eminently calculated to strengthen faith, and promote the advancement of spirituality and holiness in the soul. — *Methodist Magazine, London, England.*

Another eminently pious work from the pen of the devoted Mrs. Palmer. It breathes the same spirit as "The Way of Holiness," and cannot fail to fan the flame of devotion wherever it circulates. We would recommend all class leaders in the Methodist churches to strive to circulate both works among the members under their charge. Next to the reading of the Holy Scriptures, such works must contribute largely to the formation of all the habits of a holy life. — *Methodist Association Magazine, London, England.*

It contains gems of gospel truth, and is pervaded by a strong devotional feeling — a feeling which finds its way to the heart of every Christian reader. — *British Mothers' Magazine, London.*

The late Rev. Dr. Bond, in a lengthy and most favorable editorial notice of this work, referring to its rapid sale, says, "The work, therefore, must be extensively known and approved, and does not require any eulogy from us to commend it to the public attention. The subject, however, which the work embraces — 'Faith and its Effects' — can never be exhausted or become of less interest by its familiarity. On the contrary, it will be increasingly appreciated as we come more and more to comprehend it in all its bearings and depth of meaning. The author of 'Faith and its Effects' takes the right way to explain the nature and effects of saving faith; namely, by the Scriptures and experience. There are no metaphysical speculations employed. It assumes that God has spoken. This fact is supposed to be demonstrated by indubitable evidence, and then all that remains is to inquire what he has said, and to rely upon it as *true.* This evidence is faith. But of course the *faith* to be exercised will consist of various *acts*, each necessary to salvation, but not essentially the same act. . . . We do not wonder, then, that this little book, illustrating and making plain 'Faith and its Effects' should have had such an extensive run. We hope the demand will still increase." — *Christian Advocate and Journal, New York.*

PRESENT TO MY CHRISTIAN FRIEND; OR, ENTIRE DEVOTION. By Mrs. Phœbe Palmer. Twentieth Edition.

A charming little present for the holidays. A new edition, greatly improved and enlarged. Though presented in a new form, with a large addition of new matter, it has no new doctrines to teach. A mere announcement of the work will be sufficient to lead many to supply themselves with it. — *Western Christian Advocate.*

Well worthy a place in the Christian library, or as a travelling pocket companion. — *Christian Repository.*

We know no work of its size comprising so much that is calculated to arrest the attention, and fix the mind of the reader on the importance and attractiveness of the subject of which it treats. — *Guide to Holiness.*

This invaluable little work contains nearly double as much matter as the earlier editions. So widely is the beloved author known that any words of explanation or recommendation would be superfluous. — *Ladies' Repository.*

If public demand and extensive circulation are an evidence of value, much sterling value must be accorded to the book. — *Christian Advocate and Journal.*

In this neat little volume of 192 pages the nature of Holiness is set forth, the way of entering into the enjoyment of it plainly pointed out, and the advantages to ourselves and others described. — *Weekly Message.*

In size and style it is especially adapted to the young disciple, whom we would advise to procure and prayerfully read it. More experienced Christians, too, will find in it the sincere milk of the word, whereby they may grow. — *Christian Guardian.*

"Present to my Christian Friend." 1st English, from the 20th American Edition. This is the designation of a new work from the prolific pen of Mrs. Palmer. The amiable authoress is already known to the religious public of this country by several eminently pious and useful productions; and the work now before us is equal in merit to the rest of her valuable writings. We could wish these works a very extensive circulation among our members. — *Methodist Association Magazine, London.*

INCIDENTAL ILLUSTRATIONS OF THE ECONOMY OF SALVATION: ITS DOCTRINES AND DUTIES. By Mrs. PHŒBE PALMER. Ninth Edition.

It is got up in the neatest style of the art, and is ornamented with a likeness of Mrs. P., beautifully executed on steel. It will, no doubt, be the most popular of the author's works. It contains in an admirable degree the exciting interest of narrative with the profit of didactic reading. The articles are generally short, and furnish the richest variety, and all are pervaded by the heavenly unctuous spirit which characterizes the amiable author. There are one hundred and seventy-three topics discussed, illustrated, many of them, by the most thrilling incidents. The work is general in its character, and treats of religious doctrines and duties in their various phases. The book is eminently practical, as well as experimental. — *Northern Christian Advocate.*

It is mainly made up of facts, all tending to one great object — holiness of heart and life. Many of the "Illustrations" are beautifully simple, and told in a winning strain of touching eloquence. The book cannot fail to do good; for the blessing of the Almighty is with it. — *National Magazine.*

These "Illustrations" especially apply to experimental religion, having little to do with theoretical or speculative dogmas. The sketches and incidents are very affecting, tendering the heart, and moving the holiest affections of the soul. Reader, in all your gettings, be sure and get this book, not for yourself only, but for your household. — *Christian Advocate and Journal.*

Mrs. Palmer's pen has greatly contributed to enthrone the *living oracles* in the minds of the people. "Incidental Illustrations of the Economy of Salvation, its Doctrines and Duties," contains, of course, the same views of religious truth presented in her other writings. They are urged, however, under new aspects, and illustrated by interesting and sometimes thrilling incidents from her own observation. The style is clear, positive, appropriate. Mrs. Palmer's remarks on entire consecration as a prerequisite of faith are well worthy of notice. Salvation *through* Christ is presented continually with the utmost clearness. Many other topics of importance are glanced at which cannot here be mentioned. The whole is perfumed with that fragrance, and accompanied by that unction, which evince that the influences of the Holy Spirit have been diligently sought in secret through the blood and mediation of Jesus. Would that all of us, ministers and people, might have the same deep and comprehensive views of salvation, the zeal, the power, the success, of this Deborah of Methodism. — *Western Christian Advocate.*

This is a work from the gifted and well-known pen of Mrs. P. Palmer, of New York. Every line throbs with the pulsations of living piety, and the sole object of the writer seems to be to do good. It is written in the author's peculiarly simple and artless style. The works of Mrs. P. are singular and original. — *North-Western Christian Advocate.*

O, how the woman talks ! God has baptized her heart with his perfect love ; and she lets out from her full soul a perfect gush of thought and truth, which your faith grasps and makes blessed to your spirit. In little, short, rapid sentences, each with an idea in it that goes right home, this work tells you just what you want to know about salvation in a way that your *heart* can understand. We love such earnest books. Get one and read it. — *Memphis and Arkansas Advocate.*

While reading its instructive pages, we could not but desire our readers to enjoy with us the precious gospel truths, as here presented, illustrating the happy results of taking God at his word, and receiving whatsoever is asked in faith. — *Weekly Message.*

This volume, from a favorite author, is a beautiful 12mo volume of 380 pages, and contains a fine portrait of Mrs. P. It bids fair to have greater success than any of her former works. It has been issued only a few weeks, and the fourth thousand is being rapidly sold. This comes in part from the subject. . . . But the style and reputation of the talented authoress has something to do with its success. Mrs. P.'s former books have won for her no small fame. They have been successful in accomplishing great good. She has a place in the hearts of the multitude. Without the least effort to write fine, or what some call "impressively," she has acquired a style which is singularly adapted to convey her sentiments. She goes at once into the merits of the question, interesting head and heart. But after all, the merit of the work is the subject on which it treats. It is evangelical, not denominational. It is practical, not theoretical. There is but one aim in the whole, and that is to save souls. Let all our readers get the book for themselves. It is one of those books which you can pick up or lay down at any time. — *Beauty of Holiness.*

Dr. Cook, President of the French Wesleyan Conference, by whose advice the works of Mrs. Palmer are now being translated into the French language, says :

"I am fully convinced that they are well adapted to the actual state of French Methodism, and will meet and satisfy and develop the aspirations of many hearts. This conviction led me to procure them for myself, and prevented me from being surprised that Rev. J. W. Lelievre, who was then engaged as professor of the French language in an institution in England, was greatly quickened and successfully directed in the pursuit of Holiness while reading one of your works. I encouraged him to set about the translation of the works, and I suppose by this time one of the books is ready for publication."

TITLES in THIS SERIES

1. THE HIGHER CHRISTIAN LIFE; A BIBLIOGRAPHICAL OVERVIEW. Donald W. Dayton, *THE AMERICAN HOLINESS MOVEMENT: A BIBLIOGRAPHICAL INTRODUCTION.* (Wilmore, Ky., 1971) *bound with* David W. Faupel, *THE AMERICAN PENTECOSTAL MOVEMENT: A BIBLIOGRAPHICAL ESSAY.* (Wilmore, Ky., 1972) *bound with* David D. Bundy, *Keswick: A BIBLIOGRAPHIC INTRODUCTION TO THE HIGHER LIFE MOVEMENTS.* (Wilmore, Ky., 1975)

2. *ACCOUNT OF THE UNION MEETING FOR THE PROMOTION OF SCRIPTURAL HOLINESS, HELD AT OXFORD, AUGUST 29 TO SEPTEMBER 7, 1874.* (Boston, n. d.)

3. Baker, Elizabeth V., and Co-workers, *CHRONICLES OF A FAITH LIFE.*

4. THE WORK OF T. B. BARRATT. T. B. Barratt, *IN THE DAYS OF THE LATTER RAIN.* (London, 1909) *WHEN THE FIRE FELL AND AN OUTLINE OF MY LIFE*, (Oslo, 1927)

5. WITNESS TO PENTECOST: THE LIFE OF FRANK BARTLEMAN. Frank Bartleman, *FROM PLOW TO PULPIT— FROM MAINE TO CALIFORNIA* (Los Angeles, n. d.), *HOW PENTECOST CAME TO LOS ANGELES* (Los An-

geles, 1925), *AROUND THE WORLD BY FAITH, WITH SIX WEEKS IN THE HOLY LAND* (Los Angeles, n. d.), *TWO YEARS MISSION WORK IN EUROPE JUST BEFORE THE WORLD WAR, 1912-14* (Los Angeles, [1926])

6. Boardman, W. E., *THE HIGHER CHRISTIAN LIFE* (Boston, 1858)

7. Girvin, E. A., *PHINEAS F. BRESEE: A PRINCE IN ISRAEL* (Kansas City, Mo., [1916])

8. Brooks, John P., *THE DIVINE CHURCH* (Columbia, Mo., 1891)

9. RUSSELL KELSO CARTER ON "FAITH HEALING." R. Kelso Carter, *THE ATONEMENT FOR SIN AND SICKNESS* (Boston, 1884) *"FAITH HEALING" REVIEWED AFTER TWENTY YEARS* (Boston, 1897)

10. Daniels, W. H., *DR. CULLIS AND HIS WORK* (Boston, [1885])

11. HOLINESS TRACTS DEFENDING THE MINISTRY OF WOMEN. Luther Lee, *"WOMAN'S RIGHT TO PREACH THE GOSPEL; A SERMON, AT THE ORDINATION OF REV. MISS ANTOINETTE L. BROWN, AT SOUTH BUTLER, WAYNE COUNTY, N. Y., SEPT. 15, 1853"* (Syracuse, 1853) *bound with* B. T. Roberts, *ORDAINING WOMEN* (Rochester, 1891) *bound with* Catherine (Mumford) Booth, *"FEMALE MINISTRY; OR, WOMAN'S RIGHT TO PREACH THE GOSPEL . . ."* (London, n. d.) *bound with* Fannie (McDowell) Hunter, *WOMEN PREACHERS* (Dallas, 1905)

12. LATE NINETEENTH CENTURY REVIVALIST TEACHINGS ON THE HOLY SPIRIT. D. L. Moody, *SECRET POWER OR THE SECRET OF SUCCESS IN CHRISTIAN LIFE AND*

WORK (New York, [1881]) *bound with* J. Wilbur Chapman, *RECEIVED YE THE HOLY GHOST?* (New York, [1894]) *bound with* R. A. Torrey, *THE BAPTISM WITH THE HOLY SPIRIT* (New York, 1895 & 1897)

13. SEVEN "JESUS ONLY" TRACTS. Andrew D. Urshan, *THE DOCTRINE OF THE NEW BIRTH, OR, THE PERFECT WAY TO ETERNAL LIFE* (Cochrane, Wis., 1921) *bound with* Andrew Urshan, *THE ALMIGHTY GOD IN THE LORD JESUS CHRIST* (Los Angeles, 1919) *bound with* Frank J. Ewart, *THE REVELATION OF JESUS CHRIST* (St. Louis, n. d.) *bound with* G. T. Haywood, *THE BIRTH OF THE SPIRIT IN THE DAYS OF THE APOSTLES* (Indianapolis, n. d.) *DIVINE NAMES AND TITLES OF JEHOVAH* (Indianapolis, n. d.) *THE FINEST OF THE WHEAT* (Indianapolis, n. d.) *THE VICTIM OF THE FLAMING SWORD* (Indianapolis, n. d.)

14. THREE EARLY PENTECOSTAL TRACTS. D. Wesley Myland, *THE LATTER RAIN COVENANT AND PENTECOSTAL POWER* (Chicago, 1910) *bound with* G. F. Taylor, *THE SPIRIT AND THE BRIDE* (n. p., [1907?]) *bound with* B. F. Laurence, *THE APOSTOLIC FAITH RESTORED* (St. Louis, 1916)

15. Fairchild, James H., *OBERLIN: THE COLONY AND THE COLLEGE, 1833-1883* (Oberlin, 1883)

16. Figgis, John B., *KESWICK FROM WITHIN* (London, [1914])

17. Finney, Charles G., *LECTURES TO PROFESSING CHRISTIANS* (New York, 1837)

18. Fleisch, Paul, *DIE MODERNE GEMEINSCHAFTSBEWEGUNG IN DEUTSCHLAND* (Leipzig, 1912)

19. SIX TRACTS BY W. B. GODBEY. *SPIRITUAL GIFTS AND GRACES* (Cincinnati, [1895]) *THE RETURN OF JESUS* (Cincinnati, [1899?]) *WORK OF THE HOLY SPIRIT* (Louisville, [1902]) *CHURCH—BRIDE—KINGDOM* (Cincinnati, [1905]) *DIVINE HEALING* (Greensboro, [1909]) *TONGUE MOVEMENT, SATANIC* (Zarephath, N. J., 1918)

20. Gordon, Earnest B., *ADONIRAM JUDSON GORDON* (New York, [1896])

21. Hills, A. M., *HOLINESS AND POWER FOR THE CHURCH AND THE MINISTRY* (Cincinnati, [1897])

22. Horner, Ralph C., *FROM THE ALTAR TO THE UPPER ROOM* (Toronto, [1891])

23. McDonald, William and John E. Searles, *THE LIFE OF REV. JOHN S. INSKIP* (Boston, [1885])

24. LaBerge, Agnes N. O., *WHAT GOD HATH WROUGHT* (Chicago, n. d.)

25. Lee, Luther, *AUTOBIOGRAPHY OF THE REV. LUTHER LEE* (New York, 1882)

26. McLean, A. and J. W. Easton, *PENUEL; OR, FACE TO FACE WITH GOD* (New York, 1869)

27. McPherson, Aimee Semple, *THIS IS THAT: PERSONAL EXPERIENCES SERMONS AND WRITINGS* (Los Angeles, [1919])

28. Mahan, Asa, *OUT OF DARKNESS INTO LIGHT* (London, 1877)

29. THE LIFE AND TEACHING OF CARRIE JUDD MONTGOMERY Carrie Judd Montgomery, *"UNDER HIS WINGS": THE STORY OF MY LIFE* (Oakland,

[1936]) Carrie F. Judd, *THE PRAYER OF FAITH* (New York, 1880)

30. THE DEVOTIONAL WRITINGS OF PHOEBE PALMER Phoebe Palmer, *THE WAY OF HOLINESS* (52nd ed., New York, 1867) *FAITH AND ITS EFFECTS* (27th ed., New York, n. d., orig. pub. 1854)

31. Wheatley, Richard, *THE LIFE AND LETTERS OF MRS. PHOEBE PALMER* (New York, 1881)

32. Palmer, Phoebe, ed., *PIONEER EXPERIENCES* (New York, 1868)

33. Palmer, Phoebe, *THE PROMISE OF THE FATHER* (Boston, 1859)

34. Pardington, G. P., *TWENTY-FIVE WONDERFUL YEARS, 1889-1914: A POPULAR SKETCH OF THE CHRISTIAN AND MISSIONARY ALLIANCE* (New York, [1914])

35. Parham, Sarah E., *THE LIFE OF CHARLES F. PARHAM, FOUNDER OF THE APOSTOLIC FAITH MOVEMENT* (Joplin, [1930])

36. THE SERMONS OF CHARLES F. PARHAM. Charles F. Parham, *A VOICE CRYING IN THE WILDERNESS* (4th ed., Baxter Springs, Kan., 1944, orig. pub. 1902) *THE EVERLASTING GOSPEL* (n.p., n.d., orig. pub. 1911)

37. Pierson, Arthur Tappan, *FORWARD MOVEMENTS OF THE LAST HALF CENTURY* (New York, 1905)

38. *PROCEEDINGS OF HOLINESS CONFERENCES, HELD AT CINCINNATI, NOVEMBER 26TH, 1877, AND AT NEW YORK, DECEMBER 17TH, 1877* (Philadelphia, 1878)

39. *RECORD OF THE CONVENTION FOR THE PROMOTION OF*

SCRIPTURAL HOLINESS HELD AT BRIGHTON, MAY 29TH, TO JUNE 7TH, 1875 (Brighton, [1896?])

40. Rees, Seth Cook, MIRACLES IN THE SLUMS (Chicago, [1905?])

41. Roberts, B. T., WHY ANOTHER SECT (Rochester, 1879)

42. Shaw, S. B., ed., ECHOES OF THE GENERAL HOLINESS ASSEMBLY (Chicago, [1901])

43. THE DEVOTIONAL WRITINGS OF ROBERT PEARSALL SMITH AND HANNAH WHITALL SMITH. [R]obert [P]earsall [S]mith, HOLINESS THROUGH FAITH: LIGHT ON THE WAY OF HOLINESS (New York, [1870]) [H]annah [W]hitall [S]mith, THE CHRISTIAN'S SECRET OF A HAPPY LIFE, (Boston and Chicago, [1885])

44. [S]mith, [H]annah [W]hitall, THE UNSELFISHNESS OF GOD AND HOW I DISCOVERED IT (New York, [1903])

45. Steele, Daniel, A SUBSTITUTE FOR HOLINESS; OR, ANTINOMIANISM REVIVED (Chicago and Boston, [1899])

46. Tomlinson, A. J., THE LAST GREAT CONFLICT (Cleveland, 1913)

47. Upham, Thomas C., THE LIFE OF FAITH (Boston, 1845)

48. Washburn, Josephine M., HISTORY AND REMINISCENCES OF THE HOLINESS CHURCH WORK IN SOUTHERN CALIFORNIA AND ARIZONA (South Pasadena, [1912?])